Verify in Field

Verify in Field:
Projects and Conversations
Höweler + Yoon
by Eric Höweler
and J. Meejin Yoon

Design
Common Name

Project Management, Editing
Rae Pozdro

Copy Editing
Edith Fikes

Printing
DZA Druckerei zu Altenburg
GmbH, Thuringia, Germany

© 2021 Eric Höweler
and J. Meejin Yoon,
and Park Books AG, Zurich
© for the texts: the authors

Park Books
Niederdorfstrasse 54
8001 Zurich
Switzerland
www.park-books.com

Park Books is supported by the
Federal Office of Culture with a
general subsidy for the years
2021–2024.

ISBN 978-3-03860-224-8

Verify in Field:
Projects and Conversations
Höweler + Yoon

Eric Höweler and J. Meejin Yoon

Verify in Field (VIF) is a notational convention used to indicate that some information on an architectural drawing is incomplete, contingent, and subject to unknown conditions in the field. VIF highlights the gap between design intent and built reality. The term acknowledges both the disciplinary investment in the instruments of design and the specific processes and protocols that inflect, alter, and modify design intent. Verification may refer to a field dimension, an alignment, or survey point. It may also refer to a process of interaction and feedback where information and expertise are incorporated into the design process in ways that adapt, modify, or recast the original design intent. While VIF can be understood as architecture's fine print, the notation speaks volumes about the discipline and the profession — and, our agency to act on the physical world.

In the context of this book, we use the term *verify in field* as a lens through which to view the agency of architecture at different scales; to examine the techniques and processes that both constrain and enable us to create, make, and build today. VIF not only acknowledges the gap between the idealized realm of conception and the messy and material realm of construction, but allows the gap to be a productive space of inquiry. *Verification* involves double-checking — measure twice, cut once. Verification is about curiosity and expanding knowledge. It requires an openness to inputs. It is investigative. It acknowledges contingencies and externalities, as well as expertise that may be located elsewhere, in another discipline, or outside the realm of the experience of the designer. Verification entails doubt. Verification is essential to the translation of design from concept to construction.

Verify in Field

Likewise, we see the *field* as necessarily both territorial and operational. The field of construction and craft, of discourse and debate, or of political and environmental forces that act on the built environment. While VIF technically addresses the physical conditions of construction and shifts responsibility for executing intent from the architect to the contractor, we employ the term more expansively to frame our process and projects. Here we examine the term as an ethos — one that develops means for more agency, responsibility, and engagement.

Verification as feedback and *field* as context structure how we navigate and frame our practice. In the first chapter titled "What's the Matter?" we attempt to take the temperature of our time, asking not only: what's the matter? But also, what matters? Design as a means for embodying societal values prompts the question: what do we value? And, how can we materialize those values with design? Given the myriad, compounding crises spurred by global warming, social injustice, and political polarization, we also ask: what about matter? And, why does architecture matter? Seen as a physical manifestation and affirmation of shared values, the Memorial to Enslaved Laborers at the University of Virginia raises many of these questions. The memorial seeks to highlight difficult histories while providing a platform for learning, healing, and justice.

"Means and Methods," the book's second chapter, explores tensions between design and construction. Examining how digital workflows and deliverables challenge the compartmentalization of scope that allocates the means and methods of construction to the contractor and

A moment of reflection and protest as a woman kneels

design intent to the architect, the chapter explores how we operate and where we find agency. Verification in this context includes processes that acknowledge the gaps between concept and construction that enable feedback loops and the development of expertise. Projects included in this chapter highlight the incorporation of material systems and labor practices into their conception, and how these systems and practices contribute to material imagination.

At another scale, VIF implies an engagement with larger fields, including the social and political contexts in which we work. Beyond construction, the processes and protocols that bring architecture into being represent another scale of verification and a different conception of the field. Whether through participatory planning, community engagement, or the public approvals process, design enters a realm of negotiation between private entities and the larger public. Real estate forces, regulatory agencies, and authorities having jurisdiction (AHJ) all impact the process of design. We call this process "Going Public," and it is the subject of the book's third chapter. Verification in this context suggests a feedback loop of community engagement, negotiations with agencies, and the value management of project financing, funding, and execution. This chapter explores projects at varying scales that engage in processes of verification, validation, and valuation, and,

Signal Spire, an interactive installation at Nubian Square in Boston, broadcasts 311 data as a real time lighting display.

Double Horizon, an interactive lighting installation at the San Ysidro border crossing, signals the movement of cars across the border with a burst of light.

that speak to an expanded field that includes public space, the public realm, and public engagement.

The book's fourth chapter, "Under the Weather," expands the scope of inquiry to include embodied energy, ecosystems, and the natural environment. Human perceptions of climate and environment shape our understanding of systems we rely upon every day and ultimately influence our behavior. In the expanded context of the natural environment, the field includes the expanded space-time of the Anthropocene, and verification is the process by which environmental effects are registered and understood, as well as how a collective ecological consciousness is produced. Projects included in this chapter engage with questions of climate-responsive design, the calibration of environmental systems, and platforms designed to shift our perceptions and deepen our knowledge of urban ecologies.

Chapter five, "... In the Details," looks closely at the evolution of a single detail across three residential projects. The perceptual effects of these details ask the viewer to look twice; to verify how they perceive the architecture from outside in and from inside out. The three projects explore material and perceptual effects to encourage careful looking to determine how a building's appearance is achieved through the detailed articulation of its parts. The aggregate effect of these material manifestations across projects suggests a shift in attitudes about material design from tectonic expression to a contemporary articulation of material in the context of an image-obsessed contemporary culture.

In addition to thematic essays and projects, *Verify in Field* includes a number of conversations with friends and

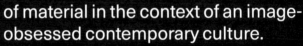

colleagues. These dialogues allowed us to develop some of the ideas that push and pull on the work in the studio, and to think through the larger contexts that influence design today. Adam Greenfield approaches the role of technology from a number of different angles ranging from the personal to the public, and at scales that vary from the individual to the global. Nader Tehrani engages with important questions raised by fabrication and construction processes and their translation. Kate Orff's perspective on the agency of design in the context of urban ecology and the roles of architects and landscape architects as advocates or activists is both grounded and provocative. Daniel Barber's conversation on comfort and climate expands ideas around architecture's role as a mediator of climate. And lastly, Ana Miljački raises complex questions around design processes, architects' understanding of precedents, the critical imagination brought to design, and the influence of image-dense media on design practice. Interspersed between chapters, these conversations with colleagues encompass topics within the field and across fields that intersect with architecture practice, design culture, and the many considerations that comprise the larger field as ideas move from conception to construction.

In our previous book, *Expanded Practice*[1], we argued for an expanded definition of architecture that would integrate projects as wide-ranging as concept clothing, interactive installations, and kinetic sculptures. We added electronic technologies, micro-controllers, and smart materials to our repertoire as architects. During this period, we argued for *media as material* for architecture. In the twelve years following *Expanded Practice*, we have seen

White Noise White Light, an interactive light and sound installation for the 2004 Athens Olympics, proposed *media as material* for architecture.

radical transformations in technology and culture. Ideas that seemed to be at the forefront of the discipline in the early 2000s are folded into mainstream practice today.

If our early work argued for *media as material*, the last decade of our work examines material after media. While the construction industry is historically slow to embrace innovation, there have been significant transformations on many digital design and fabrication fronts. Design workflows are now entirely mediated by digital technologies from early concept through prototyping, coordination, and construction. The contemporary design workflow begins as a digital model, which is then engineered via computational software, coordinated on a cloud-based building information model, transmitted to the fabricator via file transfer platforms, translated from a 3D model to a scripted tool path, milled with robotic equipment, installed with digital surveying equipment, documented and post-produced, and shared on social media. Indeed, given our experience with the impact of the digital, and in our contemplation of the post-digital, we ask ourselves: what about architecture is not media, or mediated?

At the same time, material — and the way we conceptualize material — is also rapidly evolving. Thinking materially today is less about understanding material as having essential qualities that produce inevitable correspondences between, say, bricks and arches. Rather,

It is more about understanding material qualities and potential — strength and durability, embodied energy, their upstream and downstream impacts, as well as new composites and hybrids. Material thinking in design now is a matter of expanding and recasting, using digital tools to work with existing materials in new ways, and finding productive uses for new materials. Material thinking today is thinking material after media.

Media and material are an interrelated through line for the projects in this book. The world today is more complex, and the contexts in which we work are more saturated with information and disinformation, challenging us to speculate on how to navigate contemporary fields and rethink how we act on the world.

Verification has also taken on new relevance. Not only because there are new digital tools that enable simulation, analysis, and verification, but because these digital tools enable us to doctor, modify, fake, and disseminate misinformation. The Cold War quip "trust, but verify" in the context of nuclear detente assumed that truth could be verified. There either were or were not missiles in the silos. Fifty years later, a common understanding of our shared reality, a shared understanding of truth, and the articulation of common values seem remote. The age of Post-truth coincides with Big Data and the Information Age. In theory, we have never known more. And yet in practice, the need for verification, systems of feedback, and techniques for translation, has never seemed more urgent.

Translation between the digital model in the Rhino environment and the material construction of the Memorial to Enslaved Laborers.

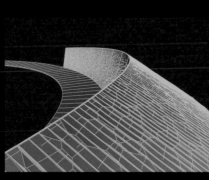

1   Yoon, J. Meejin, and Eric Höweler. *Expanded Practice: Höweler + Yoon Architecture / MY Studio.* New York, N.Y.: Princeton Architectural Press, 2009.

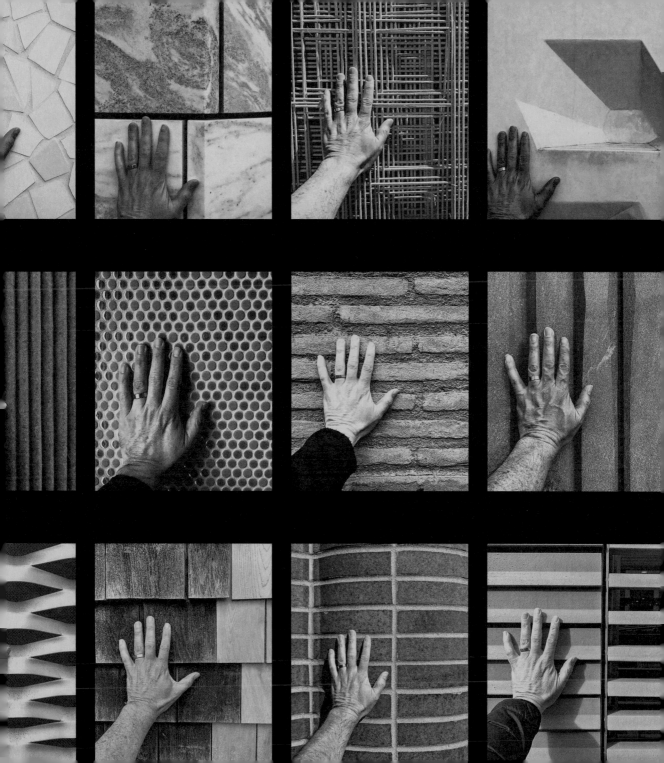

Chapter I   What's the Matter?

Surveying the contours of our uncertain present, we ask: what's the matter? The question is both colloquial and prodigious — the term *matter* references not only physical substance but also the essence of something — specifically, the essence of our problems. The problems of the moment are numerous and intersectional: the pandemic, racialized violence, divisive politics, and climate change to name a few. What are our values, beliefs, and aspirations? As architects, how do we materialize what we value? Or, how does what we build convey our values? And, how do we build what matters?

Ongoing calls for racial justice amplified by the murders of George Floyd, Breonna Taylor, Ahmaud Arbery, and many others catalyzed a national reckoning with the legacy of racialized, anti-Black violence. The COVID-19 pandemic has shut down institutions and workplaces the world over, forcing people into physically distanced isolation that opens new questions about the future of cities, public spaces, behavioral norms, and new normals. COVID-19 has impacted Black and Latino communities at disproportionately high rates, devastating families and neighborhoods, and underscoring the unequal distribution of risk and vulnerability in our society. Meanwhile, pugilistic politics has fractured the country, polarized communities, and flooded public discourse with divisive rhetoric, propaganda, and alternative facts. Prospects for controlling climate change seemed increasingly dim when the U.S. pulled out of the Paris Climate Agreement and rolled back environmental protection laws. And, the built environment continues to deplete natural resources, consume energy, emit greenhouse gases, and systematically jeopardize the near and distant future of the planet.

This partial list of crises, catastrophes, and concerns gives us reason to pause. There are plenty of things that

What's the Matter?

matter. What can architecture do? What can designers do? In 1969, the French curator Madame L'Amic interviewed Charles Eames about the nature of design. Asked to define the boundaries of design, he responded with another question, "What are the boundaries of problems?" For Charles and Ray Eames, design was about addressing problems in the world. From the design of a bentwood leg splint to reframing the world in *Powers of Ten*,[1] the Eameses designed across scales and disciplines to address the urgent and changing questions of their time.

Addressing the pressing questions of our time requires us to grapple with difficult histories, including the legacy of slavery, Jim Crow, segregation, racist planning and lending practices, and other forms of systemic racism. In many cases these histories were untold, mistold, hidden, or ignored. Contemporary historians, scholars, and researchers, however, are mining archives and public histories, and advancing scholarship that requires us to unlearn our histories in order to learn them anew.

On October 22, 2012, a University of Virginia landscaping crew discovered a site containing sixty-seven unmarked graves in a plot of land just outside the stone walls of the University Cemetery. Archaeologists believe the site to be a burial ground for enslaved Black Americans connected to the university. The number of graves suggests that the enslaved were a significant population on the University Grounds. The unmarked graves and forgotten burial ground stand in sharp contrast to the adjacent university and

Students hold a candlelight vigil at UVA in the aftermath of the Unite the Right rally in 2017.

confederate cemeteries, which are marked by engraved tombstones and statuary. The unknown and unmarked graves of the enslaved are a reminder of lives unrecorded and histories unwritten that characterize much of the institution of slavery in the United States. This vast blind spot in the history of the university prompted then president of UVA Teresa Sullivan to form the President's Commission on Slavery and the University.

The University of Virginia was founded in 1819 by Thomas Jefferson, author of the Declaration of Independence, third president of the United States, UVA's architect — and slave-holder. While Jefferson's architecture is often associated with democratic ideals, the university he founded was built on the foundations of enslavement. Today, traces of that enslavement remain legible in the institution's architecture and landscape.

The university's constructed landscape of the central lawn, with its unifying colonnade and picturesque pavilion fronts, is complemented by a series of rear yards and service areas. The lawn occupies the leveled ridge that rises to the Rotunda at its highest point. Ten classically-inspired two-story pavilions face the terraced lawn, while the view from the back side reveals that they are actually three-story buildings with walk-out basements that open into walled yards. These lower-level spaces and adjacent yards were where many of the enslaved were forced to labor for the university and its students and faculty.

UVA's serpentine walls enclosed work yards behind the pavilions.

Vigil at the African-American burial site adjacent to the UVA cemetery, after the discovery of unmarked graves in 2012.

Jefferson's design for UVA's grounds is often celebrated for the architectural composition of the lawn, rotunda, and pavilions, with no mention of the enslaved labor that produced and maintained life at the university. Historian and designer Mabel O. Wilson points out that Jefferson's use of section reveals a contradiction. Jefferson's university, and the entire way of life of the slave-owning South, was reliant on the forced labor of the enslaved, yet Jefferson, the owner of over 600 enslaved people, found the practice abhorrent and thus employed architectural and landscape design strategies to conceal it. The violence and cruelty of enslavement were hidden in plain sight.

The private gardens associated with the pavilions, which are today enclosed by serpentine walls, were used for cutting firewood, slaughtering livestock, doing laundry, and preparing meals. The bricks used to build the pavilions were likely made by hands of enslaved boys and men. The terraces of the lawn and cellars of the pavilions were dug by enslaved people. The practice of slavery, its inherent violence and systematic dehumanization of men, women, and children, is woven into the fabric of the buildings. The canonization of the Academical Village and the lawn as representatives of democratic ideals obscures the violent history of an institution founded, built, and supported by the practice of slavery.

The history of slavery at the university was not officially acknowledged until 2007 when the Board of Visitors, the governing body of the university, made an "expression of regret" that noted the presence of the enslaved on university grounds. The statement was accompanied by the installation of a stone plaque set in the brick pavers surrounding the

Rotunda. Small in scale, inappropriately sited, and inscribed with language that downplayed the role of the enslaved, the marker had the unintended consequences of sparking the student outrage that generated momentum for creating a permanent memorial. In the same year, Professor Frank Dukes and others began developing what became UCARE, the University & Community Action for Racial Equity. Among the first group of students in Dukes' class was Ishraga Eltahir, an undergraduate student pursuing dual majors in Political and Social Thought and African American Studies. In 2009, with Ishraga's leadership, the students formed an organization that was recognized by the student council as the Memorial for Enslaved Laborers, known colloquially as MEL. This group then sponsored a student design ideas competition in 2011 to raise awareness and promote interest in building a permanent memorial.

A half-decade later, in 2016, our design team responded to a request for proposal (RFP) and joined the effort to build a permanent memorial to acknowledge and honor the lives of the estimated 4,000 men, women, and children who were enslaved and worked on the university's grounds. Our collaborative design team included a range of experts in their fields: cultural historian and designer Mabel O. Wilson; landscape architect Gregg Bleam; community engagement facilitator Professor Frank Dukes; and later, artist Eto Otitigbe. Each member of the design team brought a unique perspective that was integral to the design of the memorial. Mabel's extensive scholarship on race and architecture, her design research on rendering anti-Black racism in the built environment

legible, and her own experiences as a UVA student and alum were critical to the design. Frank's engagement with students, his contributions to UCARE, his efforts on the Charlottesville Commission on Race, Memorials, and Public Spaces, lent a perspective and tone of engagement that was based on listening and building trust between multiple communities from the university and Charlottesville, including a descendant group that traces their ancestry directly to those who were enslaved and labored at UVA. Convening in Gregg Bleam's office in downtown Charlottesville early in the design process, we looked out the window at the equestrian statue of confederate general Robert E. Lee and reflected on the local debate around removing the monument.

The fate of the confederate monument lingered as we began the design process for the Memorial to Enslaved Laborers. Before we could begin to design the memorial we understood that we had to first design a process founded on deep listening that would build trust between the university, community members, and the design team. This took the form of meetings with members of the local community, including the descendant community. We met in churches and schools. We met with UVA faculty and students, alumni, and staff. We heard about the deep wounds and underlying distrust. We heard that a memorial would need to convey important dualities — the experience of pain and suffering, as well as resilience and dignity. We heard the desire for the memorial to prominently acknowledge the individuals who were enslaved on the university grounds. We heard calls for the memorial

To design the UVA Memorial, first we had to design the process — beginning with a series of dialogues and community engagements.

to be open and living, capable of capturing new scholarship as identities and histories of the enslaved were uncovered. We heard that it should lend humanity and dignity to the individuals whose names remain unknown. We heard that it should both recognize the past and be relevant to the present — that it should provide a space for coming together to do the work of "righting past wrongs," and create a space for healing.

We asked: what could a memorial be? Could it be a distributed memorial that would be scattered across the grounds? Could it be an ephemeral memorial made of planted crocus flowers that would bloom seasonally to transform the iconic green lawn into a sea of purple? Could it be an academic symposium, a series of publications, or scholarships for students? While distributed and ephemeral memorials were intriguing, the feedback we received from participants resoundingly supported the memorial as a singular physical place to gather and honor the enslaved of the past while also creating a commemorative landscape to advance racial justice today.

At the outset, there was no single site designated for the memorial. Four possible sites were studied: a parcel on the site of the Anatomical Theater, two parcels adjacent to Pavilion X and Pavilion X, and the Triangle of Grass, a wedge-shaped clearing to east of the Rotunda. Our design team sketched and discussed options for all four sites. A memorial acknowledging slavery at a university has little precedent in the U.S.. What should it look like? How could it convey the magnitude of its meaning? Was there a way to convey the violence of slavery without mimicry? How might it offer a means for healing? To what degree should the memorial be representational? How could we display the names of the approximately 4,000 enslaved if their names were largely unknown? How might it be part of the grounds, yet remain distinctly apart and in dialogue with the past and present?

Preliminary sketches were shared with the President's Commission on Slavery at the University, with the local and descendant communities, with staff, faculty, and students. Surveys were conducted online and feedback was collected during meetings and workshops. The conversation gravitated toward a scheme that was inspired by the West African ring shout ritual — a spiritual dance practiced by the enslaved in the form of a circle. A ring, a space for gathering, a void referencing the ring shout, and a place to "let freedom ring."

The final design proposal consisted of a semi-embedded ring, approximately 80' (24 m) in diameter, which is formed by a concave stone wall that rises upward as the circular path gently slopes into the ground. Two intersecting cones define the geometry of the ring. From the entrance of the memorial to the opposite corner, the enclosing wall rises to 8' (2.4 m), creating a sense of intimacy. The rising ridgeline of the enclosing wall creates a new horizon line that screens out the context, allowing visitors to contemplate the memorial and its meaning.

The circular path and center lawn are defined by a lower stone ring that displays a historical timeline. A slow stream of water runs over the timeline from a high point at the northern edge of the memorial to the entrance. The movement of the water evokes acts of

Memory marks and names on the concave wall of the memorial.

Scalloped marks on the wall's convex face.

cleansing and libation. The inscribed timeline entries recount the history of slavery at the university. Some entries are short as if an entry in a journal or log. For example, "1820–1822 Sam works for two years at the university as a blacksmith." Another entry states, "1832 Three professors purchase Lewis Commodore at public auction for the school's use. They are later reimbursed, and he becomes UVA's property." Some entries describe acts of brutality that resonate with contemporary news headlines, "1856 An enslaved eleven-year-old girl is beaten unconscious by a UVA student. Claiming his right to discipline any slave, he suffers no consequences." These terse entries make poignant the brutal acts of everyday violence and events catalogued in the historical documents of the university.

The concave inner wall facing the path is inscribed with 4,000 memory marks, horizontal lines that cut into the stone like a gash. Each mark represents an individual — enslaved, bought, sold, whipped — dehumanized. When known, names accompany the marks: Isabella Gibbons, Sally Cotrell Cole, Henry Martin, for example. Some records only note a single first name: Sammy, Old Sam, Young Sam. Other records mention the enslaved only by the tasks and labor they performed: mason, sawyer, butler. In some cases, the records consist of transactions. How to assemble from fragments of records and logs a sense of community and humanity among the enslaved people? How to convey individuality? After prolonged deliberation, the design team proposed to inscribe their names if known, their trade if recorded, and their kinship ties as interpreted from records. Experiencing the inside wall of the memorial, the sheer presence of 4,000 marks, representing

Carved stone panels depict Isabella Gibbons, a formerly enslaved person, on the outer wall of the memorial.

4,000 individual lives, is powerful. The fact that the vast majority are unnamed is also striking. Yet the genealogical cloud of names, skills, and kinship brings humanity to those whom slaveholders systematically oppressed and denied their place in history. As new names are discovered either in the archive or through genealogical research, they are carved in situ above a memory mark, rendering the memorial open-ended and unfinished, much like a living archive. Five additional names have already been identified since the memorial's construction.

While the interior of the memorial wall is smooth, the exterior of the memorial is rough and textured, as if split from a block in a quarry. The textured grooves on the inclined wall recall the drill marks made in the process of quarrying stone, while the gouged and scalloped surface evokes the rough textures of cleft stone found on local tombstones. With artist Eto Otitigbe, we explored techniques for integrating representational images into the materiality of the memorial through actions such as carving. Otitigbe's work resonated powerfully with the design team and community, and he worked with participants to develop a representational artwork for the memorial using a similar technique to that of his self-portrait, *Becoming Visible*.

The final design embeds an enlarged portrait of

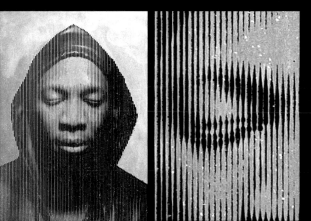

Isabella Gibbons, revealing only her eyes, into the texture of the outer wall. Isabella Gibbons is one of the few enslaved people at UVA for whom there is a photographic record. She was owned by UVA professor

William Barton Rogers and was among the very few enslaved people who learned how to read and write, a form of resistance at the time. Carving an image of her eyes, at a colossal scale, into the surface of the memorial imbues it with a haunting but subtle presence. At times, the image is hidden in plain sight and becomes visible only under certain lighting conditions or from particular vantage points. Gibbons is both witness to the violence of the past and watcher of the present.

After the Civil War, Gibbons became a teacher at the Charlottesville Freedmen's School. She wrote of her experience in the *Freedman's Record* in 1867:

"Can we forget the crack of the whip, the cowhide, the whipping post, the auction block, the handcuffs, the spaniels, the iron collar, the negro-trader tearing the young child from its mother's breast as a whelp from the lioness? Have we forgotten those horrible cruelties, hundreds of our race killed? No, we have not, nor ever will."

The dedication for the memorial, originally scheduled for April 11, 2020, was postponed due to the COVID-19 pandemic. On May 25, 2020, the world witnessed the brutal murder of George Floyd by police in Minneapolis, Minnesota. Protesters responding to Floyd's death gathered publicly in cities across the U.S. and around the world. The killing of Floyd and the many other unarmed Black Americans who face unwarranted institutional violence galvanized the Black Lives Matter movement and again drew attention to the legacy of slavery and anti-Black racism in America.

On June 4, a group of doctors, nurses, and students from the UVA Medical School were joined by the broader UVA and Charlottesville community for a White Coats for

Black Lives gathering in remembrance of George Floyd. The community took a knee for 8 minutes and 46 seconds to mark the period of time that Floyd was brutalized by the Minneapolis police officer, and as a reminder of the violence and injustices that persist in the wake of slavery. In solidarity with Black Lives Matter, the protesters found a place to gather and share their grief and outrage, and to connect past and present, at the Memorial to Enslaved Laborers.

Many stories and histories will need to be told and retold. Sited in a public space at the entrance of the UNESCO World Heritage site on the UVA Grounds en route to the Rotunda, the Memorial to Enslaved Laborers endeavors to tell a part of the story. We hope it has a capacity for consequence. When it rains, the memory marks drip as if with tears. The circular patch of grass awaits the bloom of crocus flowers at the end of winter. The memorial is unfinished and incomplete. The memorial's openness and ability to incorporate additional names acknowledges that history is incomplete and that the work for social justice continues.

And so, we ask: what is the matter? And what matters? Black Lives Matter. Social Justice matters. The history of institutionalized violence matters. The omission of histories matters. The acknowledgment of past wrongs matters. The commemorative landscape matters. Spaces for protest and gathering matter. The articulation of values through design matters. The materialization of what matters, matters.

UVA Medical School affiliates share 8 minutes and 46 seconds of silence at the UVA Memorial during the White Coats for Black Lives event.

1 Eames, Charles, Ray Eames, Shelley Mills, Lucia Eames Demetrios, Eames Demetrios, and Gregory Peck. *The Films of Charles and Ray Eames.* DVD. Chatsworth, CA: Image Entertainment, 2005.

Memorial to Enslaved Laborers
at the University of Virginia

Surveying the contours of our uncertain
present, we ask, "What's the matter?"
in order to articulate what matters.
As architects, how do we materialize what
we value? Or, how does what we build
convey our values? And, how do we build
what matters?

1619

First written
mention of
enslaved Africans
in Virginia

1705

Virginia enacts
slave codes that
formalize
race-based slavery
in American
colonial law.

1817

Ten enslaved
people begin to
clear the land that
will become UVA.

1818-1865

UVA temporarily
rents enslaved
people from a
seventy-mile radius.
This separates
families and often
forces the enslaved
to walk long
distances.

Sited within the University of Virginia grounds in Charlottesville, Virginia, the
Memorial to Enslaved Laborers honors the lives of an estimated 4,000 enslaved
men, women, and children who built and sustained UVA. Owned and rented
by the university, they constructed and maintained its grounds and structures
and labored for its founders, faculty, and students under the dehumanizing
and violent conditions of slavery from UVA's founding in 1817 to the end
of the Civil War in 1865. Following a student- and faculty-initiated effort to
critically examine the history of slavery at the university, UVA commissioned
the memorial to create a landscape of active remembrance and reflection. The
design process began with listening and learning. In public forums and intimate
conversations, in large classrooms and small chapels, students, faculty, alumni,
and community members that included descendants of the enslaved, shared
their aspirations and ideas. Historians dug deep into the archives of ledgers and
letters to uncover and tell a fuller story of this period.

1825

UVA opens for its first session with 123 white male students. 90-150 enslaved people also live on grounds.

1831-32

In the wake of Nat Turner's slave uprising, the Virginia legislature debates the fate of slavery. They choose to uphold the slave system.

1859

Abolitionist John Brown tries to seize a federal arsenal at Harpers Ferry, Virginia, as part of a plan to lead an armed slave uprising.

1861

Virginia secedes from the Union, invoking the federal government's "oppression of the slaveholding states"

1865

With general emancipation underway and the Civil War over, UVA in September begins to pay wages to those formerly enslaved.

Tanner's Boye Map of Virginia (1826) depicts the university grounds, the Academical Village with ten classical pavilions, and a colonnade framing the terraced lawn and terminating rotunda. This idyllic depiction obscures the lives and work of the enslaved people whose toil supported life on the campus. In the lower-left corner of the engraving, an enslaved woman cares for her owner's child.

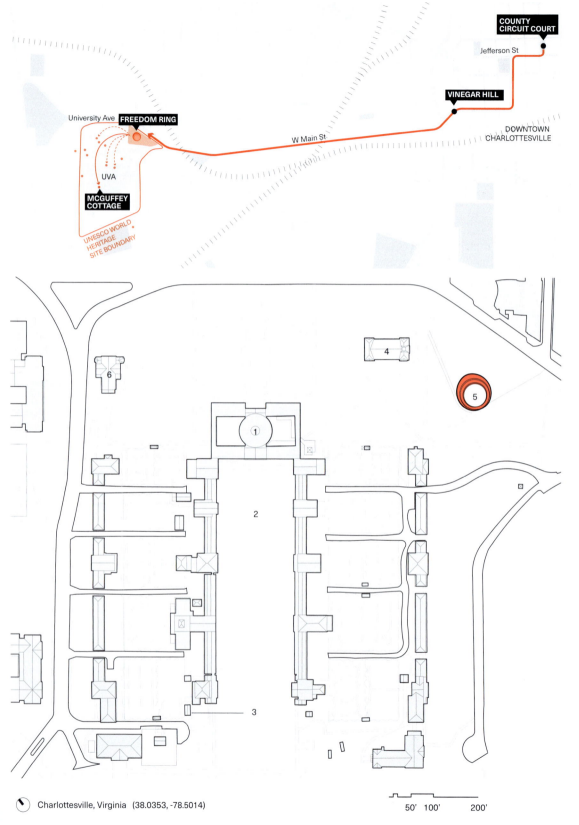

COUNTY CIRCUIT COURT

Jefferson St

VINEGAR HILL

University Ave   FREEDOM RING

W Main St

DOWNTOWN CHARLOTTESVILLE

UVA

MCGUFFEY COTTAGE

UNESCO WORLD HERITAGE SITE BOUNDARY

4

5

6

1

2

3

Charlottesville, Virginia   (38.0353, -78.5014)

50' 100'   200'

32

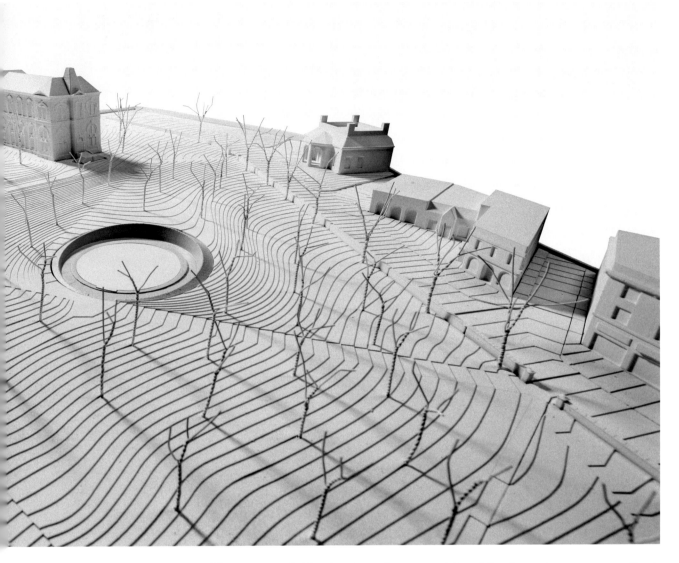

1 The Rotunda
2 The Lawn
3 McGuffey Cottage
4 Brooks Hall
5 Memorial to
   Enslaved Laborers
6 University Chapel

The memorial is sited on the east side of the lawn in an area called the Triangle of Grass, just beyond the university's iconic rotunda and within UNESCO World Heritage Site boundaries. Located at the threshold between the UVA's grounds and downtown Charlottesville, the memorial serves as a gathering space along the Liberation and Freedom Day walk, a community march from the slave auction block marker in the town square to the university grounds that takes place every year on the third of March to commemorate the end of slavery in Charlottesville.

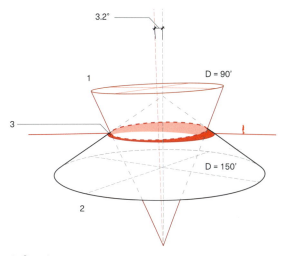

3.2°

1

D = 90'

3

D = 150'

2

1 Cone 1
2 Cone 2
3 Intersection

The memorial's circular form, inspired by the ritual ring shout dance and the term "let freedom ring," is carefully nestled into the landscape. The ring-like form is calibrated to mediate the site's sloping landscape and the scale of the human body. The geometry is determined by two intersecting cones three degrees off-axis, resulting in a tilted crescent figure that rises from the ground to 8' (2.4 m) at the highest point of its sweeping ridgeline. The open bowl-like landform measures 80' (24 m) in diameter, equivalent to the interior dimensions of the Rotunda. However, in contrast to the closed sphere of the Rotunda, the memorial creates a public space for gathering that opens, reveals, and invites.

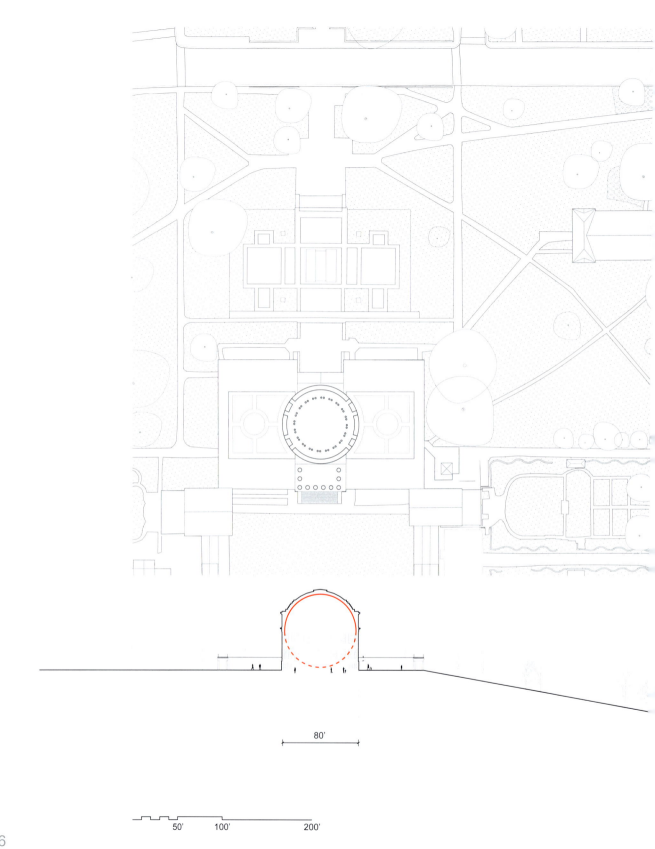

80'

50'   100'   200'

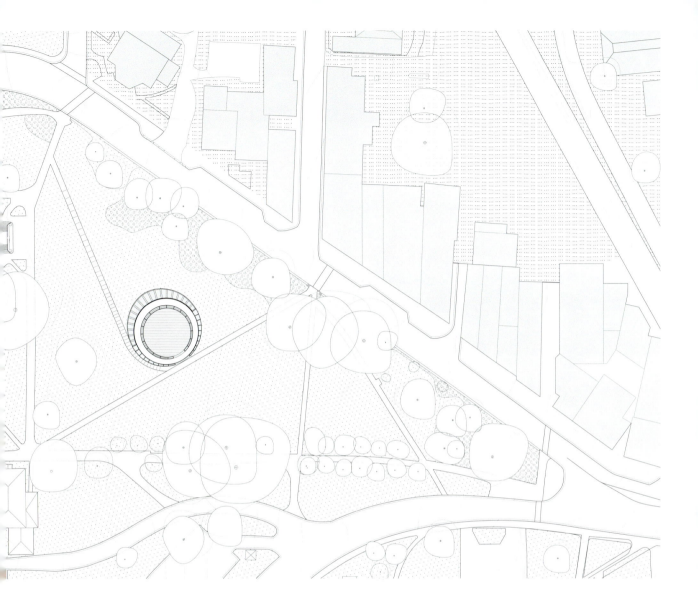

80'

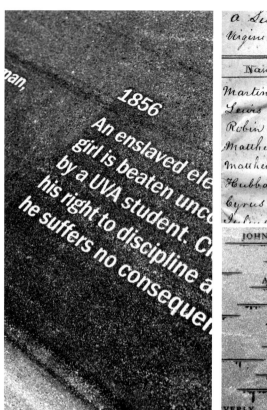

1856
An enslaved ele[ven]
girl is beaten unc[...]
by a UVA student. C[...]
his right to discipline a[...]
he suffers no consequen[...]

2

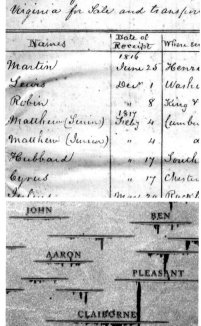

A List of Slaves and Free [...]
Virginia for Sale and transp[...]

Names	Date of Receipt	Where se[...]
	1816	
Martin	June 25	Henr[...]
Lewis	Dec. 1	Wash[...]
Robin	" 8	King [...]
Matthew (Senior)	1817 Feb.y 4	Cumb[...]
Matthew (Junior)	" 4	a[...]
Hubbard	" 17	South
Cyrus	" 17	Chester
[...]	[...]	Roch[...]

3

JOHN   BEN
AARON   PLEASANT
CLAIBORNE
SON
[...]VERLY   LEWI[...]

4

The memorial, which consists of concentric granite rings, expresses many dualities as it opens a space for collective commemoration and personal contemplation. The memorial encourages multiple visitor experiences by layering imagery, form, and aspects of the African diaspora ranging from the ritual ring shout dance to hush harbors to the horrors of the middle passage. The central circle is the gathering space; this inner ring has a timeline of historical events inscribed on a low water table; the concave surface of the inner wall acknowledges a community of individuals both known and unknown; the convex surface of the outer wall creates a canvas for an artistic representation of a community matriarch.

From the rough-hewn, cleft finish of the exterior surface where vertical grooves reference drill patterns in quarried stone, to the precise cuts in the smooth honed interior surface, the memorial aims to express the humanity of the enslaved community and render palpable the injustices and violence they endured.

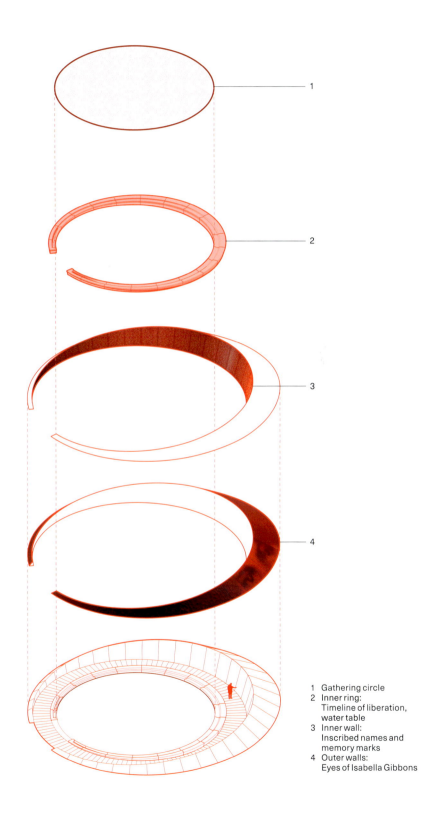

1 Gathering circle
2 Inner ring:
  Timeline of liberation,
  water table
3 Inner wall:
  Inscribed names and
  memory marks
4 Outer walls:
  Eyes of Isabella Gibbons

As visitors walk along the memorial's interior path, the granite wall rises to create a new horizon line that screens out the surrounding context and focuses attention inward. The path gradually declines nearly 2' (60 cm) from the beginning to the center, while the ridgeline ascends to 8' (240 cm) at the wall's highest point.

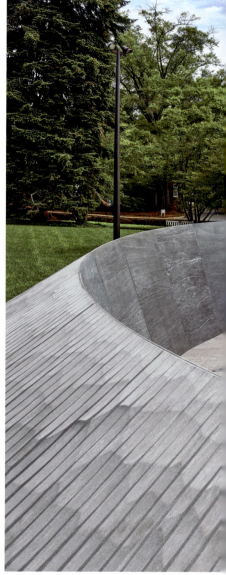

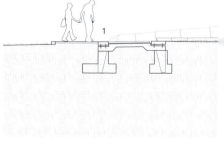

Section

2'   5'   10'

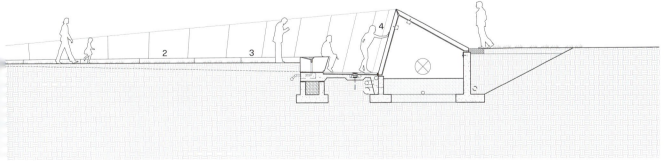

1 Entrance
2 Sloped ledge
3 Water feature
4 Concave stone face
with engraved names

A cross-section through the high point of the memorial shows
the geometry of the landform, its inclined walls, circular path, and
timeline. The section inscribes the human body into the memorial.
The water table timeline set low encourages visitors to bow their
heads as they read the timeline, and the concave interior wall leans
back, encouraging visitors to extend their arms in order to touch
the surface. The convex exterior surface mediates a change in the
ground plane, allowing visitors to see into the memorial's open
bowl from higher ground.

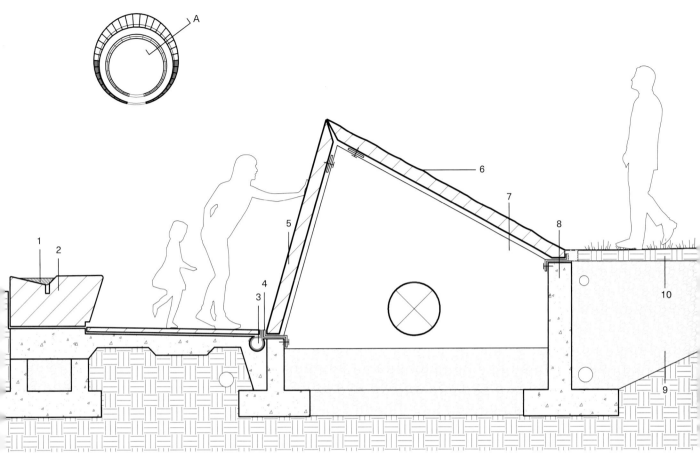

Section Detail A

6" 1'   2'   4'

1   Water feature
2   Stone ledge
3   Gutter
4   Metal clip securing stone
5   Concave stone face with
     engraved names
6   Convex stone face with
     CNC-milled artwork
7   Concrete buttress
8   Concrete retaining wall
9   Compacted structural fill
10 Planting soil

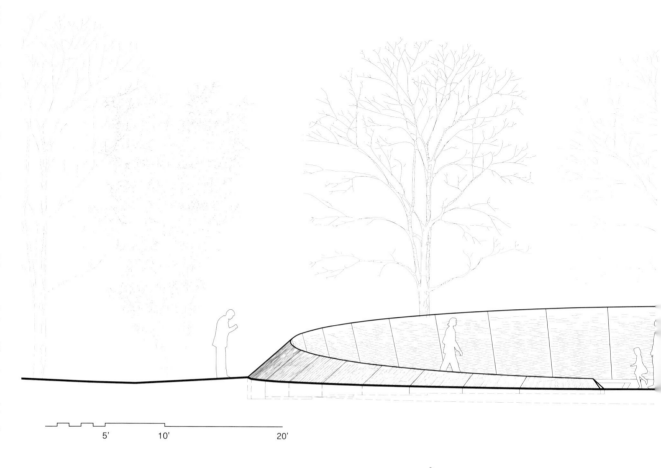

Historians estimate that approximately 4,000 enslaved individuals labored on UVA's grounds between 1817 and 1865, though little detail is known about their lives. While transactional records and accounts of the kind of labor performed exist in archives, identity and humanity are largely absent for many of the enslaved. For approximately 3,000 enslaved persons, the archives include no first or last name. Partial names are known for 577 people, and the record contains few full names. The remaining individuals are known only by their trade and kinship relations.

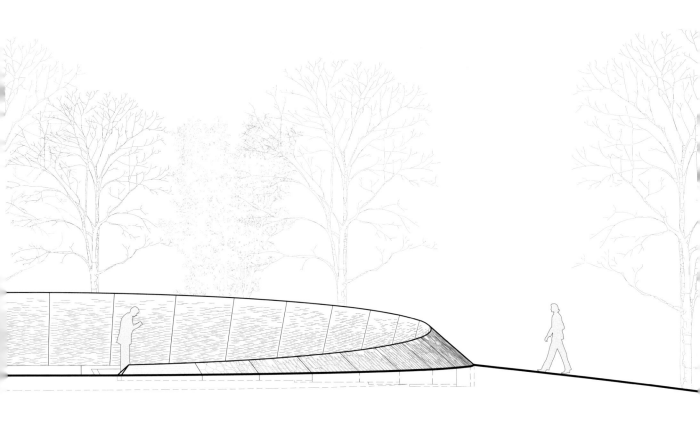

4,000 memory marks underscore the magnitude of slavery at the university. Each mark, representative of an individual life, is carved into the honed granite surface at varying lengths. Known names, kinship relations, trades, and skills are added above the memory marks, creating a genealogical cloud that stretches across the memorial's inner surface. The wall of marks and names functions as an incomplete archive. As new names of the enslaved are discovered and confirmed, they are added above an open memory mark. Five additional names were carved in situ in January 2021.

The central ring combines a water feature and historical timeline of slavery at the university. Seventy entries, beginning with the arrival of enslaved people to Virginia in 1619 and ending with Isabella Gibbons' death in 1890, portray the everyday events, transactions, and the daily violence of slavery at the university. The timeline concludes with Gibbons' words. Running water evokes libation rituals, creating a steady stream that washes over the entire arc of the timeline. The memory marks themselves also hold water — after a rain, water held in the crescent-shaped carvings runs down the memorial wall.

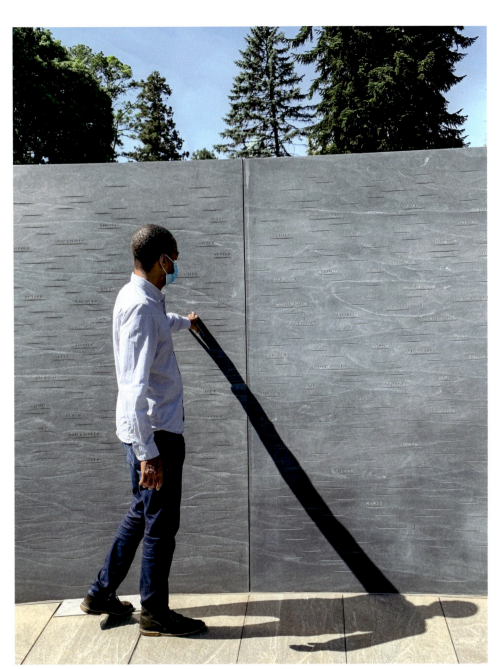

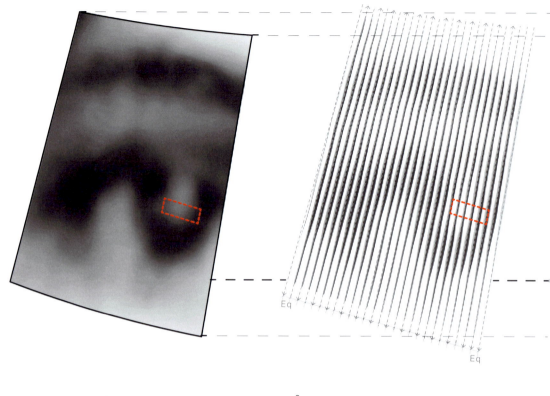

1
Sample

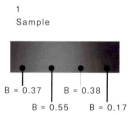

B = 0.37   B = 0.38
     B = 0.55   B = 0.17

2
Section

D = W

W

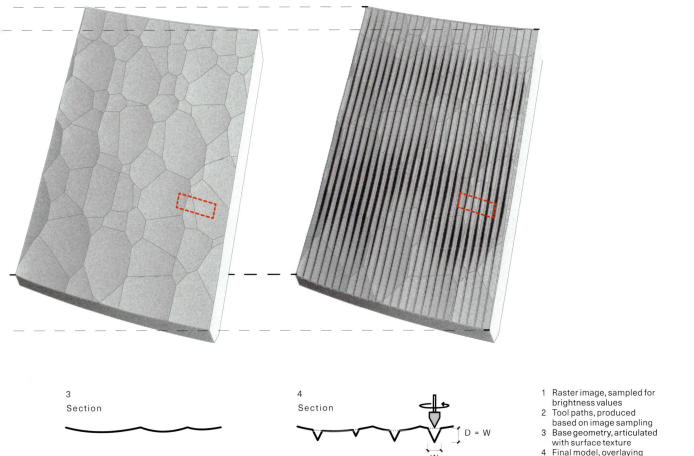

3
Section

4
Section

D = W

W

1 Raster image, sampled for brightness values
2 Tool paths, produced based on image sampling
3 Base geometry, articulated with surface texture
4 Final model, overlaying multiple techniques

Engraved on the northeast side of the outer wall is the likeness of Isabella Gibbons, an enslaved woman who defied the laws of her time by learning to read and write. Gibbons is one of few enslaved people for whom there exists a record of her full name, date of death, a photograph, and an account of her experiences in her own words. Visual artist and collaborator Eto Otitigbe references the eyes of Isabella Gibbons as found in her portrait. A linear milling technique translates her likeness from a raster image into a series of parallel grooves of varying depth. The rough, cleft, and grooved texture of the exterior surface recalls hand-tooled, unmarked cemetery headstones from the period. The image of Gibbons' eyes is inscribed by varying the depth of the grooves in the stone to create an optical effect whereby viewers see the image only from specific perspectives and under certain lighting conditions.

The construction of the memorial required close coordination between the stone fabricator and the general contractor. Using CNC fabrication, each stone was robotically milled to a high tolerance of less than 1/16" (1.5 mm). Each of the seventy-five stone components was carved, finished, and measured before delivery and installation.

Only days after the removal of the construction fence around the memorial, the UVA Medical School's White Coats for Black Lives group organized a gathering and knelt for 8 minutes and 46 seconds in remembrance of George Floyd, a reminder of the racialized violence and injustices that persist with the legacy of slavery. The Memorial to Enslaved Laborers is rooted in a community's collective desire to face the past and advance a more just future. The openness of what is very much an unfinished memorial acknowledges that history is incomplete, and that the work for racial justice is ongoing.

Memorial to Enslaved
Laborers at the University
of Virginia

Location
Charlottesville, Virginia, USA

Team Members
Eric Höweler
J. Meejin Yoon
Namjoo Kim
Caroline Shannon
Anna Kaertner
Alex Li
Julia Roberts
Caleb Hawkins
Boris Angelov

Collaborators
Dr. Mabel O. Wilson (Cultural
Historian and Designer)
Eto Otitigbe (Artist)
Dr. Frank Dukes
(Community Engagement)
Gregg Bleam
(Landscape Architect)

High & Low, Fast & Slow
Conversation
with Adam Greenfield

Writer, designer, and urbanist Adam Greenfield discusses architectural applications of technology as a way to encourage interactive behavior in the public realm.

ERIC
Design culture today seems preloaded with ideas of oversaturation, the digital realm, and their effects on architecture. Technology has permeated our methodologies in design as well as our behaviors and aesthetics.

MEEJIN
To that end, I'm curious how you think the 'digital' installation architecture of the '90s and early 2000s differs from the way digital technology is affecting design today? That moment felt transformational for the discipline. There was significantly more investment in digital technology and interactive media as an aesthetic project than there seems to be today.

Gartner Hype Curve

ADAM
The Gartner hype curve shows us which technologies are the most hyped at the moment, which are being whispered about or emerging from military or corporate R&D, which are robust, and which are fully assimilated. You might begin to hear a lot of chatter about 'direct magnetic levitation' or something like that and then there is this explosive spike in hype around it. Suddenly, everyone you know is talking about it, and entrepreneurs and inventors associated with the development of the technology are on the cover of *Wired*, *Business Week*, and *Forbes*. Then, toward the end of the spike, there is generally a moment that we might call 'mass adoption' as a technology's commercial potential is actualized. And then there's this long, slow curve, which varies for different technologies, toward obsolescence and the cliff-edge where popularity drops off completely.

MEEJIN
Until there is a retro-tech comeback.

ADAM
The weird thing is that very few technologies actually disappear completely from everyday life. The telegraph probably finally disappeared thirty years ago, but in my childhood, you could send a Telex telegram. We've completely assimilated this function into new technologies, like text messaging. In 2001, you may have had academic conferences about text messaging, and these days that just makes us chuckle to even think about. Once all the techniques involved have been mastered, they show up again in a different form, like a kind of ghost haunting the expressive repertoire of the world.

MEEJIN

Maybe that's what happened with interactive architecture. As microprocessors and sensors were becoming available, many designers started asking: what can I do with this? Years later, when we were designing Signal Spire for Boston's Dudley Square, we proposed addressable LED lights as an evolving data map of Boston's neighborhoods. There was pressure to offer interaction with users in a literal way, to make it 'tweetable.' The original moment of surprise produced by dynamic lighting turned into on-demand entertainment.

ADAM

The data underpinning Signal Spire could be transmitted on a personal device. But clearly, the experiential qualities begin to eclipse the purely informational qualities.

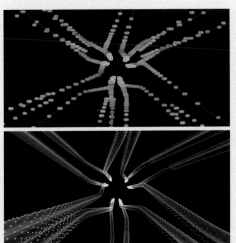

Signal Spire. Höweler + Yoon. Boston, Massachusetts. 2016

ERIC

The question is then about what we expect from that experience. How does it hold our attention? If we aren't satisfied with a broadcast of the everyday performance of the city, then we're looking for entertainment. It becomes a visual spectacle.

MEEJIN

Architecture doesn't have to do what a media device does. Its value is its spatial and material experience, not its entertainment value.

ADAM

A dynamic signaling medium like this is, by definition, a time-based medium, and attention over the lifespan of Signal Spire becomes an acute issue. Everything is flattened into the interface, which has its own prerogatives and constraints. The immediate engagement with the interface is mapped onto every other experience in life.

When the interface becomes spatial, it requires a certain amount of patience, even if you're provided a legend for decoding what's happening. You watch patterns emerge over time, and it may be beautiful, but it's also operating against the logic of the moment. What I've always loved about your practice is that you allude to a time when space itself would evolve in response to use. You create new kinds of affect and possibilities for the people moving through and occupying space.

As practitioners, can you tell me if clients ask for that anymore? Or, why aren't we seeing more of that? Is it simply because it is too expensive? Or, maybe it isn't all that interesting anymore.

ERIC

I think there was a moment when people asked us for work that looked 'high-tech.' For example, in the early 2000s, we were doing design work for a telecom company who asked us to design and configure elements that looked like very advanced technologies for their property. At least in that case, 'media as material' wasn't seen as a public project, but a branding opportunity. It made us question whether blinking and flickering LEDs were the best modes of broadcast.

We are interested in the informational and atmospheric effects of lighting — what effects can come from lighting and sensors — but for us, it is still important to create experiences and behaviors, more than images and graphics, in the public realm. We are interested in how media can integrate with space to create a sonic effect or a playful behavior. Public behavior is largely conditioned to comply with certain norms. If you walk down the street you are going to behave a certain way, and when you get home you might behave entirely differently.

Aviary. Höweler + Yoon. Dubai, UAE. 2013

ADAM

One thing I'm interested in is how suddenly and totally the word 'playful' seems to have cropped up, similarly to the way a given technology shows up on the hype curve. I wonder why it is necessary that a public space be 'playful,' of all things?

We emphasize these things so much because we no longer know how to do them. It's a return of the repressed because we don't ourselves have the time or the energy to play. Our lives are a crushing routine of progression through time, space, and contexts in which we never have enough energy or time to care for ourselves or the people around us.

MEEJIN

That is probably why Swing Time has been so popular. It is deliberate in making a space for play.

ADAM

Yes, the demand to play in public cuts against our routines in some weird ways. But Swing Time carries other associations, too. I mean, this is not an accidental motif. This is the tire-swing-tied-to-the-tree of childhood. This is a technological take on something that is universal in the North American childhood of our generation — something we could associate with carefree moments of summertime. These are potent

Swing Time at the Lawn on D. Höweler + Yoon. Boston, Massachusetts. 2014 indexes of experience. But, because it's technological, it presents the potential for upgrade and adaptation. Its behavior can change. You can almost retrofit the entire environment with a new capability. Maybe the swings now have a gyroscope in them and move on a different axis — or maybe the lighting works differently. Maybe some percentage of the LEDs need to be swinging for any of them to light at all. Software gives you the freedom to modify the behavior of the whole system with relatively low investment. That to me is an arc that extends through the future of all of these discussions.

MEEJIN

That brings me back to your question: did interactive technologies and media as material stop being interesting to us? Not necessarily. Instead, we were suddenly confronted with projects with programs that are meant to communicate in very different ways. The Collier Memorial explicitly needed to be symbolic and representational. Memorials transcend function. Their effect lives outside of what you're asked to do. That was the moment where it seemed like the technology couldn't measure up to the medium of architecture — technology as a medium couldn't quite manage to actually create affect and evoke emotion. In a sense, we are still in transition because we haven't found projects that tie back to the early work yet.

Collier Memorial fabrication. Höweler + Yoon with Quarra Stone. 2015

ADAM

That's a confession, right? A pretty powerful confession.

I would be tempted to live in the transition; not try to force a linkage, but rather to make use of that rupture. I'm going to kind of put words in your mouth right now. This is just me, but it's the confession that traditional tools for modulating built form are still more powerful and communicative to bodies moving through space and time than anything digital technology lets us do.

In the case of the Collier Memorial, you used algorithmic means to shape the space, to choose the contour. If I remember correctly, that was all computational blocks — something that wouldn't have been possible to design or fabricate without computation — but now, computation is buried several levels deep in form. What I see happening in your practice is that technology is being folded in. I see a digital aesthetic, but a less naïve, more mature digital aesthetic. The computation is entirely self-evident to those who know what to look for but may not be as apparent to people occupying the space.

ERIC
Digital fabrication has completely incorporated the highest resolution means to measure and cut stone. Collier was modeled in a digital environment, but it employs the most archaic structural system: a load-bearing arch. Going back to the Gartner curve, it is a technology that is now obsolete because nobody knows how to do it anymore. We needed sophisticated digital means to design one of the oldest structural systems. Just like the telegram and the text message, the arch had to be subsumed by a newer technology in order for us to make it today.

MEEJIN
It bears the traces of technology but also tectonics — hundreds of thousands of years of pressure to create the structural density of stone.

ADAM
That's what happens with things when they're at the fore-end of the hype curve. We learn how to integrate them. We don't need to wear them on our sleeves. That's when it gets interesting — when attention is kind of shifted away from novelty.

MEEJIN
Now that I'm reflecting on it, Collier is similar to White Noise White Light because both, at certain moments, utilized technology that was newly accessible. We happened to do White Noise White Light just as microcontrollers were becoming affordable, and we used them in an original enough way for it to become a project. The same thing happened with the Collier Memorial. We used Grasshopper to customize software to be adaptive for the design of the structure, and new CNC technologies to carve the stone. Synthesizing technologies in a timely way has been critical to our projects.

White Noise White Light. Höweler + Yoon. 2002

ADAM
This difference is the product of a mature industrial capability. Presumably, there are elaborations yet to come as some of that capability is folded back into the design process. But the fluency to work deftly in material is something that arises at a later stage of the evolution of this technology. Before, everything was clunky, clumsy, needy, temperamental — but now, it's far more stable. It's a proposition you can assimilate as a whole because, probably at this point, there are ten years of experience with this technology.

MEEJIN

I think it goes back to your point about how quickly technologies lose their novelty. Architecture is a slow technology, and its power has a different response time. Once you understand what it can do and what it cannot do, that duration can create different effects than responsive media can.

ERIC

We've landed at a place where applied and integrated technology can be quite powerful. For the Collier Memorial, we thought about whether there was a purely technological or ephemeral proposal. I remember seeing a bus go by right after the marathon with an LED banner that read "Boston Strong." DOT traffic signs said, "Remember Fallen Heroes." What's a memorial if not a mnemonic device? What are these displays if not a collective means of broadcasting? They can broadcast "Lanes Closed from 6–7 p.m.", or they can broadcast "Remember Fallen Heroes." All the same, the messages on these devices seemed fleeting because they are continuously replaced by new content. It accelerates the cultural amnesia, and this didn't seem appropriate for the Collier Memorial. In a way, stone has the opposite effect as it tends to create a durable collective memory.

MEEJIN

You could also say that stone can be used as a signboard, just as much as LEDs can be used as a signboard. The difference is that the Collier Memorial creates a space.

ERIC

Which is the oldest architectural goal.

Boston DOT traffic signs

ADAM

Technologies evolve at different rates. Some things move at the speed of stone, others don't. The LED sign is at risk of making the memorial banal by mixing it in with lane-change announcements on the freeway. But because it is so unexpected, it has this capacity to snap you back to the moment. What's important is that you're contributing to the vocabulary of memory in a pretty powerful way. And now that I reflect on this, it's astonishing that your practice excels in these two completely, almost diametrically, different registers — the playful and the memorial.

Chapter II   Means and Methods

On June 4, 1937, a small crowd gathered in Racine, Wisconsin to watch a structural integrity test performed on a full-scale concrete column. The unusual column was only 9" (23 cm) at its base and tapered slightly to its top, where the column flared out to a large disk measuring 18' (540 cm) in diameter. The column, designed by Frank Lloyd Wright for the SC Johnson Wax Administration Building, had been rejected by the Wisconsin Industrial Commission due to its unusual design. The small diameter of the column did not conform to the code as written. Determined to demonstrate the capacity of the dendriform column, Wright had a full-scale mockup built and loaded beyond its design load. The column withstood the load of the 6 tons (5,400 kg) that was required and the 12 tons (11,000 kg) to include the safety factor. The members of the commission were satisfied, but Wright insisted on continuing to load the column. "Keep piling," he shouted. The column was loaded to 30 tons (27,000 kg), and then 60 tons (54,000 kg) (ten times the required amount), before it was toppled. The story of Wright's dramatic structural test, a theatrical display of the architect's "truth against the world" attitude, is now part of the mythology of modern architecture.

The full-scale mockup is a provisional architecture; a partial construction of the future whole, built to test qualities that exceed what can be drawn, calculated, or simulated. The mockup is part of the range of tools — along with drawings, models, material samples, prototypes, and simulations, among others — that precede the building. Together, these anticipatory tools are the instruments of design that inform architectural conception before construction. In the process of translation from drawing to building, myriad tools are used to yield feedback about the

Means and Methods

design prior to selecting a material. The act of design is a foretelling of a materialized future.

The mockup test performed by Wright to demonstrate the structural capacity of the column would be hard to imagine in today's risk-averse culture that strictly separates the domains of architect, contractor, engineer, and Authorities Having Jurisdiction (AHJ). According to the American Institute of Architects (AIA) the contractor "shall be solely responsible for, and have control over, construction means, methods, techniques, sequences and procedures, and for coordinating all portions of the Work under the Contract." In contrast, the architect's role, as defined by the AIA, is concerned primarily with the design intent, the *what,* but has little to say about the specifics of the *how*. Allocating the means and methods by which a building is constructed to the scope of the builder narrows the architect's scope to solely design intent. The separation of intent from implementation, and its legal rationale, reflects the evolution of architectural practice in the context of construction litigation and the emergence of what sociologist and theorist Ulrich Beck calls "risk society."

Even as risk mitigation pushes design away from issues of execution and implementation, digital workflows and Building Information Modeling (BIM) press design toward greater integration with fabrication and construction. As the medium of conveyance for design intent, architectural drawings and digital models are acknowledged as instruments of service to the architect.

Yet, contemporary developments in design software, BIM, project delivery modes, and digital fabrication have blurred the boundaries between representation and execution, disrupting traditional workflows, and creating significant implications for risk and responsibility. Digital documents, where the 3D model is the deliverable, transfer design intent from concept to construction with little need for drawings. The instrumentality of digital design offers opportunities for greater architectural agency while simultaneously requiring new mechanisms for risk management, quality assurance, and verification.

Contemporary processes by which architecture is conceived, modeled, and mocked up illustrate the messy process of translation from concept to construction. How do we leverage the capacities of computational tools (and formats) for fabrication against the backdrop of a risk-averse construction industry and a litigious society? How do we tailor design to the situational context of construction even as we practice in an increasingly globalized world with uneven distributions of technology, skill, and labor? And how do we apply design and its expanded capacities in service of larger questions such as environmental responsibility, social justice, and fair labor practices? If architecture is to have greater agency in addressing the many challenges encompassed by the built environment then questions of material procurement and reuse, embodied energy, and building trades and craft cannot be separated from design.

On the cold, wet morning of April 9, 2015, a small group gathered on the corner of Main Street and Vassar Street in Cambridge, Massachusetts to watch the removal of the scaffold under the Collier Memorial. The construction team had been laboring through a winter of record-breaking snowfall to erect an unusual structure made entirely of solid stone blocks. The blocks were set on a framework of scaffolding, beginning with a central five-sided keystone, and were then placed along their radii proceeding outwards toward the edges. This morning, the scaffold was slowly and carefully lowered from under the keystone, 1/8" (3 mm) at a time. As the threaded sections of the scaffold supports were lowered, the weight of the massive blocks of stone was transferred to each adjacent stone. The scaffold had been constructed on an array of industrial scales to monitor the load transfer from block to block. As the keystone's supports were lowered, the reading on its scale decreased as the reading on the adjacent scales went up. Observing the weight of the blocks transferring from the center to the perimeter, the team determined that the load transfer was occurring as calculated. After eight hours of painstaking work lowering the threaded segments of the scaffolding, 190 tons (170,000 kg) of stone arranged in an asymmetrical arch were unsupported for the first time, and structural engineer John Ochsendorf announced, "We have arching action!"

The industrial scales under the scaffolding were not the only measurement, test, and verification instruments applied to the memorial structure. A team of researchers at MIT also installed strain gauges at the joints between stones to measure displacement during the final phases of construction. The unusual nature of the project, its highly

The design team working through the memorial's assembly sequence.

Lowering the scaffolding at the Collier Memorial and real time verification of load transfer measured on scales.

atypical construction, and compression-only structure transformed the memorial into a design-research project. The Collier Memorial served as a full-scale test case for contemporary design, fabrication, and construction processes that challenged conventional construction sequences and design workflows to realize an unprecedented structure. Combining advanced robotic fabrication and age-old structural principles of masonry vault construction, the project highlights many issues raised by the contemporary digital workflow and provides insights into the iterative process of translation from design through fabrication and construction.

Conceived as an asterisk-shaped form with a void at its center, the memorial forms a vaulted structure that conveys a sense of absence in remembrance of MIT officer Sean Collier. In conceiving of the memorial as a solid stone structure in the earliest stages of design, the initial concept transformed from a geometrical definition of surfaces into solid masses. Conceptualizing the memorial as an irregularly shaped, solid compression vault gave the memorial structural parameters and real constraints. The horizontal thrust of the arch is resisted by the buttress walls, where the length of the wall is proportional to the thrust it is resisting. The buttress walls are arranged to open toward Vassar Street and two of the walls frame a view of the site where Officer Collier was shot, resulting in the asymmetrical geometry of the buttress walls. The keystone at the center is an irregular five-sided polygon that takes its geometry from the perpendicular planes of the force vectors of the buttress walls. The specific geometry of the memorial is a translation from force to form. The horizontal proportion of the arches resulted in high thrust values as well as displacement sensitivity. 1" (25 mm) of displacement laterally would lead to 6" (150 mm) of displacement vertically. To ensure load transfer from block to block, the two faces had to be absolutely parallel to avoid load concentrations. The displacement sensitivity and the need to uniformly transfer loads from one block to another necessitated an extremely precise fit between each block, making precision and near zero tolerance a structural necessity.

Working with Quarra Stone as fabricator and Phoenix Bay State as installers, the design team mapped out a strategy to fabricate thirty-two unique blocks and a sequencing plan to set the stones on site. We reversed the traditional construction sequence and started with the placement of the keystone at the center. We then worked outward so that tolerance could be shed to the edges. First, the keystone was set precisely on scaffolding and located via GPS surveying equipment. The five adjacent ring stones were then fit to the keystone, and eventually, the buttresses were added to complete the memorial. The

entire memorial was assembled in the air, lifted on scaffolding and shims, before the buttress walls were installed to ground the structure.

As a discipline, we have great confidence in digital tools. As digital workflows evolve to turn digital models from tools of conception into instruments of execution, it is easy to overestimate the precision implicit in our tools. With this comes an expectation of perfection and an intolerance for material deviations from the digital ideal, a condition that architect and theorist Francesca Hughes calls the "fetishization of precision."[1] For Hughes, the evolution of the instruments of measurement, design, and fabrication has created expectations between models and material that recategorize much of the physical world as imprecise and nonconforming. An expanded understanding of precision is needed to realign disciplinary thinking around our obsession with precision in the digital age. We have a set of X-Y-Z coordinates that tell us the precise dimensions of a 3D model. In translating the digital model to a material like stone we think we know where the stone is supposed to begin and end.

How can we be sure of the exact limits of the stone when we are not sure of the exact limits of the tools carving the stone? The stone is carved by the robotic diamond-tipped saw, and the saw is also worn down by the stone over time. The stone yields to the saw as material is removed, and the diameter of the saw is also diminishing. These questions about digital processes, precision, material, and means of measure illustrate Hughes' argument about exactitude and error. In questioning the precise limits of the stone relative to the diameter of the saw, we challenged our fundamental understanding of precision in digital fabrication. Both the stone and the saw are material artifacts with particular properties of density and hardness. And, both materials wear, albeit at different rates, creating a cumulative imprecision that requires regular

Engineer John Ochsendorf with circular block saw equipment.

recalibration of the saw to verify its actual dimensions, and accordingly, regular updates to the tool paths.

The unusual means and methods applied to the Collier Memorial called for careful coordination between the design, fabrication, and installation teams. The process of structural design raised critical questions for providing redundancy in an all-compression structure. The fabrication specifications for the stone necessitate unique processes for precise fabrication, quality control, and verification to ensure that the unique blocks fit together precisely on site. And finally, the erection plan requires a rethinking of the construction sequence to manage the tolerance from center to perimeter. At each step, field conditions exert pressure on the design and provide continuous feedback from processes of peer review, instrumentation, measurement, monitoring, and confirmation — all of which impact the design intent as well as the means and methods of fabrication and construction.

While the Collier Memorial takes advantage of state-of-the-art modeling and fabrication technologies, the Sky Courts project, in Chengdu, China, addresses a different set of questions regarding construction, labor, and translation for a project built across great geographical distance. Sky Courts challenged us to address the

client's desire to evoke traditional Chinese architectural and material qualities in contemporary ways.

The design was organized around a series of outdoor courtyards and employed local gray brick as a base material punctuated by a pattern of windows with tapered weathered steel surrounds. In communicating with the Local Design Institute (LDI) and the contractor, our two sheets of brick detail drawings described the simple logic for laying bricks: orient them to the cardinal directions, as if each had an internal compass. This rule, applied to the most basic unit of construction, transformed the appearance of the building in dramatic ways. As the walls turn corners and the plan geometry deviates from the orthogonal, the brick pattern maintains its global orientation, resulting in a serrated brick pattern on the oblique walls.

Sky Courts tailors a design strategy to the capabilities of local bricklayers to translate from design intent to built reality. The logic of brick orientation provided a rule that was easily translatable to the local brick masons in the field. The design intent anticipates the means and methods of construction and encodes those constraints in the design. In recognizing that the field is indeed a global practice, the Sky Courts project acknowledges that parameters include local labor, available materials, and cross-cultural communication.

Operating within a very different kind of field, the historic fabric of Boston's Bay Village neighborhood and local unionized labor markets, 212 Stuart Street employs a different set of contextual strategies and constructional logics that highlight the push and pull between design intent and the means and methods of construction. The

Transition in the brick wall at Sky Courts.

nineteen-story residential tower is sited on the edge of the historic neighborhood and is subject to the Boston Landmarks Commission. The façade design consists of bundles of fluted precast concrete piers that give the tower a solid appearance and resonate with the masonry detailing of nearby historic structures.

We initially assumed the number of unique molds would drive the cost of the project. The precast piers, produced from a set number of unique molds, are interchanged to create variation and repetition. The piers are two and three stories tall to save time in the erection process. The combination of limited molds and multi-story piers sought to optimize the design based on those variables. Feedback from the construction manager and the precast fabricator suggested that the real driver of cost is the time it takes to pick and place piers in the field. Equipped with this information, we redesigned the façade composition to create panels optimized for crane capacity and the erection schedule as opposed to the number of unique molds.

The fluted vertical pattern of the precast panels contrasts with the taut glazing infill between them. The fluted precast piers form a concave profile that is 12" (30 cm) deep at the edges and 5" (12 cm) deep at its narrowest point. The depth of the piers creates an articulated pattern on the façade and the shadows cast by the piers animate the building's elevations. The weight of the

precast panels is carried by the concrete slabs, transferred to the columns, and brought down to the foundation. Throughout the process of value engineering, we sought to reduce the cost of the project by making the panels lighter, the slabs thinner, and the foundation shallower to reduce the weight and overall project cost. The final design represents a trade-off between the amount of surface articulation, the weight of the precast piers, the thickness of the concrete slabs, and the depth of the mat foundation.

The design for 212 Stuart Street was calibrated to the mechanized means and methods of high-rise construction in Boston, where time and labor are at a premium. What is true in politics is also true in construction: all construction is local. Every project, whether it is built in Boston or Chengdu, Somerville or Shanghai, must engage in the specifics of context, including available materials, processes and sequences, labor, skill, and trades. By incorporating information about procurement and processes, architects can reclaim both instrumentality and innovation — and therefore, agency — through the design process.

While the means and methods of construction are, strictly speaking, the responsibility of the builder, a holistic approach to conceptual design cannot ignore implementation. Questions of sequencing, constructability, and tolerance are integral to a comprehensive design process. Limiting liability has

Installing multi-story "fluted" precast concrete panels at 212 Stuart St.

distanced designers from the processes of construction, ceding authority over materials and methods, the very medium of architecture. At the same time, the digital design processes, as well as the applicability of digital tools in fabrication and construction, shifts toward more integration of conception and construction. The contingencies of construction, as articulated in the verify in field notation, necessitate the development of techniques for absorbing and incorporating contingency. They call for new strategies that allow verification, integration, and tolerance to become drivers of design. By maintaining a comprehensive view of the design and construction processes, architects can ask urgent questions facing the built environment today. Questions calling for designers to better understand the *what* and *how* — and critically, the *why* of our choices.

Even as we work to develop designs tailored to specific contexts and capabilities for construction, it is important to distinguish means from ends. An integrated approach to assembly and sequencing might yield an innovative structural solution and expand the material imagination, but the means and methods of that process are still the means to an end. How materialized concepts interact with a public, how they serve their communities and transform the lives of their occupants, is the product of all preceding design and construction processes. Only by thinking through the physicality of architecture, the matter and medium of our material imagination, can we reclaim agency and realign disciplinary thinking so that architecture is the means by which we make a meaningful impact on the world.

1. Francesca Hughes, *The Architecture of Error, Matter, Measure, and the Misadventures of Precision*, MIT Press, 2014, p.5.

Sean Collier Memorial

If architecture is to have more agency in addressing the challenges of the built environment — from climate change to labor practices — then questions of material procurement and reuse, building trades and craft, and embodied energy, cannot be separate from design.

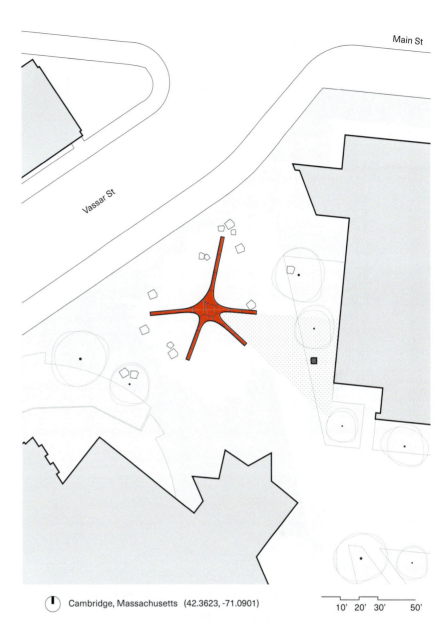

Cambridge, Massachusetts (42.3623, -71.0901)

10' 20' 30'   50'

The Collier Memorial, built in memory of MIT officer Sean Collier who was killed by the perpetrators of the 2013 Boston Marathon bombing, takes the form of a vaulted five-pointed figure. Located at the site of the tragedy on MIT's campus, the memorial is a sculptural form that represents loss and absence as well as strength and unity.

Hollowed out of a five-pointed figure is a central void. This conspicuous absence is legible through the subtraction of one volume from another. A Boolean difference operation subtracts an ovoid figure from the five-pointed figure to create a space of remembrance, permit passage, and frame views. The central void is further differentiated by contrasting stone finishes: smooth, honed stone is found on the inside while a rough, flamed finish covers the memorial's exterior.

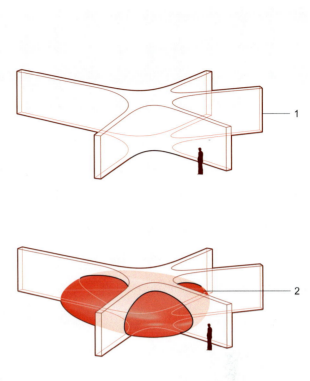

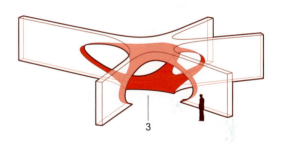

1   Five-pointed extrusion
2   Solid figure
3   Void space

The five-pointed figure that results from the carving process forms an irregular arch and stone vault supported by each block that transfers force through a fully compressive structure. A design workflow combining digital models and custom computational tools allowed the design team to calibrate the form and calculate the structure simultaneously.

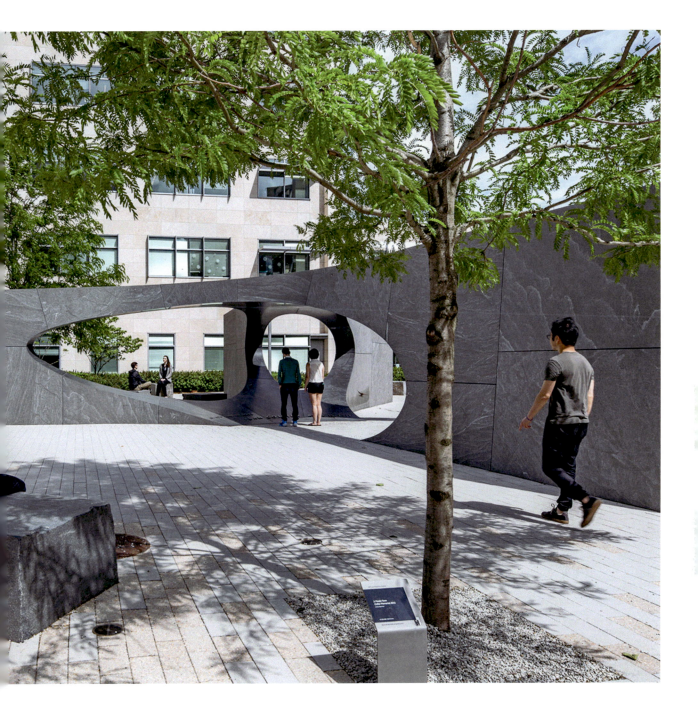

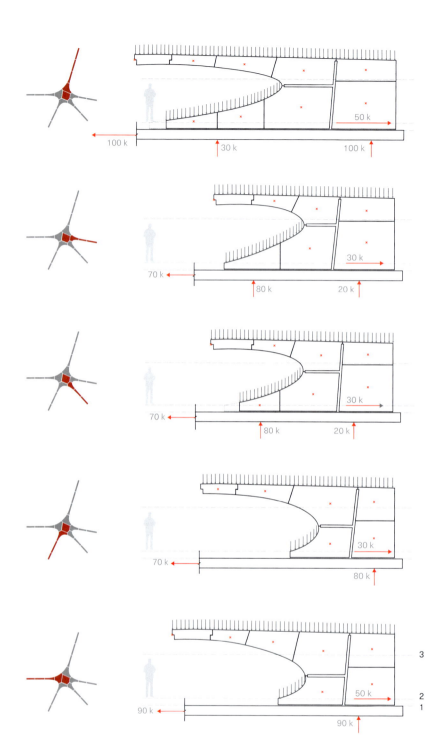

1   Gradebeam level
2   Ground level
3   Head height clearance

*all forces noted in Kips

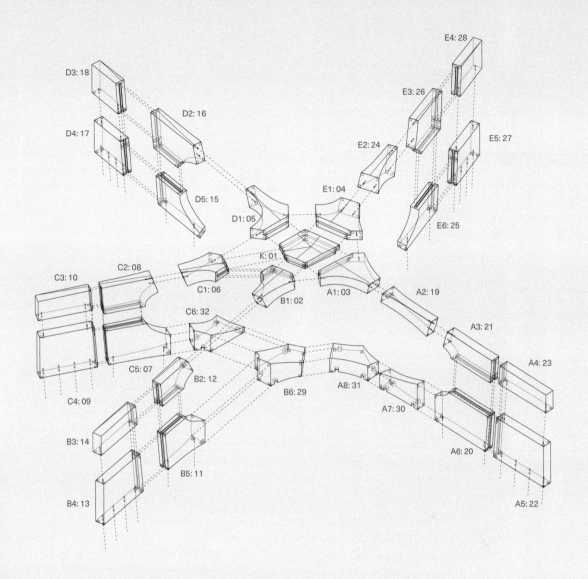

Typically understood in two dimensions, compressive arches transfer loads from the keystone through consecutive stones until forces are resolved at the ground. In this irregular configuration, each buttress wall carries force through the consecutive blocks to the ground, with longer buttress walls corresponding to higher thrust vectors. The individual design of each stone foregrounds the part-to-whole relationship. Angled joint lines in the elevation index the perpendicular force trajectories of the stone blocks, rendering the structural thrust legible within the monolithic figure.

89

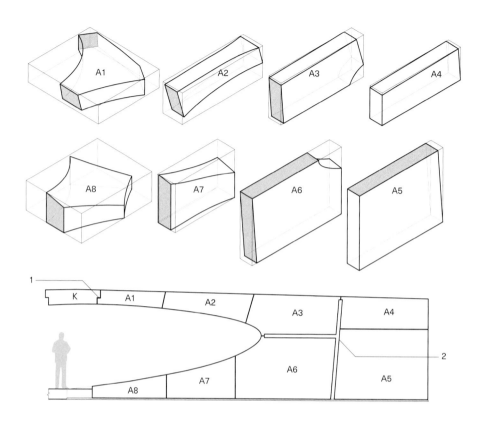

Fabrication of the Collier Memorial's unique blocks required the use of a diverse array of fabrication tools including saws, CNC mills, and multi-axis industrial robots. The carving process began with a rough stone block that became a bounding box onto which the final geometry was superimposed.

1 Shelf connection
2 Keyway joint

Consecutive cutting operations removed material with increasing degrees of precision. A near zero dimensional tolerance ensured the load transfer between blocks of the stone arch. Joints between stones were designed to be 1/4" (6 mm) wide, requiring extreme precision in both fabrication and installation. Each stone was lifted into position and supported by scaffolding while the stone's precise location was verified by digital surveying equipment.

Traditional arches are built with scaffolding and falsework, sequencing assembly from the buttresses to the center with the keystone completing the arch. However, the precision required at the Collier Memorial necessitated a reverse process, starting with the keystone and working outward so that any tolerance would be driven away from the center. The five-sided irregular keystone was set first, followed by the five adjacent ring stones that are fitted to the keystone.

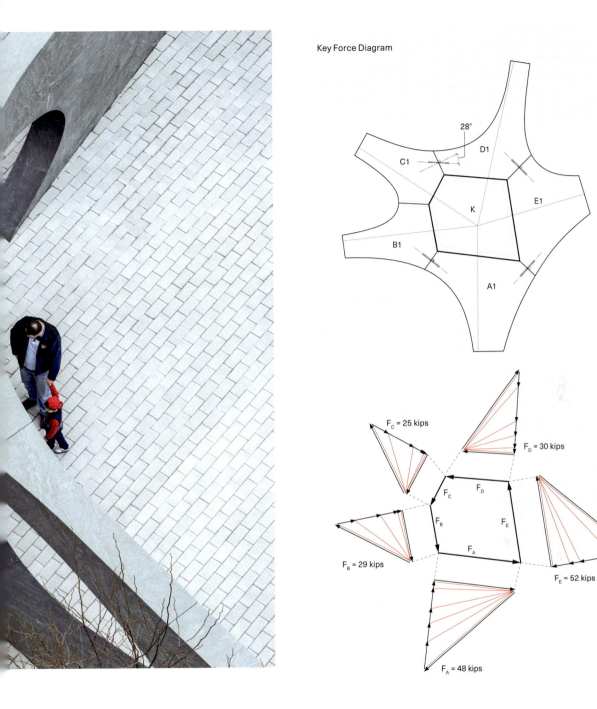

Key Force Diagram

$F_C = 25$ kips

$F_D = 30$ kips

$F_B = 29$ kips

$F_E = 52$ kips

$F_A = 48$ kips

The geometry of the keystone derives from the irregular angles of the five buttress walls, and the faces of the keystone are perpendicular to the thrust vectors of each wall.

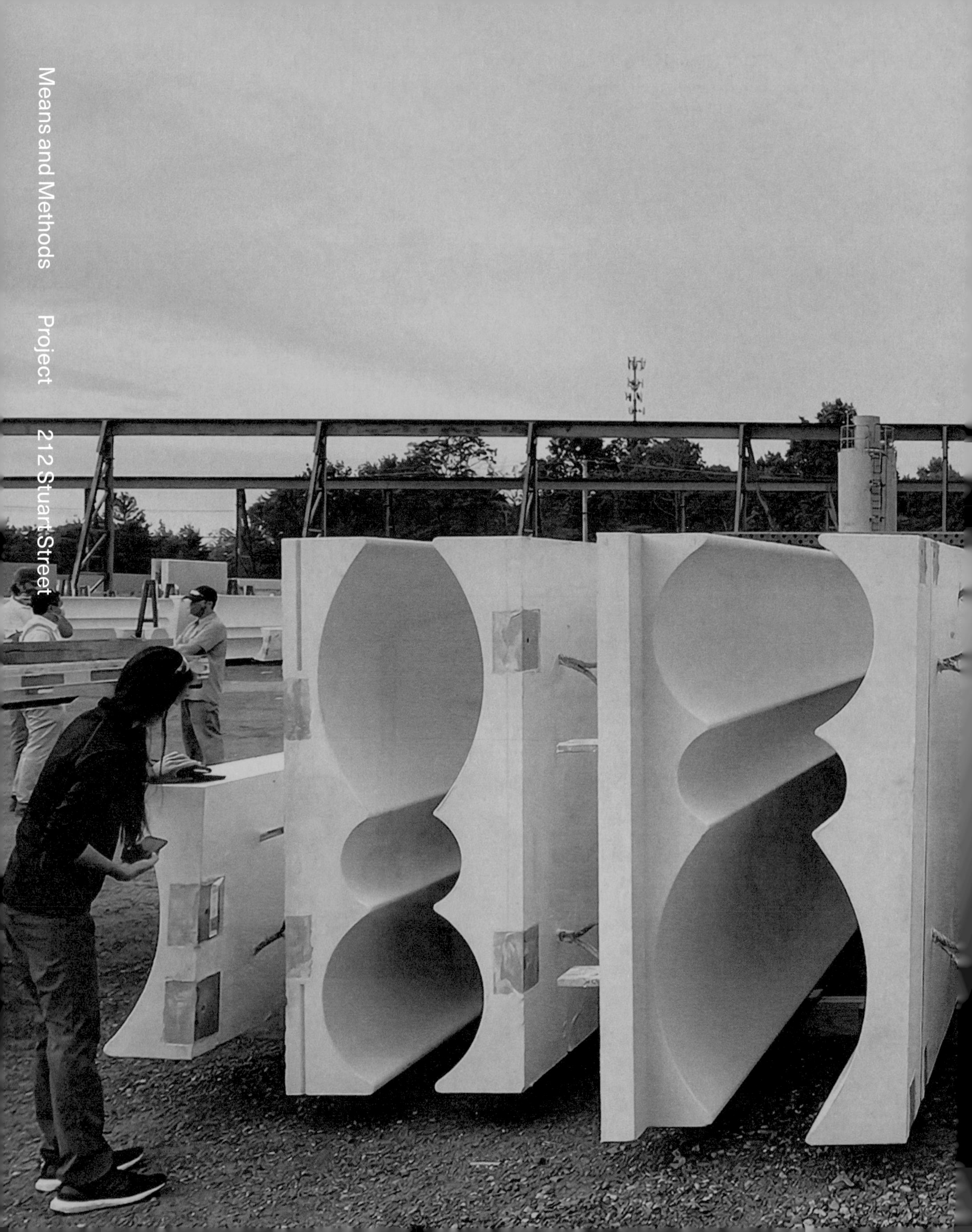

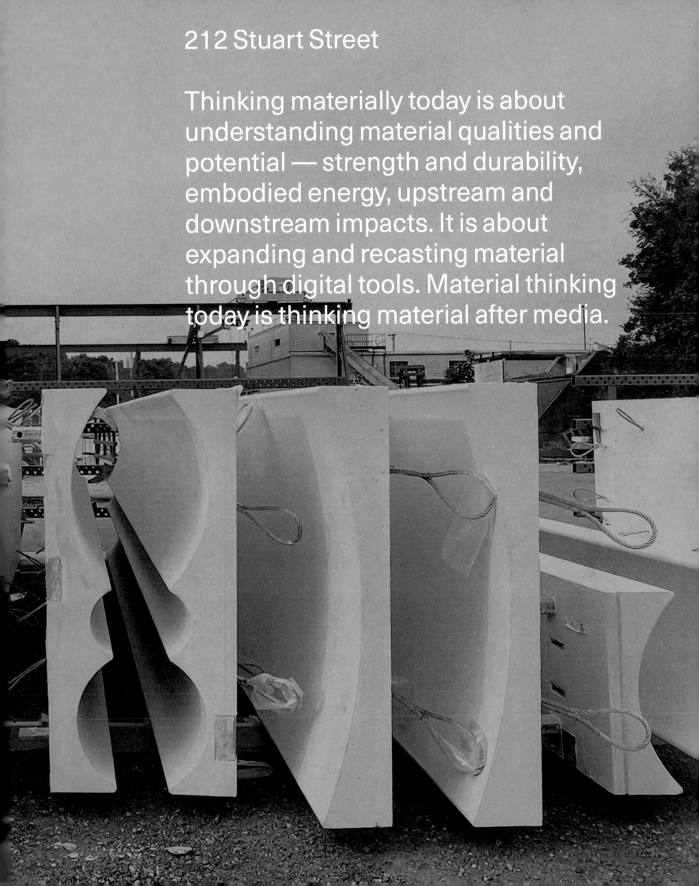

212 Stuart Street

Thinking materially today is about understanding material qualities and potential — strength and durability, embodied energy, upstream and downstream impacts. It is about expanding and recasting material through digital tools. Material thinking today is thinking material after media.

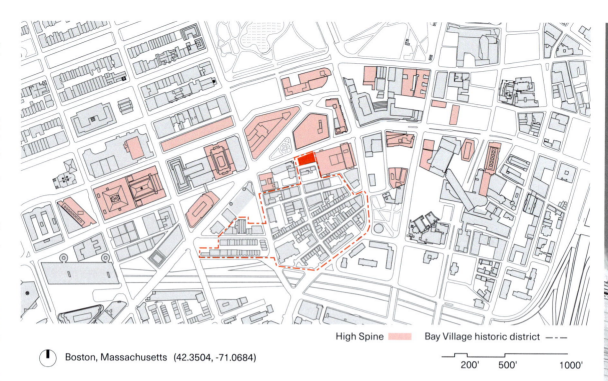

High Spine ▭   Bay Village historic district ———

Boston, Massachusetts (42.3504, -71.0684)

200'   500'   1000'

212 Stuart Street employs classical elements, like fluted piers arranged in horizontal courses, to create contemporary effects that resonate with its historic context. Situated at a threshold between two neighborhoods, the design of the building negotiates the intimate, fine-grain residential scale of Bay Village and the monumental scale of buildings along Boston's High Spine.

Ground Floor Plan

1 Retail space
2 Residential lobby
3 Townhouse unit one
4 Townhouse unit two
5 Pedestrian promenade
6 Stuart Street
7 Shawmut Street

5' 10' 20' 50'

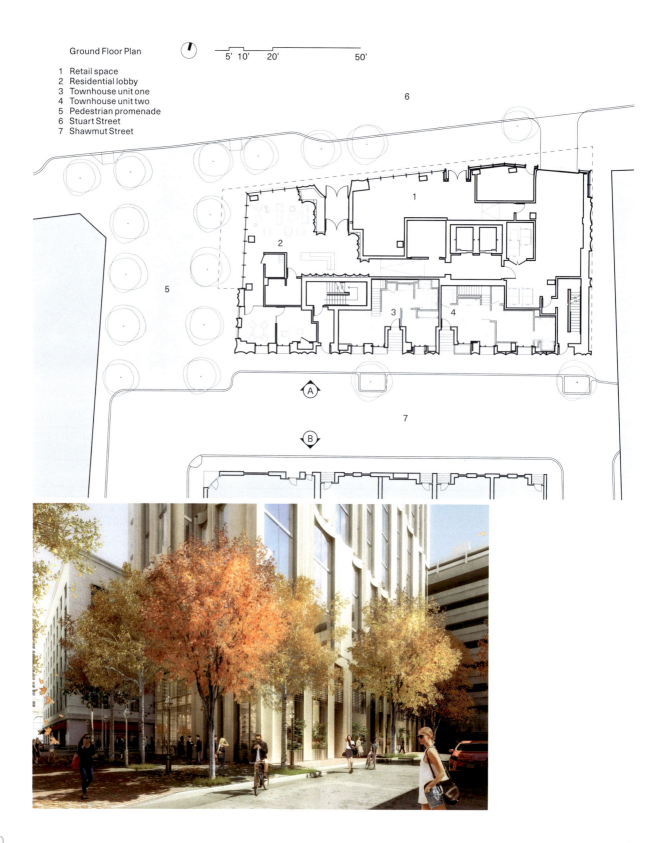

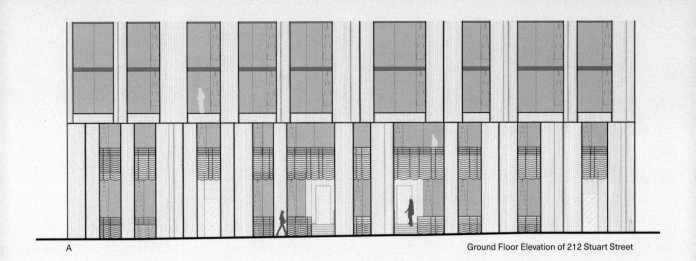

A

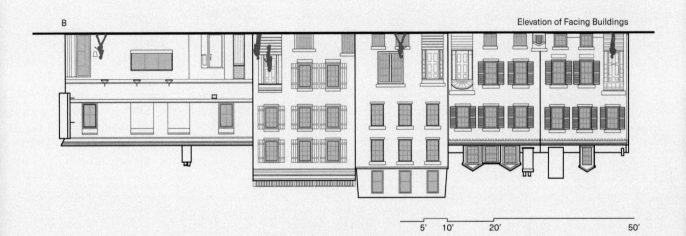

B

Elevation of Facing Buildings

5' 10' 20' 50'

212 Stuart Street operates at several scales in the city. When viewed from a distance, the building meets the sky with a distinctive silhouette and adds to the composition of the Boston skyline. At the street level, the building meets the ground in a way that immediately engages with the sidewalk and streetscape as stoops, planters, and decorative ironwork create a dialogue with the residential context of Bay Village. This nineteen-story building also contains two townhouses that complete the north side of the Bay Village streetscape.

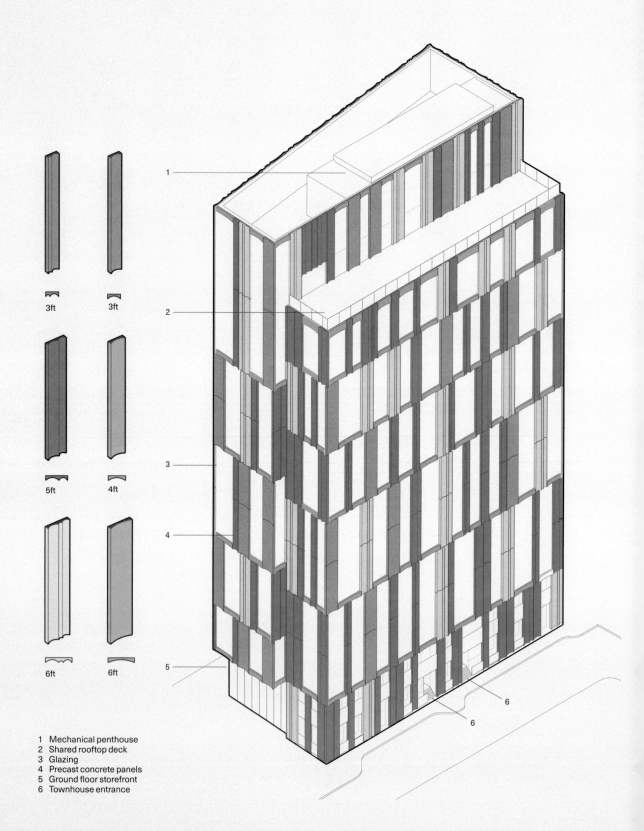

3ft   3ft

5ft   4ft

6ft   6ft

1 Mechanical penthouse
2 Shared rooftop deck
3 Glazing
4 Precast concrete panels
5 Ground floor storefront
6 Townhouse entrance

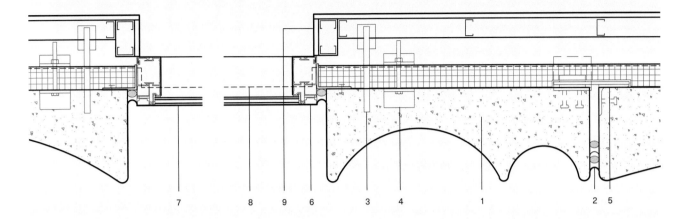

1 Multi-story precast concrete panel
2 Two lines backer rod and sealant
3 Precast gravity connection
4 Precast lateral connection
5 Slab cover precast gravity connection
6 Window wall jamb mullion
7 Face of glass
8 Edge of slab
9 Interior finish

Plan Detail

3" 6"   1'   2'

Organized into discrete packages of two, three, four, five, and six stories, the façade expression diminishes its apparent height while emphasizing the vertical grain of the building. The façade consists of irregularly spaced opaque panels and the window wall glazing which occupies gaps between the panels. The number of concave profiles was optimized to reduce reliance on unique molds yet maintain the appearance of a highly varied façade pattern. The width of the modules was optimized to limit the number of crane picks needed to erect the façade. The building envelope was coordinated with precast concrete fabricators and façade installers in early phases of design and construction.

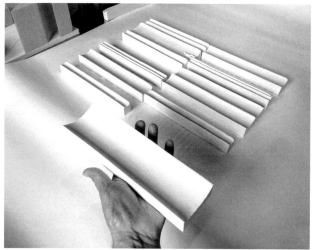

The façade features custom, fluted multi-story precast panels with a concave geometry. Preliminary studies in plaster and limestone tested the effect of light and shadow on the concave geometry. A series of full-scale mockups in EPS foam were used to test and develop the final geometry of the concavities and module sizes. Additional precast concrete visual mockups were produced to verify the final precast color mix, finish, and texture.

The installation of multi-story precast concrete panels minimized on-site construction time. We worked with the local precast manufacturer to optimize the panel geometry for weight and depth in order to reduce the dead load on the slab edge while amplifying the visual effect of shadows on the façade.

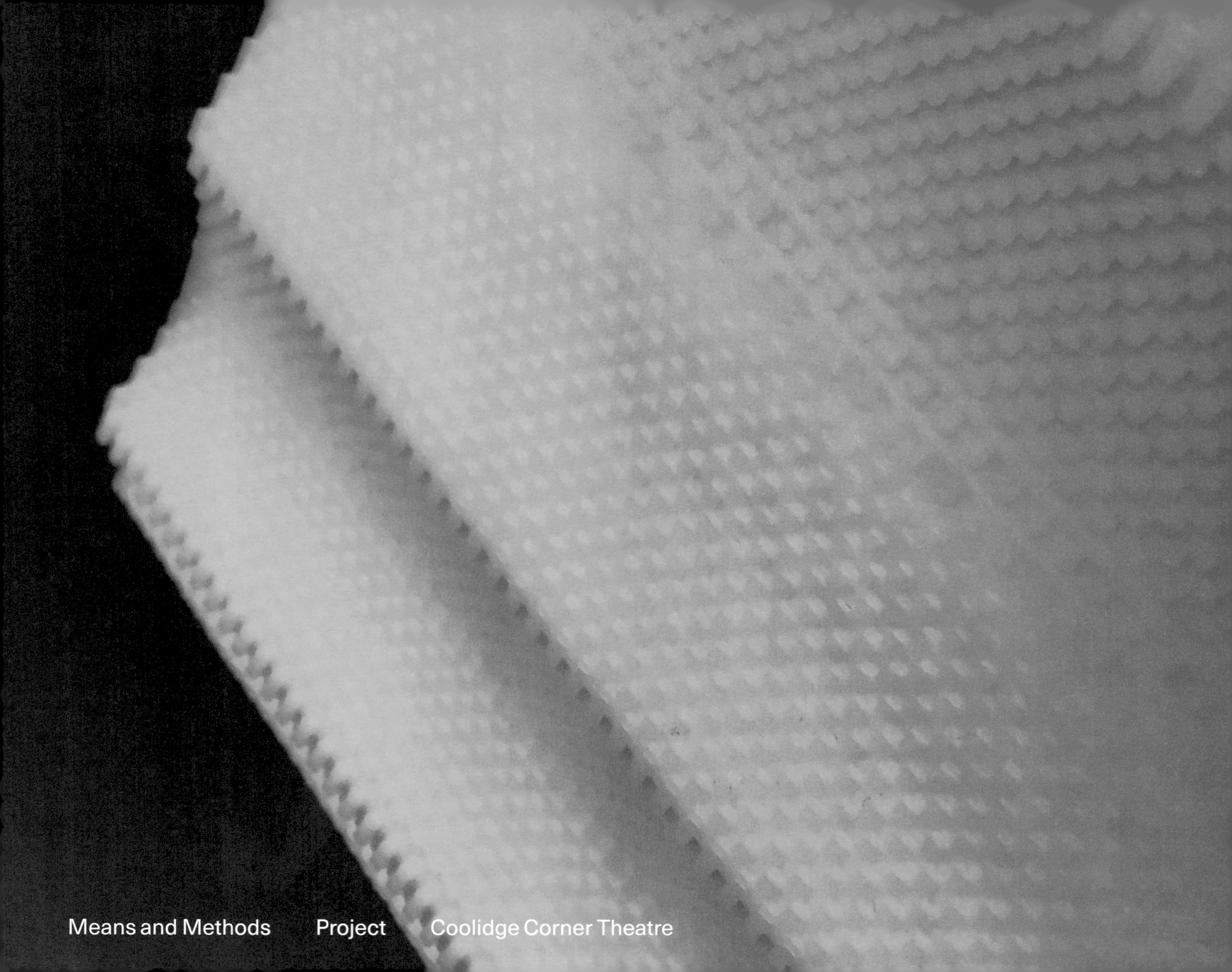

Means and Methods Project Coolidge Corner Theatre

Distinguishing means from ends —
and process from impact — material
decisions and construction processes
determine how a concept interacts
with a public, serves its community, and
affects the lives of its occupants.

Harvard St

Beacon St

Brookline, Massachusetts (42.3427, 71.1225)

20' 50'   100'   200'

The Coolidge Corner Theatre is a nationally renowned independent nonprofit cinema in Brookline, Massachusetts. The 14,000 square-foot (1,300 sq m) addition to the original 1933 art deco building reconfigures and expands this beloved community institution. This project turns the back of the theater into a new front, doubling the lobby's square footage and adding two new theaters, a community room, and a film library.

The addition expands the historic building within the constraints of its irregular and narrow site. Built on what was previously a parking lot, two new theaters cantilever over the new south-facing entrance.

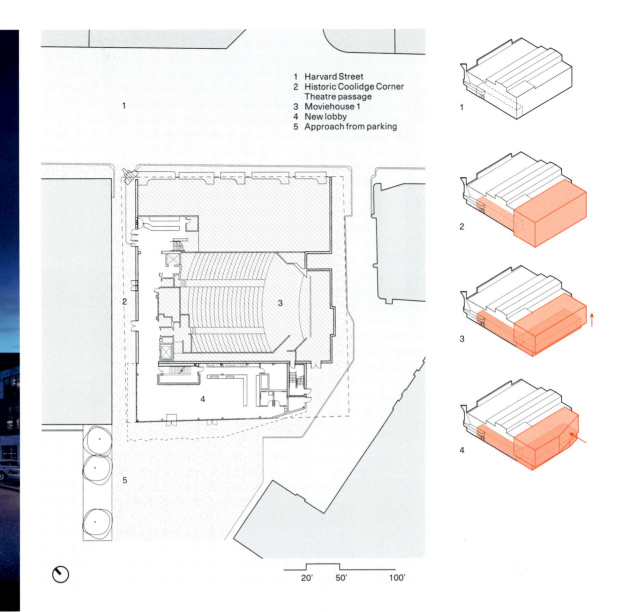

1 Harvard Street
2 Historic Coolidge Corner
  Theatre passage
3 Moviehouse 1
4 New lobby
5 Approach from parking

20' 50' 100'

1

2

3

4

Rather than queue for tickets in the side alley, the new lobby draws guests across the site and reorients the moviegoing sequence. The site includes a parking area that can transform to host outdoor community events and movie screenings.

The addition is articulated as a distinct
volume on the building's exterior. Preliminary
studies of the building massing reflect
textures and patterns derived from the art
deco motifs of the original 1933 building.

1 Multipurpose room
2 Brick "curtain" façade
3 Moviehouse 5
4 Existing theater
5 New lobby

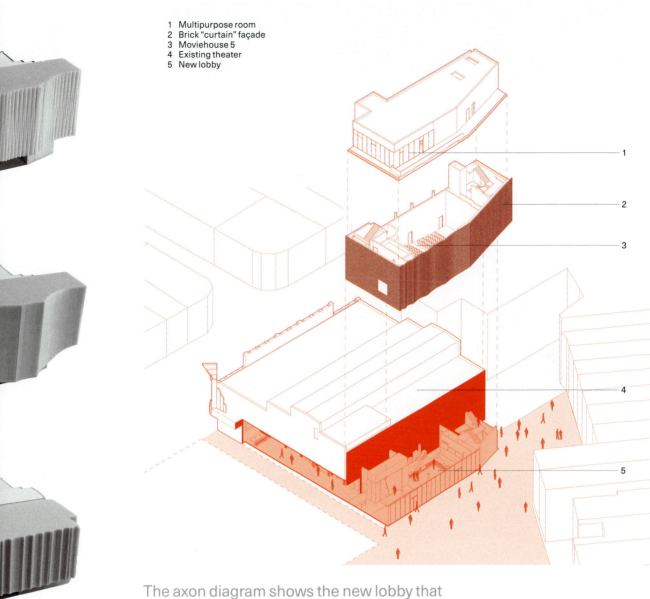

The axon diagram shows the new lobby that connects to the original lobby at grade and the setback volume of the community room located on the third floor.

A

Section A

5'   10'   20'

The Coolidge hosts more than 200,000 guests annually.
To meet this demand, the project adds two theaters
(approximately 200 seats) to the existing four movie houses,
allowing the Coolidge to expand and diversify its film
offerings. The second-floor plan includes a new 150-seat
theater and board room. The third-floor volume is set back
from the volume below and contains a fifty-seat theater, a
community room, and a catering kitchen.

Plan Level 03

1 Moviehouse 6
2 Multipurpose room
3 Catering
4 Corridor
5 Bathroom
6 Outdoor deck
7 Elevator
8 Stair
9 Roof of existing theater

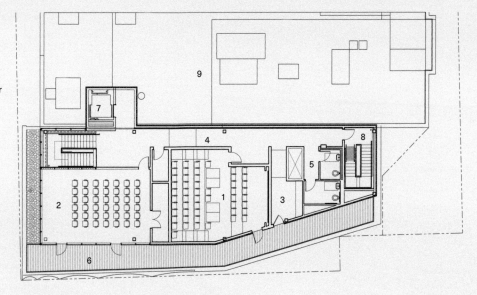

Plan Level 02

1 Moviehouse 5
2 Board room/Library
3 Corridor
4 Bathroom
5 Elevator
6 Stair

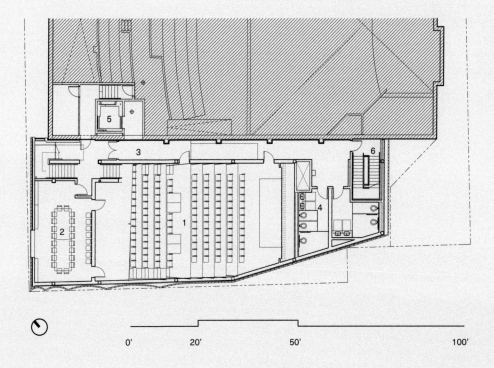

0'   20'   50'   100'

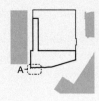

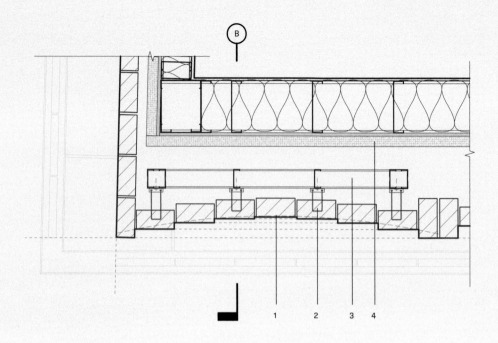

Plan Detail A

1 Stepped brick wall
2 Masonry wall ties
3 Metal framing
4 Mineral wool board insulation

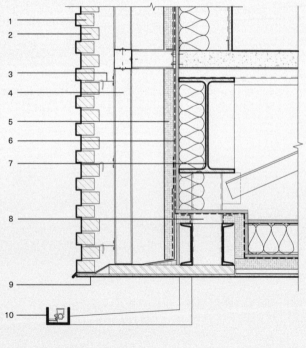

Section Detail B

1 Brick course A
2 Brick course B
3 Masonry wall tie
4 Metal framing
5 Mineral wool board insulation
6 Vapor barrier
7 Steel beam
8 Steel post
9 Custom steel relieving angle
10 Continuous tray for adjustable
   LED fixture

3" 6"   1'   2'   3'

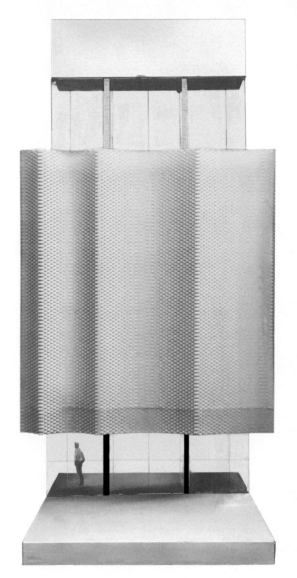

The articulated brick façade plays on the art deco motifs from the original building. A series of large concave profiles accentuate the corner while the scale and texture of the individual bricks is retained, giving the overall texture a deliberate granularity that subtly affects perception and scale.

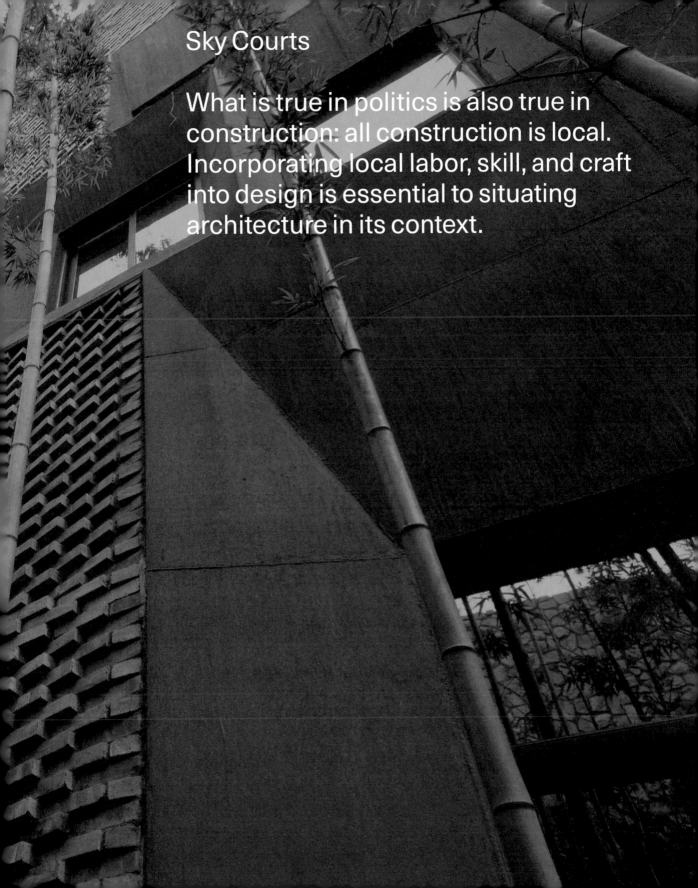

Sky Courts

What is true in politics is also true in construction: all construction is local. Incorporating local labor, skill, and craft into design is essential to situating architecture in its context.

Chengdu, Sichuan Province   (30.6676, 103.9322)

10m 30m 50m   100m

Sky Courts exhibition hall houses a variety of aggregated
exhibition galleries and programs in one large building.
Located in the IIC Park in Chengdu, China, the building
uses strategies from traditional vernacular courtyard
typologies to create a range of open spaces within the
interior of the deep floor plan.

1 Brick wall (west-southwest)
2 Brick wall (north)
3 Brick wall (west)
4 Brick wall (north-northwest)
5 Weathered steel window frame
6 Entrance
7 Courtyard gardens

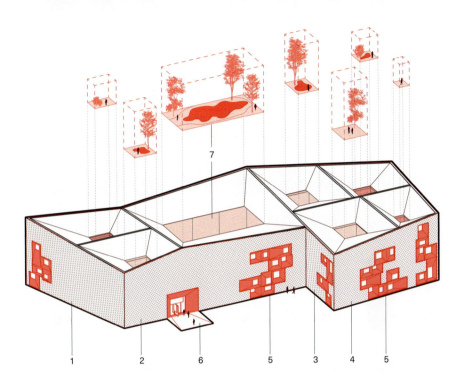

Subdivided into a series of exhibition halls wrapped
around exterior spaces, the design introduces seven
courtyards to bring natural light and air deep into the
plan. Each gallery encloses a courtyard and negotiates
between the space's orthogonal geometries and the
oblique perimeter geometries. The organization of
the interior galleries and exterior gardens produce an
exhibition hall that is at once open and divided. The
sequence through these wrapped perimeter gallery
halls creates a series of layered spaces that visitors
can see through — from one courtyard to another, and
another — from inside to outside, to inside again.

Plan Level 02

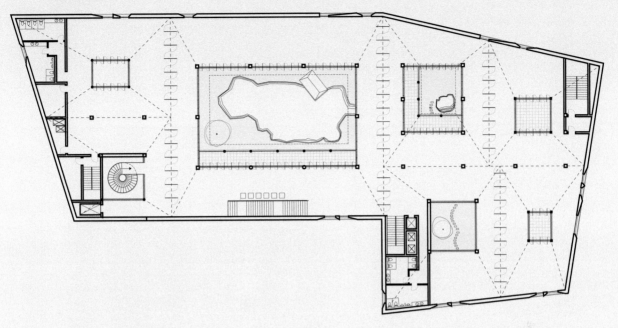

Plan Level 01

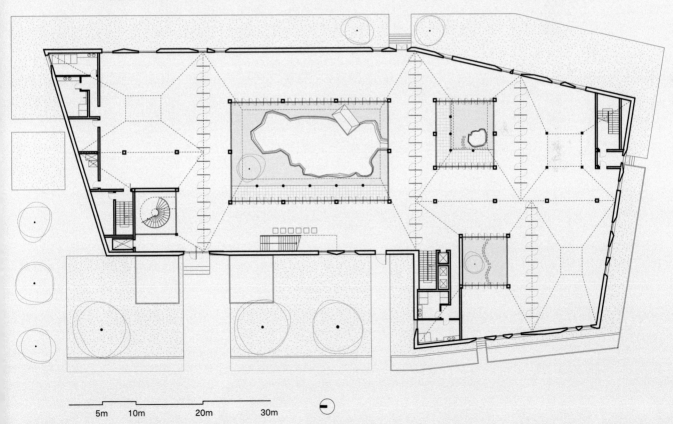

5m   10m   20m   30m

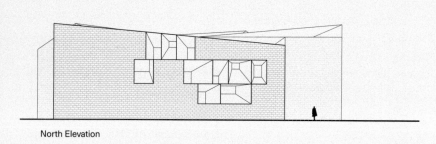

North Elevation

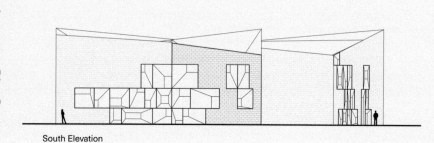

South Elevation

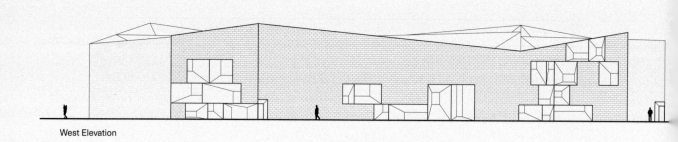

West Elevation

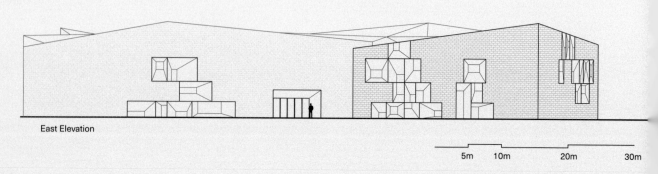

East Elevation

5m   10m   20m   30m

The ridge lines between courtyard cells produce inflection points on the profile of the exterior wall, which rises and falls to create a distinctive silhouette. The composition of the windows forms clusters that combine small punched windows and operable doors. Weathered steel window surrounds organize the windows and doors, strategically creating an intermediate figure that negotiates between the scale of a window and the scale of the building massing.

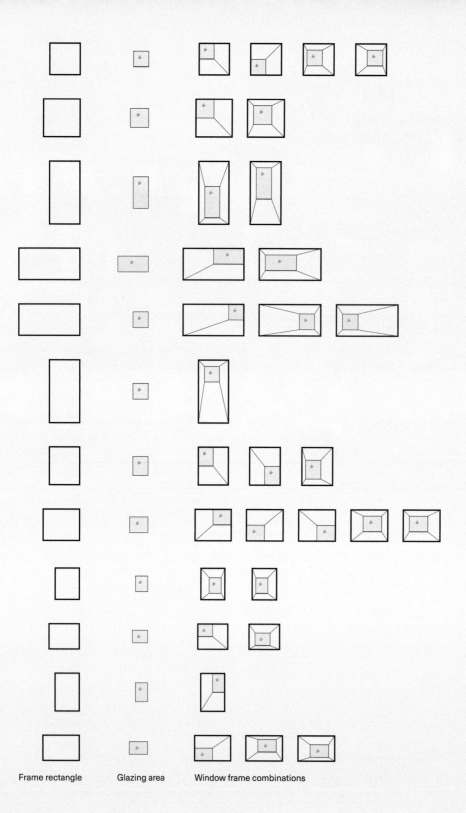

Frame rectangle   Glazing area   Window frame combinations

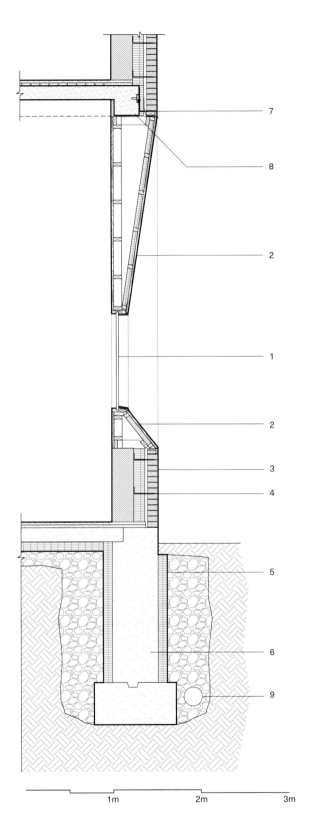

The building's façade emphasizes the depth of the wall and amplifies the scale of the windows with the tapered geometry of the window surrounds. Ten different window sizes, combined with ten larger rectangular frames, create thirty-one unique window surround types based on the placement of the window within the frame. The oxidized weathered steel surrounds offer a sharp contrast in color and texture against the locally produced gray bricks.

7

8

2

1

2

3

4

5

6

9

1m   2m   3m

Section Detail

1   Inset window
2   Weathered steel window surrounds
3   Brick façade
4   Masonry tie
5   Rigid insulation
6   Concrete footing
7   Steel shelf angle
8   Concrete beam
9   Drainage pipe

All of the building's bricks are oriented along the cardinal directions, producing a staggered texture on the façade's oblique faces. The articulation of the brickwork gives the building its distinct appearance and negotiates the local condition of the brick with the universal geometry of the site. Corners between smooth and textured faces signal a transition from cardinal to diagonal geometries. The detailed brick pattern was tailored to the available skill and labor in Chengdu and a simple set of rules contributed to its successful execution. The combination of smooth and textured bricks offers subtle cues for visitors and helps create a sense of orientation around the building.

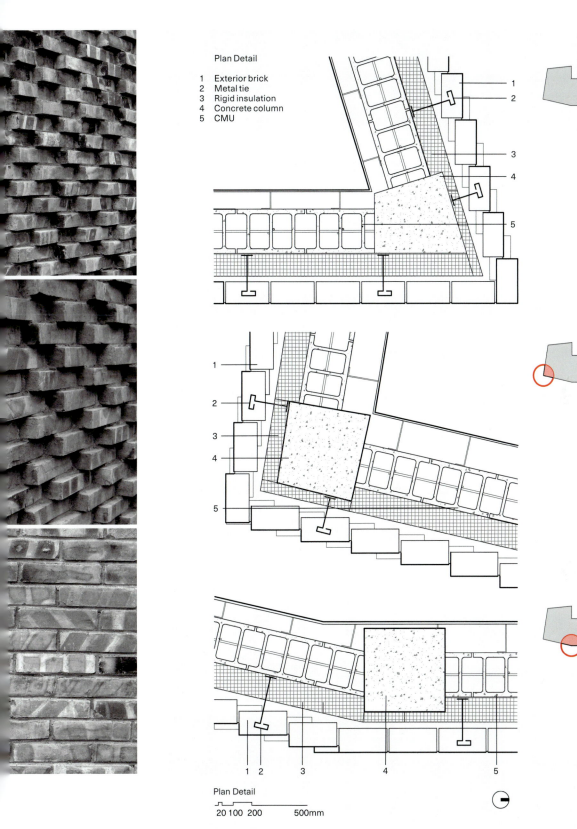

Plan Detail

1 Exterior brick
2 Metal tie
3 Rigid insulation
4 Concrete column
5 CMU

Plan Detail

20 100 200   500mm

131

Lithos Hotel

While limiting liability has distanced designers from construction processes (means and methods), the pervasiveness of digital tools in design and fabrication compels greater integration of concept and construction.

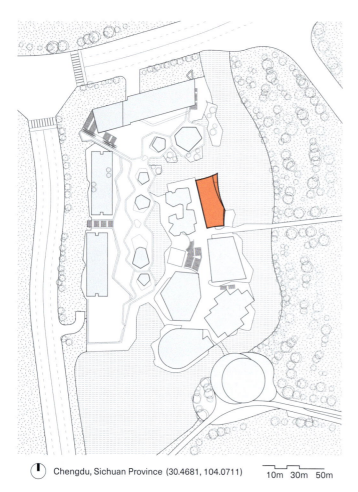

Chengdu, Sichuan Province (30.4681, 104.0711)

10m 30m 50m

Part of a new development in the southern district of Chengdu, the sculptural form of this eighteen-room boutique hotel and wellness center differentiates public spaces such as the lobby and waterfront amphitheater from the private spa and rooms above. Taking cues from the surrounding landscape, the building is shaped by a series of concave excavations that define public spaces as contoured landforms.

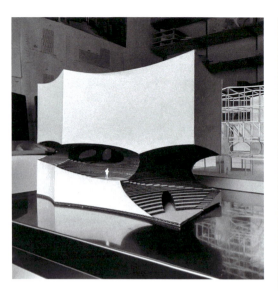

The lobby and public terrace are shaped by the sculptural void that carves out both interior and exterior spaces. The 'topography' of the lobby extends to the rooftop terrace. The volumes of the hotel rooms are shown in conceptual models as solid and devoid of fenestration.

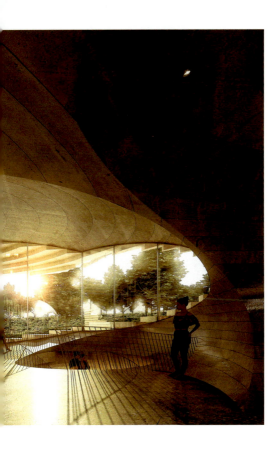

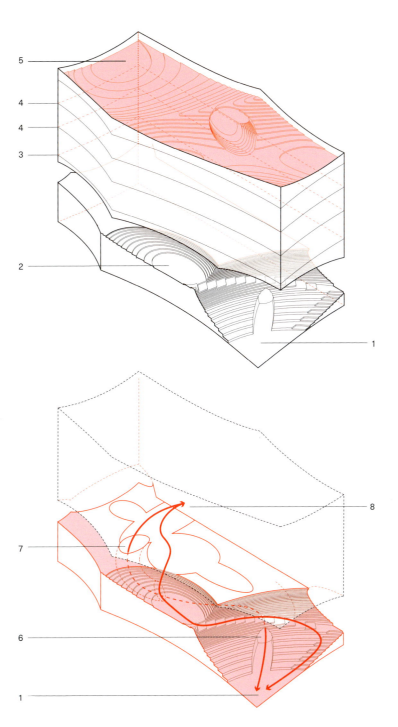

1 Arrivals level
2 Terrace and lobby level
3 Spa and yoga studio level
4 Hotel room level
5 Roof bar
6 Connection to restaurant
7 Interior stair connection
8 Connection to street level

Plan Level 04

Plan Level 03

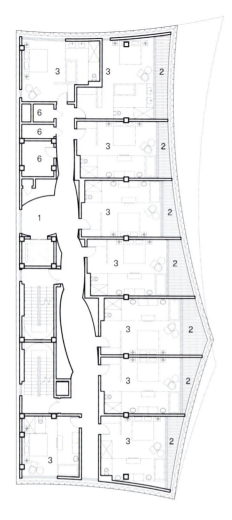

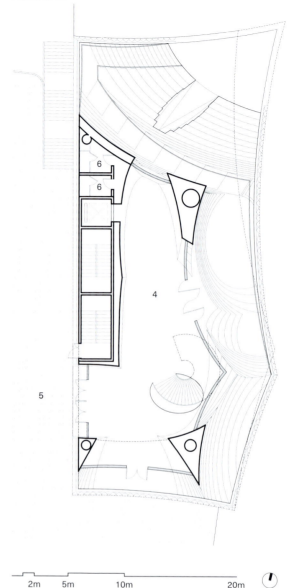

1 Elevator lobby
2 Private terrace
3 Hotel room
4 Reception and retail
5 Street level
6 Mechanical and service

2m   5m   10m   20m

Hotel guests arrive at the hotel by boat, under the cantilevered
volume of the hotel above. Contoured steps bring guests up to the
lobby level. The third floor includes a spa and yoga studios as well
as the mega-truss that supports the cantilever. The hotel's guest
rooms are located on the upper floors.

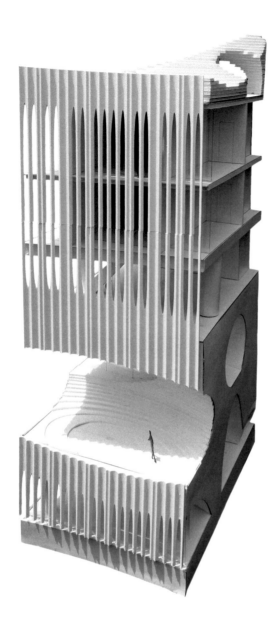

The façade uses a dense vertical screen of extruded aluminum profiles to accentuate the contrast between the sculptural void of the lobby level and the monolithic expression of the building mass. Oblong cutouts in the vertical profiles reveal the hotel room windows and balconies. The building section reveals the mega-truss level on the third floor that coincides with the spa and yoga studio program.

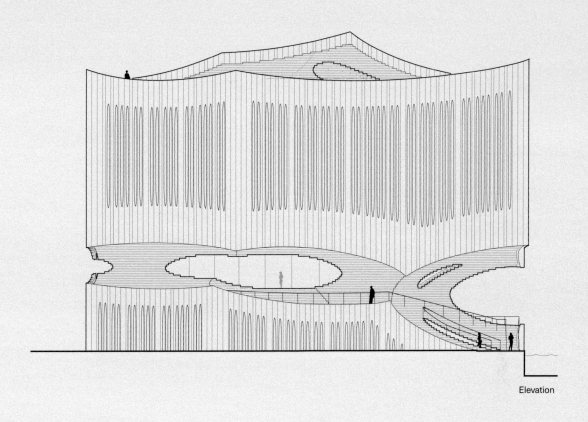

Elevation

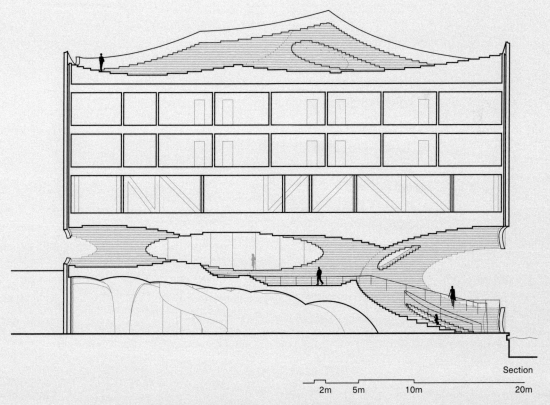

Section

2m   5m   10m   20m

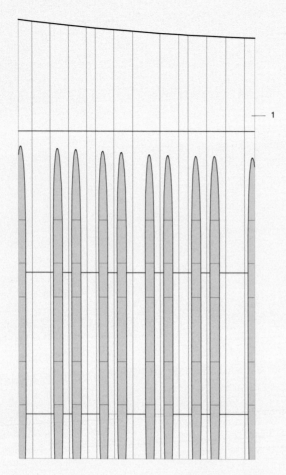

Exterior Elevation

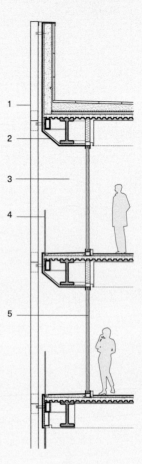

Wall Section

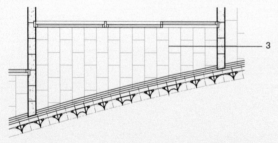

Terrace Plan

1m   2m   5m

1   Extruded aluminum rain screen
2   Metal panel
3   Occupiable balcony
4   Glass balustrade
5   Sliding glass door

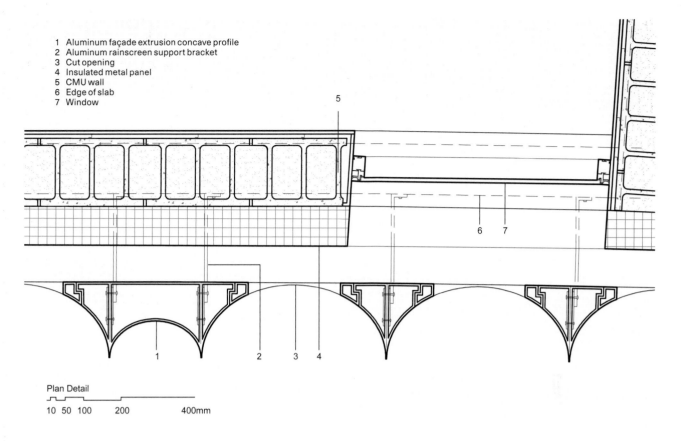

1 Aluminum façade extrusion concave profile
2 Aluminum rainscreen support bracket
3 Cut opening
4 Insulated metal panel
5 CMU wall
6 Edge of slab
7 Window

Plan Detail

10 50 100   200   400mm

The façade consists of a rainscreen system, made of extruded aluminum profiles, that shields the hotel room balconies. The dense pattern of vertical extrusions masks the punched windows behind, allowing views to the surrounding landscape while rendering the building monolithic in appearance from the exterior.

Sean Collier Memorial

Location
Cambridge, Massachusetts, USA

Team Members
Eric Höweler
J. Meejin Yoon
Yoonhee Cho
Paul Cattaneo
Sungwoo Jang
Anna Kaertner
Estelle Yoon

Collaborators
Richard Burck Associates (Landscape Architect)

212 Stuart Street

Location
Boston, Massachusetts, USA

Team Members
Eric Höweler
J. Meejin Yoon
Kyle Coburn
Jacob Bruce
Sarah Martos
Caleb Hawkins
Sophia Juneau
Daniel Fougere

Collaborators
Sasaki Associates (Architect of Record)

Coolidge Corner Theatre

Location
Brookline, Massachusetts, USA

Team Members
Eric Höweler
J. Meejin Yoon
Jonathan Fournier
Caroline Shannon
Namjoo Kim
Karl Heckman
Elle Gerdeman
Daniel Fougere
Pak Cheun Chan
David Hamm
Sungwoo Jang
Caleb Hawkins

Sky Courts

Location
Chengdu, Sichuan Province, China

Team Members
Eric Höweler
J. Meejin Yoon
Meredith Miller
Ryan Murphy
Cyrus Dochow
Matt Chua
Casey Renner
Parker Lee
Jennifer Chuong
Nerijus Petrokas
Saran Oki
Thena Tak

Collaborators
China Railway Engineering Design Institute Co. Ltd (Local Design Institute)

Lithos Hotel

Location
Chengdu, Sichuan Province, China

Team Members
Eric Höweler
J. Meejin Yoon
Sungwoo Jang
Ching Ying Ngan
Jonathan Fournier
Elle Gerdeman

Collaborators
Chengdu JZFZ Architectural Design Co. Ltd (Local Design Institute)

Fabrication and Fabulation
Conversation
with Nader Tehrani

Nader Tehrani, founding principal of NADAAA and Dean of the
Cooper Union's Irwin S. Chanin School of Architecture, discusses
how our mutual interest in fabrication might inform the way we see
the architect's role in the construction process.

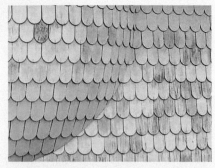

Jacob Harder House. Bruce Goff.
Mountain Lake, Minnesota. 1971

Holy Innocents Church. Ernest Coxhead.
San Francisco, California. 1890

ERIC
I have a question about fabrication and construction in general. To me, fabrication tends to be one material worked by one trade, whereas construction is the orchestration of multiple trades. It's a part-to-whole relationship. A carpenter obsesses over a wood detail, but construction puts it all together.

It requires a different organizational attitude, whether it's top-down or bottom-up. You can start with a shingle, like Bruce Goff, and use that detail to create a whole. A single element can scale up to create an architectural experience. This seems to be how fabrication migrates into a building. A laser-cutting technique can scale up to wrap a building. But this doesn't work so well on the typology of, say, the atrium building that imposes a logic from the top down. It requires much more choreography to coordinate than simply a folding of material.

NADER
I think it's very clear the way you put it, and behind that are the historical tensions that play through Gesamtkunstwerk and the architect's compulsion to control everything, irrespective of scale, down to your clothes and your shoes. It's a model of thinking in which the generic, the off-the-shelf, and the conventional are absorbed for critical reasons, not for acquiescent ones. Sometimes it's more critical to work with the world as it is, and re-tweak it in more subtle ways.

MEEJIN
Do we accept 'off-the-shelf' solutions for reasons of scale or politics?

NADER
It's an intellectual position. I am sure that questions of scale and politics do come into play, but if architects like us have a compulsion to control everything, it didn't advance us strategically in the ways we thought it would. In contrast to our trajectory, I love Lacaton & Vassal because of the way they have positioned their work. They are maniacal in a different way. They're consistent about not demolishing things; the addition is their M.O. I genuinely like the practices that think through systems and redeploy rather than reinvent.

ERIC
Architects are taught to reinvent. Maybe this is a disciplinary holdover from modernism. The idea of rupture and reinvention. But inventing things from scratch, or believing in tabula rasa, is also problematic.

NADER

Have you seen the work of Scarpa in person? I've revisited various projects because with all the pleasure that they give, they can be oppressive in the circumstantial nature of the bespoke. Despite my early infatuation with the bank in Verona, it is somewhat nauseating at the end. Maybe this is why — with all the criticism out there — I enjoy the diagrammatic clarity of OMA or BIG. Sometimes the presence of a dumb-big idea demonstrates the power of discipline over obsession at the nano-scale. Castelvecchio may be able to bridge the two approaches — it allows the existing conditions to serve as a foil for his interventions that often reconcile local contingencies: symmetries, alignments, added functions, etc.

> **ERIC**
>
> Scarpa's work often seems unrestrained, articulating many individual elements. He was on a job site every day working with craftspeople, he would continue to design even beyond the handover of the building or the constraints of the budget. It's a long way from Rem, who said, 'no money, no detail!'

NADER

It's a deeply ideological question: if Rem had all the budget in the world, would he not still behave in the way that he does? To contain the detail, to dumb it down, to subtract rather than to add? Or alternatively, would he become like Scarpa? I suspect not.

> **ERIC**
>
> I think he would impose constraints.

NADER

It comes back to the whole question of means and methods: the way in which something is fabricated. Our generation has heard stories about how Frank Gehry completely changed the relationship between the architectural discipline and the metal industry through the specification of his metal-shingled façades. He adopted an existing trade but activated the industry. He taught them to redeploy their details, or else coerced them, and worked with them to extend their yield thresholds, their tolerances, and eventually, to transform their standards.

Yet what is fascinating about Gehry is the sheer lack of discipline in what he did from a computational point of view in those initial years. Our intellectual point of departure was this: the work of art on the one hand, and the work of technology on the other, without any correspondence or reciprocity. How does architecture bring those

Castelvecchio Museum. Carlo Scarpa.
Verona, Italy. 1959-73

into critical alignment? In our work, we pushed formal speculation while disciplining it with certain fabrication protocols; the two worked in tight reciprocity.

A lot of our early projects were about the precision of systems and their ability to address broader architectural mandates. For instance, the sidewall in Casa la Roca is not about the figure of the curtain per se, but its ability to provide lateral stability and environmental porosity within the grain of its bonding system. The wall solved structural, environmental, and illumination issues with one gesture, in a space that would otherwise be completely hermetic. The system itself created the spatial and environmental conditions of that space.

Casa La Roca. Office d'A. 1995

ERIC

There are two moments in architecture's mythology that come to mind. The first is Thom Mayne's story about arriving at the site of one of his early houses and finding the concrete work shoddy. He rented a jackhammer and demolished the concrete, made new formwork, and re-cast it to show the contractor how it was supposed to be. That's the myth of the architect as a Howard Roark type who is both a heroic designer and a capable builder — rebuilding the contractor's imperfect work.

The other moment is Frank Gehry's own house. He built a series of additions over time, taking on the means and methods at the residential scale. This pushed the industry toward fabrication and inexpensive materials. There's a mythology about the architect who experiments with cheap materials to change the way he lives. In Postmodernism, Frederic Jameson sees Gehry's house as "thinking a material thought," creating a political stance for space through material means. While he is not an architect, it is an interesting suggestion that the architect's control over material also gives access to the political dimension of architecture.

MEEJIN

Nader, you are still thinking material thoughts, but in general, architects are losing control of material in their design process. Regarding the legal scope of an architect's responsibility, there is a liability for Gehry, for your practice, and all practices when they work directly with materials. Architects are not supposed to define the means and methods. But when the design requires something atypical, how do you respond?

Mantra Restaurant. Office d'A. 2001

NADER

We have done that in several ways. For the Mantra Hukkah-den, we took on its fabrication responsibilities, shop drawings, liabilities, and in turn, we also shared its profits. It was small, it was effectively an installation, and we were confident we could pull it off.

> **MEEJIN**
>
> The scale of Mantra allowed for in-house fabrication, but that doesn't really scale up when you're talking about projects you can't build yourself. How have you confronted this issue in your larger projects?

NADER

In Toronto, I was boarding a flight to Melbourne when I was told that the roof [of the Daniels Building at the University of Toronto] was gone, value-engineered out because it was over budget! With a concrete shell, you would have the formwork and then the construction, which is admittedly costlier than a flat roof. We asked, what would happen if you take the concrete system out, and do it in steel instead? They said the surface is not buildable. And we said, why not? It's a ruled surface, and that means we can even use sheet material to clad it. We had already sent them the model, but they said the model was too small to prove the point. So, we built it at full scale in the office. In the end, it was purely a rhetorical exercise. You don't need to build it to demonstrate it's buildable, and yet you have to do it as a shot across the bow.

> **ERIC**
>
> I remember going into your office and seeing all these drywall surfaces hanging from the ceiling. Prototyping can be a way to play an active role in conversations about material and assembly, without having to build everything yourself.

> **MEEJIN**
>
> Do you think architects could direct the means and methods of construction? What would the consequences be?

NADER

It's very hard to turn back the hands of time. Construction is simply much more complex today between systems, products, labor, and liabilities. We can't make the building industry less specialized at this point — the way we insulate buildings, embed technologies into buildings, waterproof them. Compared to contempo-

Prototype for Daniels Building ceiling. NADAAA.

Daniels Building, University of Toronto.
NADAAA. Toronto, Canada. 2018

rary buildings, modern buildings of the 20th century were quite archaic. Even as we accrue knowledge, new projects demonstrate how little we know about other systems, with new technologies emerging every day.

Another conundrum behind means and methods is the specter of unions and labor laws. You can't undertake certain material strategies in a city because each city is somehow 'owned' by interests that impose the use of steel or concrete based on political advantages from a labor perspective, rather than technological qualification for that particular project.

The main difficulty is that the profession has broken down the process of project and construction management, quantity surveying, and the many other specialties into different disciplines. In being proactive about key details, systems, and unconventional applications of products we have been able to address some of these issues internally.

290 Mulberry Street. SHoP. 2009

MEEJIN
I'm curious to know what you think about SHoP Architects creating a construction company in parallel to their practice. It seems like they're trying to solve the question of the boundary of an architect's responsibility at a much larger scale in-house.

NADER
I believe SHoP took on some construction manage-ment scope, effectively coordinating the cladding scope of a project, even if they do not actually build it themselves. Imagine a construction manager charging an arm and a leg for the management of a process that you would rather do in-house. I think this is the realization that SHoP came to, and they eventually took the bull by the horns. But to do that, one needs to bring on the construction and assembly expertise that practitioners sometimes lack in the design studio. All of that expertise pays off in terms of the risk and liabilities one inherits, if one has enough work to warrant such a team. I think that's intelligent, and for the scale at which they operate, possibly affordable.

ERIC
There's also the architect-led design-build model represented by Peter Gluck. He offers construction services to his clients, and he's been quite successful.

NADER
By the way, many other countries do this already. The Peter Gluck model sounds kind of extraordinary in the United States, but that's how all of Iran works.

152

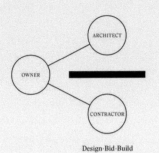

Design-Bid-Build

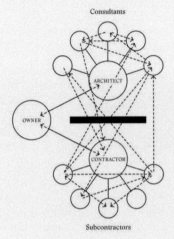

Design Build Diagram. Gluck+

Architects basically take on the responsibilities of the construction process. Some of the great works in China, Chile, Mexico, and other countries also benefit from this process because, in addition to the difference in the architect's responsibilities, the programming and the development of projects are also different in those countries. There's a model of practice in Iran called 'bessaaz befroosh,' which translates as 'build-sell,' where an architect designs speculative projects and sells them for a good profit. Most projects in Iran are the result of this model, and for good architects, it has also become a productive avenue for research.

ERIC
This makes me wonder how we can instill in young designers not only the sensibility for material properties, but also a way of thinking material thoughts? One difference with our students going into practice today is that the material palette has expanded to include polymers and hybrid materials and has gone beyond the material toward the immaterial with technologies that allow responsiveness and performance in real time.

NADER
Certainly, the work of the next generation reflects expanded possibilities of material speculation. Projects like David Benjamin's bio-engineered-bricks, or Neri Oxman's silkworm dome all suggest that there are ways to work outside the industry products, sheet materials, and standard requirements. Once 3D printing becomes a more viable fabrication strategy, it will inevitably be tested for performance at the scale of the wall section and compared to what we achieve through many layers of material now.

MEEJIN
There are alternate ways besides working in fabrication for an architect to take responsibility for material and construction at a large scale. The next generation is looking at a totally different approach to building — 3D printing, self-assembly, and synthetic biology. My question is: will that change the industry?

NADER
It depends on whether the next generation of innovative designers entertain building practices that get their hands dirty with the politics of commissions. But I do think the arena of work they undertake will impact us all going forward; we will all be building differently.

Hy-Fi, MoMA PS1. David Benjamin. 2014

153

Chapter III   Going Public

Beyond the scale of site and building, how might the terms *verification* and *field* offer insights into design where the scope and impact of a project take on cultural and political dimensions? We use the term *public* to describe this expanded territory encompassing communities and stakeholders, processes, and protocols. Community engagement and advocacy shift the notion of verification from a dimensional and technical register to a social and political one. Likewise, the notion of field is expanded from the literal field of construction to the field of social and political conditions in which we work. This expanded field is where architecture and the built environment can be thought of as 'going public.'

In the world of business, the term signals a moment when a private business entity agrees to sell shares to outside investors to raise capital as it also accepts larger responsibilities. For us, 'going public' is a shift toward thinking about architecture and the built environment as having greater responsibilities beyond themselves, and of design as a process that engages with civic practices, policies, and politics to reinscribe an evolving conception of publicness. Civic structures represent a shared or common amenity as well as a collectively agreed upon investment — something worth funding — and a common set of values. We can agree that a public park is a valuable amenity for all. It is a common good and represents common values. Hence the name of some of our oldest parks are referred to as commons; Boston Common, Cambridge Common, and even the Ithaca Commons.

Demarcations between public and private realms present challenges and defy architectural typologies because their boundaries can be blurred, shifting, and porous. Gianbattista Nolli's 1748 map of Rome represents 18th-century Rome as a figure-ground in black and white poché while rendering the interiors of churches in full detail as extensions of the public realm. Nolli's cartographic invention maps not only Rome's extents and coordinates, but the *experience* of the city. In rendering interior spaces as extensions of the public realm, Nolli also articulates an essential quality of the Catholic Church as a public institution.

Vito Acconci's 1969 *Following Piece* performs a similar cartography of the public realm, though rendered in a different medium. As a work of conceptual performance art, Acconci used his own body as the measure of public space by adhering to a set of rules. Acconci selected a person at random on the streets of New York City and followed them along their path through the public realm. He stopped when the subject's entry into a private space presented him with a barrier. Acconci's itinerary through the city was limited by locked doors, restricted access, and costs of admission. Whereas Nolli employed the tools of a surveyor and cartographer, Acconci *performed* his survey of the city, mapping the contours of his experience as well as the unwritten rules of social codes. Both the Nolli map of Rome and Acconci's mapping of New York City survey interfaces of public and private realms, acknowledging their edges and contours as well as blurred, shifting, and contested relationships.

Architecture as such can be understood as an interface. As a medium of spatial definition, a

Vito Acconci's performance, *Following Piece*, maps the limits of public space. Photo courtesy of Maria Acconci.

boundary between realms and enclosures, it delimits inside from outside, mine from yours, public from private. Yet these boundary conditions between public and private are constantly shifting as conditions of publicness, privacy, and property are entwined with cultural and political practices. Acconci's *Following Piece* tested the limits of what was considered accessible at the time. For example, he would follow his subject into the subway but did not enter private lobbies. The contemporary public realm assumes implicit and explicit codes of acceptable behavior. It is informed by shifting cultural norms, as well as the presence of new technological interfaces. Nonbinary definitions of public and private, accessible and exclusionary are sites of continuous definition and negotiation. The processes of working within these protocols is the subject of this chapter. Projects presented in "Going Public" conceptualize the field as a space of processes, approvals, jurisdiction, access, encroachment, and negotiation.

New York City's 1961 zoning resolution was the first to introduce the concept of incentives and trade-offs in order to encourage private developers to provide public amenities in exchange for development square footage. The emergence of public-private partnerships resulted in spatial phenomena that scholar, urban planner, and lawyer Jerold Kayden calls POPS, or Privately-Owned Public Spaces, which blur the line between public and private realms. Decades before Kayden coined the term, Mies van der Rohe's Seagram Building served as a model for the 1961 zoning resolution by providing a generous plaza space as part of a setback along Park

Mies van der Rohe's Seagram Building plaza produced a new paradigm for public space in New York.

Avenue. Mies's thirty-eight-story tower rises without setback and occupies only twenty-five percent of the building site. If you were standing in the plaza and tried to photograph Mies's iconic outside corner, you might be informed by a security officer that the plaza is in fact not public. It is "private space with public access."

Myriad projects following the Seagram Building benefited from incentives included in the city's 1961 resolution and building owners agreed to grant access to private land for public use as part of the negotiation process. Buildings were to make improvements to the public places adjacent to their property as part of an entitlements process. Private money paid for an improvement to the public realm in exchange for development rights in excess of what is considered "as of right."

A more recent case of a negotiated public realm can be found in Boston's Downtown Crossing, located one block from the Boston Common. The Millennium Tower was completed in 2016 on the site of the former Filene's Basement department store. As part of negotiations with the city, the developer, Millennium Partners, agreed to repave the streets around the tower and reconstruct a narrow park known as Shopper's Park. The 684-foot tower houses condominiums and relies on a drop-off area along Franklin Street. This drop-off at

the base of the tower is essentially an example of private use of public land. As part of the approvals process, we were brought on to design the park and provide a public amenity that integrates the tower into its context and facilitates a negotiated trade-off between public and private uses.

As part of the design of the Downtown Crossing Plaza, we proposed paving the street and the sidewalks with the same pavers and eliminating curbs. In doing so, the plaza is unified across a single plane, encoding the plaza as a pedestrian zone. This single-surface approach to urban space slows traffic and prioritizes pedestrians and cyclists. The continuity of the pavers and elimination of curbs makes the plaza feel more expansive, stretching from building face to building face.

The plaza redesign also included the construction of a new subway headhouse for the Downtown Crossing Station in the form of an amphitheater. The amphitheater is sloped to parallel the interior stair and escalator from the platform below, and it faces Washington Street, which is experienced as a venue for urban public theater. The amphitheater provides a mediating, or *middle*, scale between the residential tower and the improved streetscape pavers, planters, and street trees. As a privately funded urban amenity, the amphitheater paved the way for an approvals process that allowed the project to proceed. The 1,000 square-foot (92 sq m) amphitheater

Bird's eye view of the new Downtown Crossing Plaza.   Downtown Crossing T subway entrance.

produced a new public realm above the subway entrance and served as a trade-off with the adjacent private drop-off.

The Downtown Crossing Amphitheater piggybacks a public amenity on the public infrastructure of the subway system. We often think of parks and streets when we think of the public realm, though infrastructure is also public. In fact, one definition of infrastructure is not based on typology (bridges, tunnels, rails), but rather is based on its status as a common good. The subway system, like public transit, is a commons, just as the Boston Common is a commons. Commons are defined as what we value collectively. The privately built public perch above the public transit system is an example of design as a field of negotiation between degrees of publicness, access, and benefits. The field in this case is not simply the footprint of the tower and the extents of the park, but the public realm as a space of negotiation.

POPS (Privately-Owned Public Spaces) that enhance the public realm are achieved via trade-offs between private and public interests. Civic institutions like libraries, museums, and community centers define and delimit public access, choosing to open their doors to the public while setting the terms of accessibility. A museum as a civic institution can be accessible to the public, yet the price of admission introduces a paywall that defines a limit. These terms govern and regulate access to interior spaces that offer varying degrees of publicness.

The Boston Society of Architects (BSA) was the recipient of a Chapter 91

Public performance at the Downtown Crossing Amphitheater.

lease, which takes advantage of a historic law ensuring that waterfront properties maintain a degree of public access. The Chapter 91 lease allows the not-for-profit membership institution to lease space in the Atlantic Wharf development for a discounted rate in exchange for providing public amenities such as gallery spaces and information points. It also marks a shift in the mission of the BSA from a private membership institution to a public organization that actively advocates for the value of design in the built environment.

The design of the BSA Space, which was won by public competition in 2010, addresses questions of public interface through a series of key design moves. The bulk of the BSA Space is on the second floor, with a small footprint space on the ground floor. How to make a public-facing institution visible from the street? How to get the public up to the second floor? How to create an iconic new image for a membership institution that is 150 years old? The design of the BSA Space addresses all three questions with one answer. Recognizing that the ceiling of the second floor is the most visible part of the interior when viewed from the street, the ceiling acts as a kind of fifth façade, turning the green soffit into a feature that corresponds with the public gallery program. The soffit folds down to form a sculptural stair, announcing the access point to the second-floor spaces, and produces a bold icon for the BSA. The design does triple duty as a connector, icon, and billboard. Architectural strategies responsive to the policies and economics of public space can

transform constrained sites into instruments for public visibility, access, and exchange.

The new home of the MIT Museum is another example of a project that offers a point of access and window into the institute where the public can engage with the research and culture of MIT. Its new location on Main Street in Kendall Square places it adjacent to the Kendall/MIT subway entrance, and across the plaza from the new MIT Forum, a convening space for institute events and visitors. Like the BSA Space, the MIT Museum occupies the second and third floors of the building, with a relatively small footprint on the ground floor. To draw the public up to the galleries, we organized the museum program along a spiral-shaped sequence of galleries that double as circulation spaces and wrap the central service core.

A grand stair and bleacher extend the public realm into the interior of the museum with a free public gallery before the admission paywall on the second floor. By following the spiral around the core on the second floor, and proceeding up another bleacher on the opposite side of the core, the visitor completes a 360-degree rotation on three levels. This gallery spiral draws the public up all three floors and allows for support programs to occupy spaces adjacent to the galleries as the gallery program climbs the section. The oblique grand stair and cascading section eliminates the front-of-house versus back-of-house relationships typically found in museums and proposes instead a *side-of-house* relationship to the galleries. This new lateral adjacency

reframes the public's relationship to the collection spaces and the museum's education and programs departments. This subtle shift in organizational logic sets the terms and frameworks of access to the museum content, recasting the institution's relationship to the larger public.

Both the BSA Space and the MIT Museum function as accessible public interfaces to private institutions. They are like POPS in that their role as public amenities are a negotiated part of the approvals and entitlements process. In the case of the BSA Space, the Chapter 91 laws prioritize public amenities and public institutions along the Boston waterfront. Similarly, the MIT Museum serves as a public-facing component of the MIT campus and creates an accessible interface with the City of Cambridge and the larger public.

In "Going Public," we shift our reading of projects as isolated works of architecture to broader frameworks of design, including neighborhoods and communities, where engagement with stakeholders, zoning codes, and cultural norms maps out an expanded field of practice. This shift entails a broadening of scope that operates at the scale of the neighborhood and the surrounding community as well as the regulatory agencies that have jurisdiction (AHJ) over them. This engagement refers to communities, histories, and statutory and regulatory bodies. The act of design in these contexts is an act of negotiation. *Verification* in this context takes the form of a feedback loop of participation and

The "new normal" of social distancing restructured
social interactions during the COVID-19 pandemic.

engagement. The *field* mapped out by these projects includes public processes, public access, public image, and public opinion.

The contested territory between public and private realms is culturally encoded, blurred by technologies, and modified by cultural practices, norms, and behaviors. Vito Acconci not only stopped at physical barriers, he also stopped following his subject when his pursuit could be deemed inappropriate, impolite, or uncomfortable. Social and cultural barriers are equally as delimiting as physical barriers. At the same time, the extent of public and private realms are actively redefined by technologies of surveillance and control. Gilles Deleuze has theorized a "society of control," where monitoring and information tracking technologies extend the logics of a "disciplinary society," by nonphysical means. Chain link fences and credit histories redefine boundaries in societies of control. And, throughout the COVID-19 pandemic, much of our social and cultural life has migrated to Zoom calls and virtual conference rooms, leading some to question the necessity of office spaces, theaters, and museums. Indeed, social and physical distancing enforced over the course of the pandemic has brought the public realm into sharp focus and has forced a reconsideration of many of our assumptions about social space, shared space, and public life — just as public health has brought new urgency to the public realm and the values that underpin it.

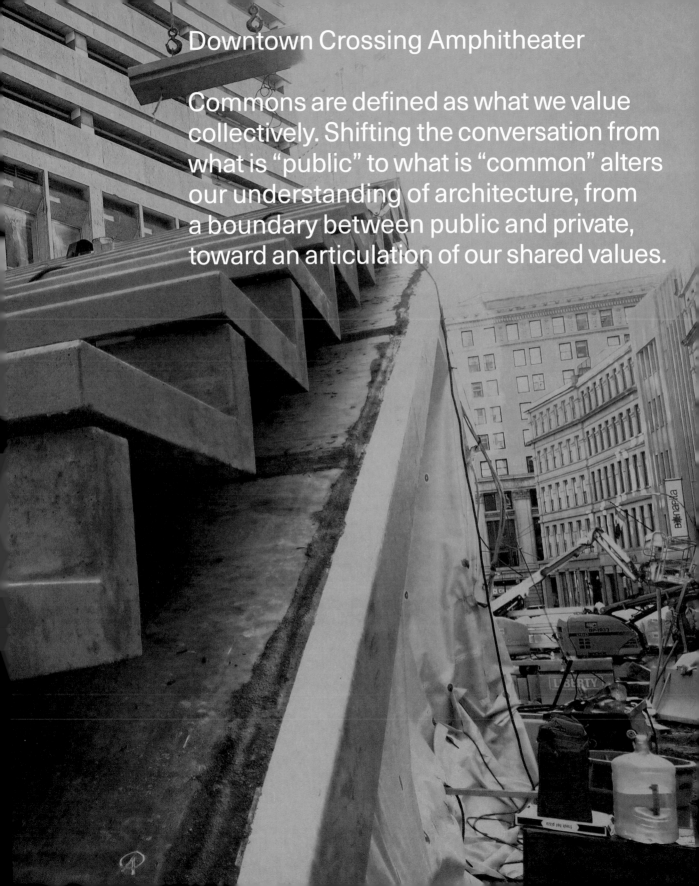

Downtown Crossing Amphitheater

Commons are defined as what we value collectively. Shifting the conversation from what is "public" to what is "common" alters our understanding of architecture, from a boundary between public and private, toward an articulation of our shared values.

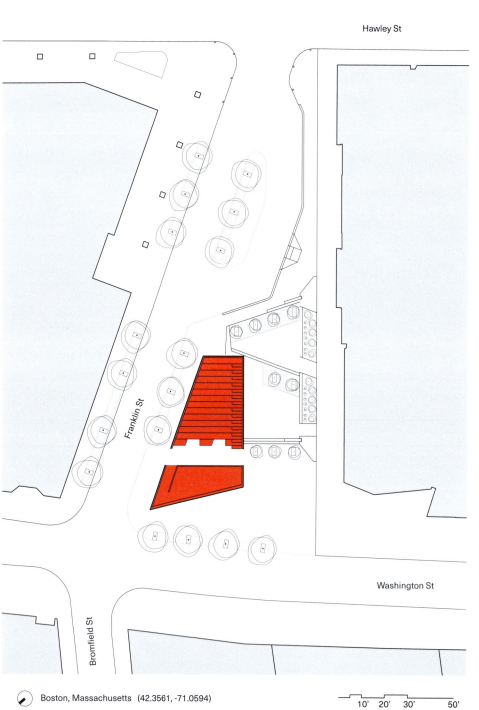

Hawley St

Franklin St

Bromfield St

Washington St

Boston, Massachusetts (42.3561, -71.0594)

10' 20' 30' 50'

The new amphitheater at Downtown Crossing repurposes an existing subway headhouse to create a 'middle-scale' urban place adjacent to Millennium Tower. Born of a public-private agreement between the project's developer and the City of Boston, the introduction of the amphitheater, stage platform, and extended plaza pavers coincides with the transformation of Boston's downtown shopping district into a vibrant pedestrian realm.

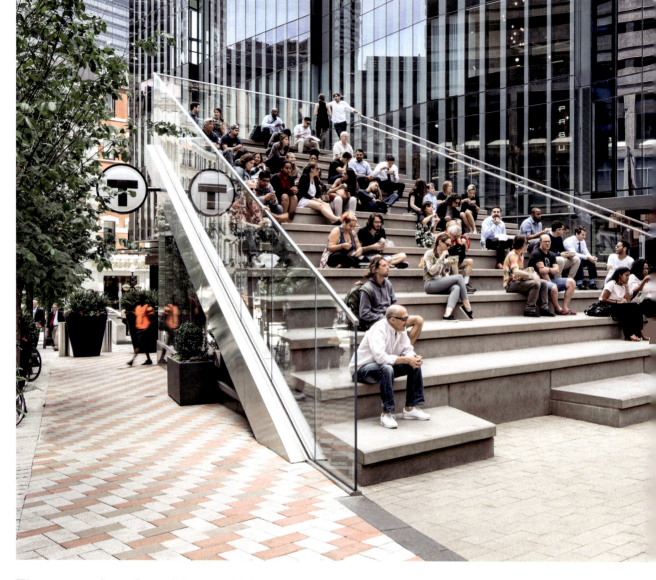

The terraced seating of the amphitheater is used for
scheduled and impromptu musical performances,
group yoga, and people watching along one of Boston's
busiest shopping streets. The amphitheater replaced
an unwelcoming 1970s subway headhouse with a new
stepped urban surface that negotiates with private
development in exchange for use of a public site.

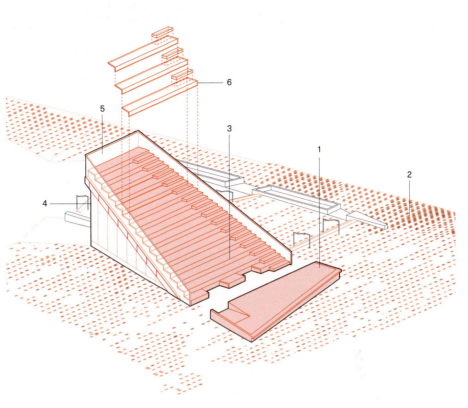

1 Stage area
2 Accented herringbone paver pattern
3 Amphitheater steps
4 Downtown Crossing T-stop
5 Glass guardrail
6 Precast concrete step

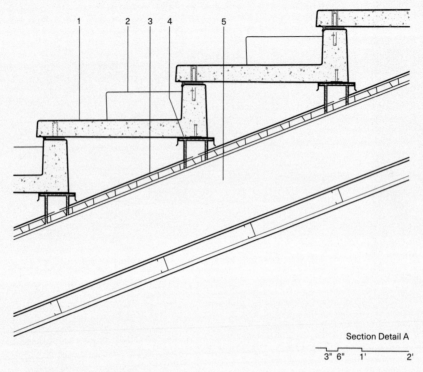

Section Detail A

3" 6" 1'   2'

1   Precast concrete stair profile
2   Precast solid intermediate stair step
3   Steel deck with water-proof membrane
4   Steel support with flashing and drip edge
5   Steel beam

An amphitheater over a subway entrance draws a relationship between the performance program above and the transit infrastructure below. Precast planks with an upturned beam profile span steel raker beams to create the amphitheater's surface. The edge of the amphitheater is clad in stainless steel panels to emphasize the thin edge of a planar surface that is seemingly 'peeled up' from the transit station below.

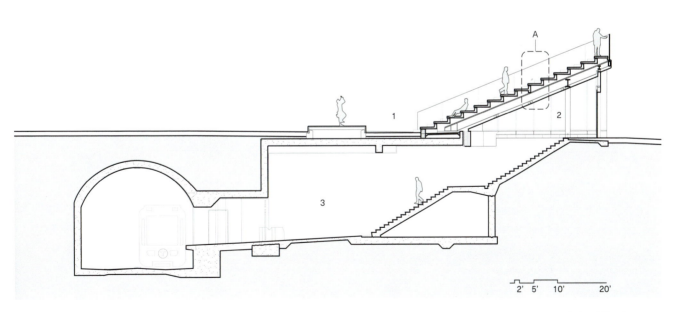

1 Amphitheater
2 Subway entrance
3 Subway platform

BSA Space

Interfaces between public and private realms are thick and blurry, often negotiated via zoning regulations, incentives, and mandated hours, resulting in new spatial and temporal concepts of access and exchange.

Boston, Massachusetts (42.3529, -71.0523)

150' 250'　　500'

BSA Space houses the Boston Society of Architects and its public programs in 16,000 square feet (1,400 sq m) of renovated additional public space at Atlantic Wharf in Boston. The space provides meeting rooms as well as 6,000 square feet (550 sq m) of exhibition space dedicated to architecture and design. BSA Space benefits from Chapter 91 legislation which ensures public access to waterfront sites in the City of Boston.

In spite of its small footprint on the ground floor, the storefront view of BSA Space captures the eye of visitors and amplifies the presence of the gallery space.

1 Feature ceiling
2 Reception plywood desk
3 Conference rooms
4 Exhibition space
5 Grand stair
6 Concierge plywood desk
7 Lobby

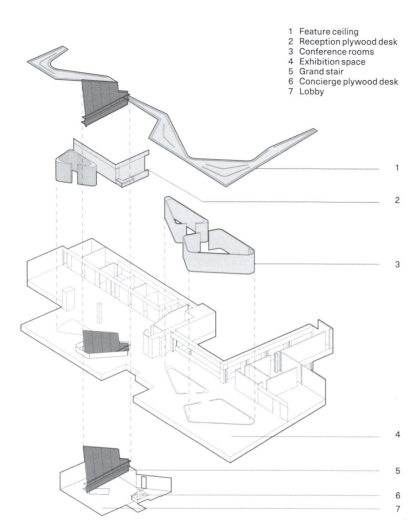

Conference rooms are distributed throughout the open gallery on the second floor, forming an 'archipelago' of administrative programs within the public gallery space. This program arrangement increases contact between the BSA members, visitors, and members of the general public. Visible from the sidewalk below, the bright green soffit on the second floor acts as an interior façade. Drawing the public up to the second floor, a grand stair appears to drop down from the ceiling above and provides a fluid transition between floors with a single gesture.

The stair is made of 3/4" (19 mm) steel plate and gives the impression of thinness and lightness. It acts as the main icon for the BSA Space, creating a strong sculptural figure behind the glass that attracts attention, offers a means of circulating to the gallery level, and connects to the gallery soffit elements.

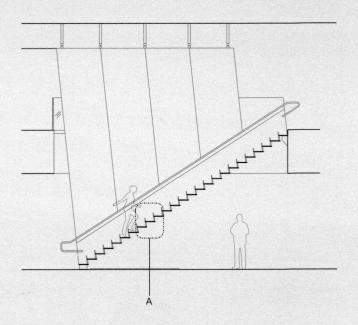

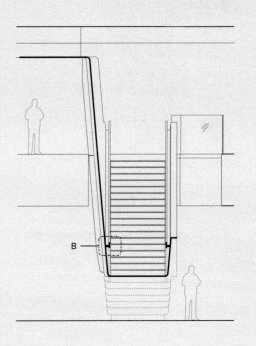

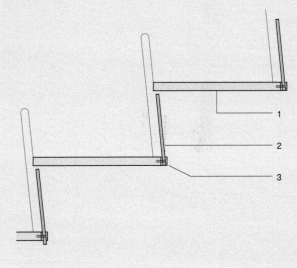

1 3/4" Steel stair tread
2 Laminated glass riser
3 Continuous clamping bar

Section

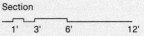

1' 3' 6'   12'

Section Detail A

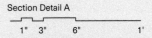

1" 3" 6"   1'

In addition to inviting visitors from the street up to the second-floor galleries, the stair functions as a billboard. At times used as a magnetic board or projection surface, the stair participates in the exhibits and broadcasts happenings from the BSA Space to the street.

MIT Museum

The contested territory between public and private realms is culturally coded, complicated by technologies, and modified by social norms. A recent focus on public health has also brought the public realm into sharp focus and forced a reconsideration of many of our assumptions about social space, shared values, and public life.

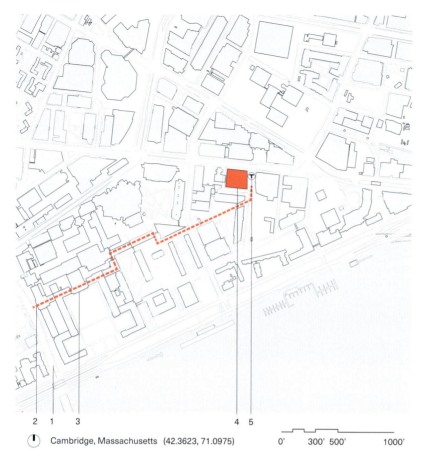

Cambridge, Massachusetts (42.3623, 71.0975)

2 1   3   4 5

0'   300' 500'   1000'

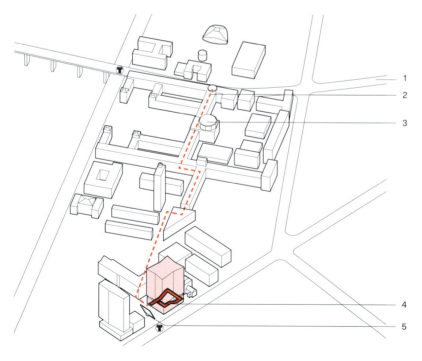

1
2
3

4
5

1 Massachusetts Avenue
2 MIT's 'Infinite Corridor' (Building 7)
3 MIT's 'Great Dome'
4 MIT Museum
5 MIT Gateway Kendall T Stop

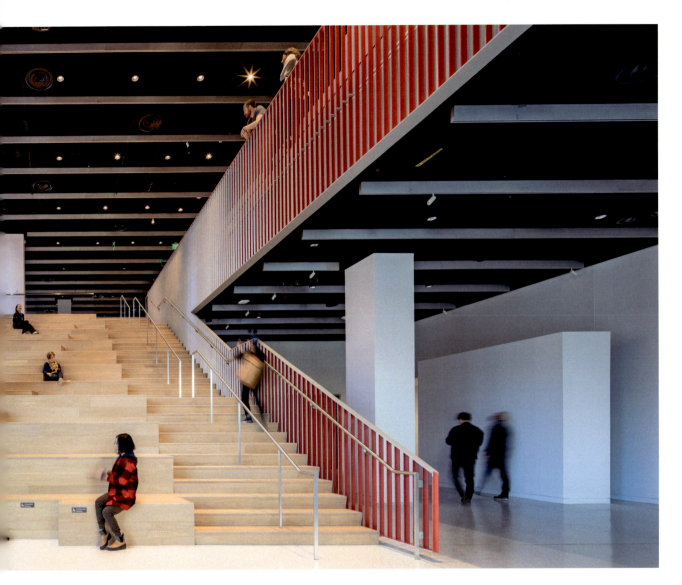

The new MIT Museum in Kendall Square provides a window into MIT, a glimpse into the artifacts of research and the stories behind them. Located on the ground, second, and third floors of a new building, the museum anchors MIT's East Campus and forms a new gateway to the institute. An early concept diagram for the museum imagines extending the famous Infinite Corridor into the MIT Museum, connecting the institute's historical 77 Massachusetts Avenue entry to the new gateway at the Kendall T subway station. Could the new museum — with its galleries, seminar rooms, and collections spaces — anchor the route's east end? The museum's organizational diagram creates a continuous spiral of public circulation around the building core, drawing the visitor up a large public stair to the second- and third-floor galleries, and terminates in the museum collections.

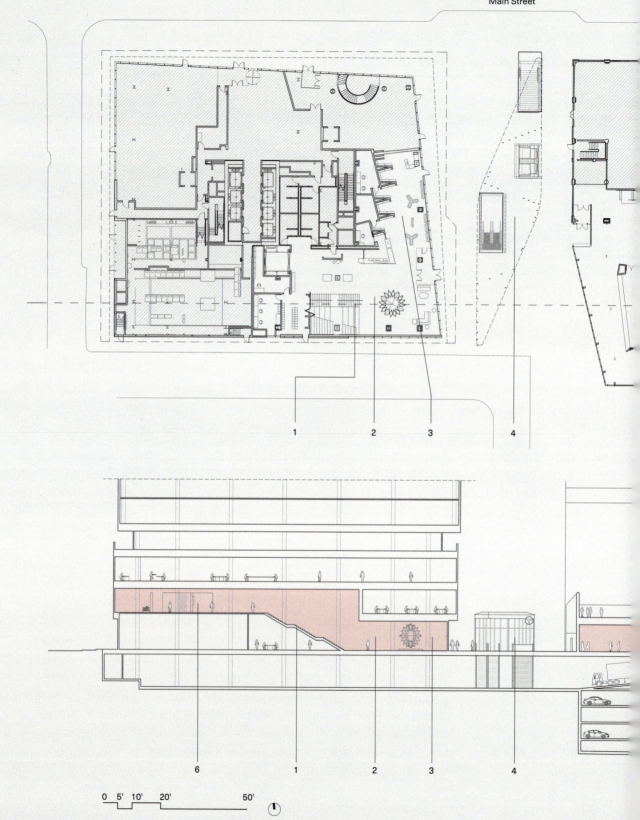

1   2   3   4

6   1   2   3   4

0   5' 10'   20'   50'

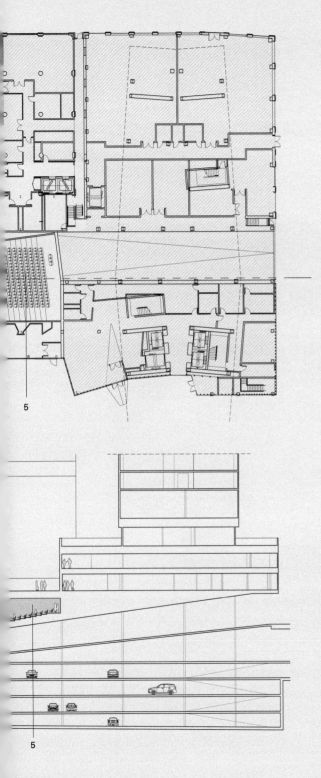

The MIT Museum and the MIT Welcome Center frame the Gateway Plaza, presenting programs that interface with the public. The plaza is also an entry to the Kendall Square T subway station, the institute's main point of access to public transit. The museum's grand stair gestures out across the plaza, extending the public museum program from the plaza up through three floors of the museum.

1 Grand stair
2 Museum lobby
3 Museum store
4 MIT Gateway Kendall T stop
5 Auditorium in MIT Site 4
6 Gallery

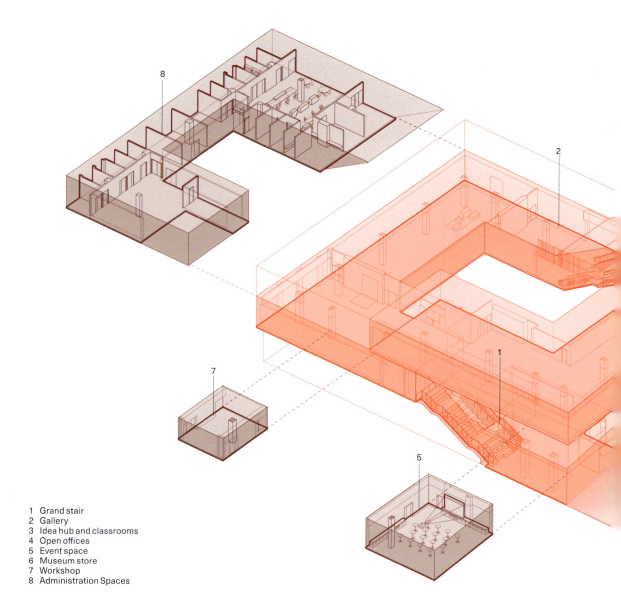

1 Grand stair
2 Gallery
3 Idea hub and classrooms
4 Open offices
5 Event space
6 Museum store
7 Workshop
8 Administration Spaces

The MIT Museum collects and preserves artifacts significant to the life of MIT as well as exhibition content aligned with MIT's mission, and convenes and engages the wider community to share MIT's scholarship. Its galleries, workshops, and classrooms facilitate the interpretation of the institute's contributions from past to the present day. The museum's gallery sequence forms a continuous spiral, connecting the pedestrian plaza and ground floor lobby to the second- and third-floor galleries. The spiral organization dispenses with traditional front-of-house and back-of-house separations and instead offers new adjacencies through a 'side-of-house' placement of education and curatorial spaces along the length of the coiled gallery. Adjacent to the galleries, the museum's workshop, classroom, seminar, and Idea Hub spaces benefit from increased foot traffic and visibility.

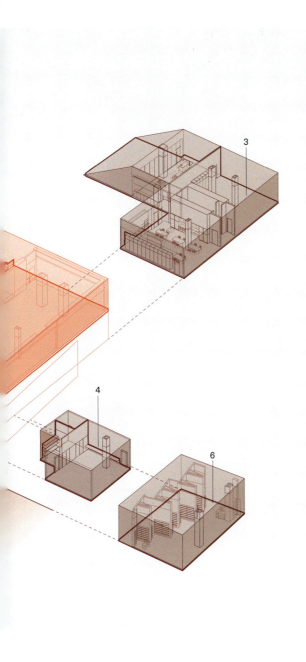

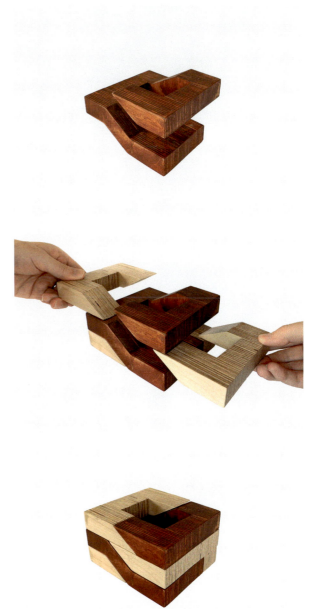

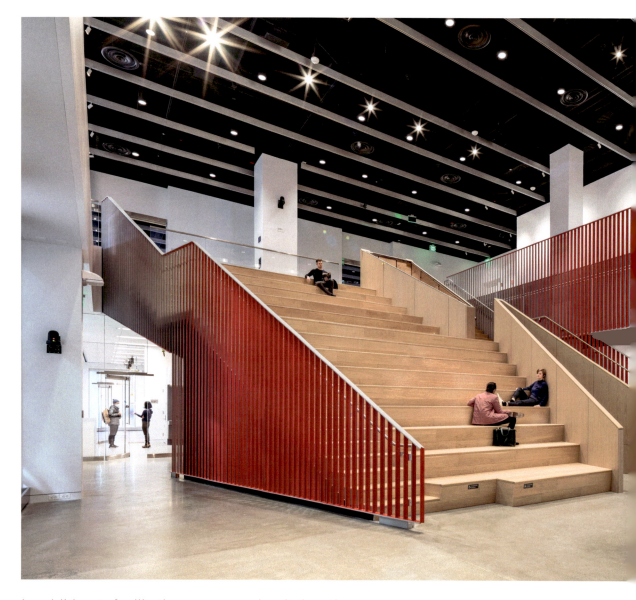

In addition to facilitating museum circulation, the Exchange Space is a large, terraced public stair that doubles as stepped seating for visitors to gather for presentations, lectures, exhibitions, and celebrations. The flexibility of the space allows visitors to connect to the gallery spiral while creating views into adjacent programs such as the Idea Hub, seen through the openings in the steps.

10'   25'   50'

The gallery spaces are highly functional, with robust ceiling infrastructure designed to accommodate the varied, changing demands of art and exhibits over time. A system of customized aluminum baffles combines power, lighting, and hanging requirements into a single, extruded profile of integrated infrastructure. When arrayed in a north-south orientation, the baffles form a distinct grain, orienting visitors within the gallery spiral while concealing MEP, AV, and structural systems above. The new MIT Museum creates a public interface for the institute, showcasing its distinct collection and hosting a range of events unique to MIT.

Moongate Bridge

Infrastructure is not only about bridges and roads. It is broadly defined as that which is shared and where different publics meet. Parks and plazas are also infrastructures — social infrastructure, environmental infrastructure, and public infrastructure.

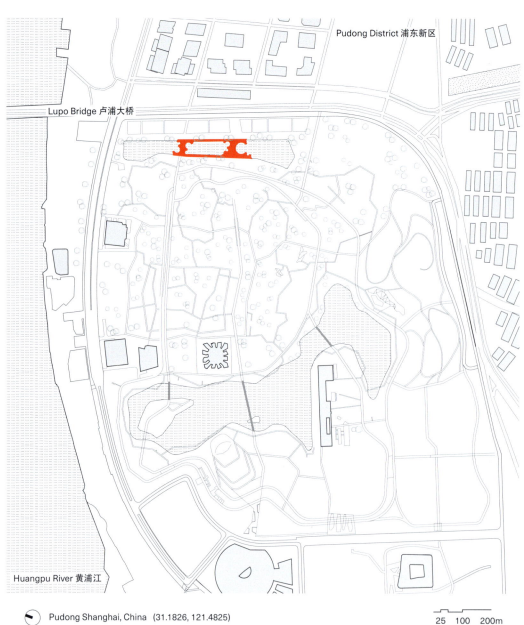

Pudong District 浦东新区

Lupo Bridge 卢浦大桥

Huangpu River 黄浦江

Pudong Shanghai, China   (31.1826, 121.4825)

25   100   200m

Located in the Houtan area of the Pudong District in Shanghai, the former 2010 Shanghai Expo grounds are undergoing a radical transformation to become a new urban public park and cultural center for the city. The site has evolved over several decades from a natural wetland, to an urban industrial zone, to a World Expo site. The transformation of the former World Expo landscape into one of the largest public parks in Shanghai again reimagines the site and redefines the role of a cultural park and landscape for the metropolis.

Moongate Bridge sits at the main entrance to the Shanghai Expo Cultural Park and connects two waterfront edges to form a pedestrian plaza that frames the water in a reinterpretation of landscape strategies used in traditional Chinese gardens. The resulting landscape offers a series of viewing platforms, meandering paths, and reflection points.

1 Pedestrian path (light pavers)
2 Pedestrian lookout (medium pavers)
3 Connecting path (dark pavers)
4 Waterway
5 Glass guardrail
6 Park entrance

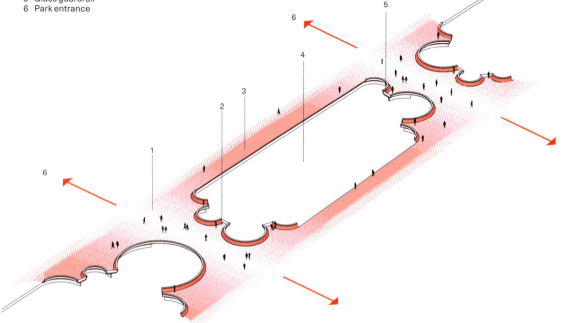

Situated at the park's northern boundary, adjacent to two subway entrances, Moongate Bridge marks the gateway to the new People's Park. The form of the bridge conceptualizes two separate pedestrian bridges as a conjoined pedestrian plaza. Inspired by traditional Chinese moongates that frame the landscape to alter perceptions of scale, distance, and nature, Moongate Bridge employs a similar technique though rotated in plan to frame the water and its reflection of the sky.

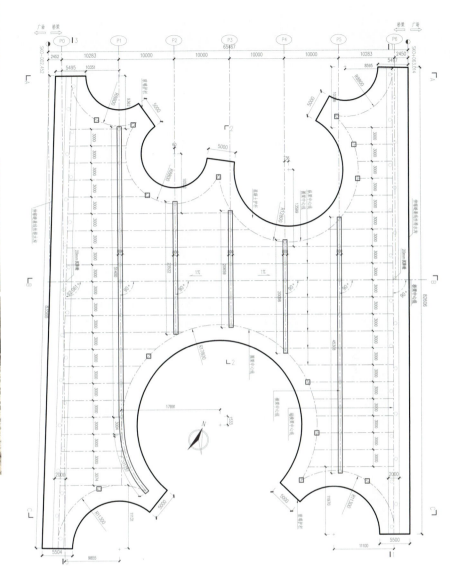

Structural Plan

5m   10m

Moongate Bridge features multiple lookout points, places to linger, and places to gather. The bridge is paved in different shades of gray granite, which indicate areas for movement and slowing down. The texture of the interior of the balustrade reveals the grain of the masonry blocks while the bridge's exterior is smooth site-cast concrete.

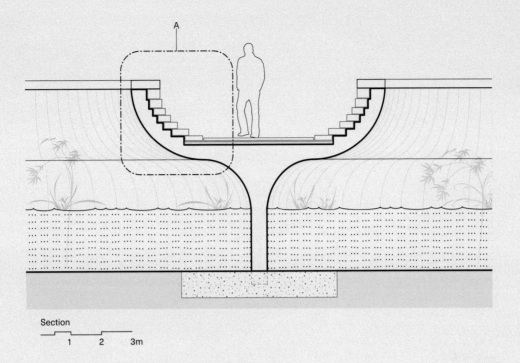

Section

1   2   3m

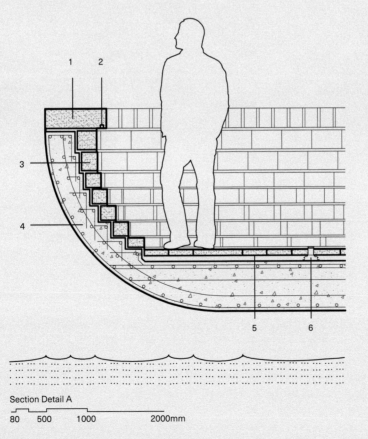

1 Granite coping
2 Recess for LED strip
3 Granite blocks
4 Site cast concrete
5 Granite paver
6 In-ground marker light

Section Detail A

80   500   1000   2000mm

The traditional Chinese garden is understood as a series of
relationships between elements. Moongate Bridge provides
multiple vantage points that create a network of relationships
across the body of water. The end grain of the bridge profile
expresses the contrast between interior and exterior textures.

A full-scale mockup is used to test the stone setting technique and confirm the relationships between stone, site-cast concrete, and the glass guardrail channel.

Downtown Crossing Amphitheater

Location
Boston,
Massachusetts, USA

Team Members
Eric Höweler
J. Meejin Yoon
Kyle Coburn
Cyrus Dochow

Collaborators
Richard Burck Associates (Landscape Architect)

BSA Space

Location
Boston,
Massachusetts, USA

Team Members
Eric Höweler
J. Meejin Yoon
Parker Lee
Thena Tak
Cyrus Dochow
Ryan Murphy

MIT Museum

Location
Cambridge,
Massachusetts, USA

Team Members
Eric Höweler
J. Meejin Yoon
Hari Priya Rangarajan
Namjoo Kim
Jacob Bruce
David Tarcali
Ching Ying Ngan
Joann Feng
Neil Legband
Elle Gerderman
Cyrus Dochow

Moongate Bridge

Location
Pudong Shanghai,
China

Team Members
Eric Höweler
J. Meejin Yoon
Ching Ying Ngan
Di Wang
Elle Gerdeman

Collaborators
Shanghai Landscape-Architecture Design and Research Institute Co., Ltd. (Local Design Institute)

Eco-Logics
Conversation with Kate Orff

Kate Orff, founding principal of SCAPE, Professor at Columbia GSAPP, and Director of the Urban Design Program at Columbia GSAPP, discusses the role of design in providing ecological education and literacy by offering new ways to understand our ecological circumstances.

ERIC

Kate, you have been examining the relationships between systems at large and small scales. Your work makes me wonder, how do people read their environments, and how do we better equip them to read their environments? If you could communicate a theme through the designed landscape, what would you broadcast to people?

KATE

We must go beyond the notion that somehow energy exists somewhere outside of our immediate environment. It can exist in micro-adjacencies in our immediate spatial context. Micro and distributed energy is our shared future. We need a new agenda for the designed landscape. Eco-literate design practices should attack the notion of large, centralized energy systems, which are dependent upon invisible and extractive feedstocks. We are conditioned to plug into a socket that masks the coal-burning plant behind it, and to pump gas from a nozzle that is disconnected from the extractive carbon industry that enables it. Energy doesn't feel visceral and all around you. Only people in sacrificial zones like stripped mountain tops or fence-line communities in regions like Houston or New Orleans see and feel its true impact. There's a lot to be gained from introducing energy, or energy awareness, into everyday spaces. We must lose that perceptual distance from our energy systems and bring them into closer view.

Hurricane Harvey devastated Southeast Texas. 2017

ERIC

It's very difficult to make energy more present and less remote, partially because people seldom visit the sites of energy production and our idea of energy is so abstract. It's always 'elsewhere.'

MEEJIN

It is interesting to see how your research works to visualize energy systems in a way that makes those distances evident. For architects, landscape architects, and students our toolset can be leveraged to shift public understanding. It seems to me that your practice can shift representation toward action.

KATE

Landscape is ultimately about the interdependence of systems, and I think we've lost our way. A big part of our work at SCAPE has been to visualize systems and reconceive how design can reset connections and reconnect fragmented systems between social life and the landscape in a way that is spatial and meaningful. To that end, the book *Petrochemical America* is a statement about the purview of landscape and its relationship to extraction and energy.

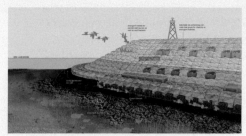

Living Breakwaters. SCAPE. New York City

MEEJIN
Petrochemical America does such an amazing job tracing patterns of energy extraction that can seem invisible. It has been hugely influential in starting a conversation among designers about the trickle-down effects of energy sourcing in this country. How do you see that research migrating into acts of design?

KATE
We've tried to advance the Living Breakwaters project, which emerged from the Rebuild by Design process and has federal funding through HUD, by expanding the notion of its performance as a pilot project. The concept of the pilot is so strong because it can evolve any kind of legal or regulatory process from the inside. A pilot is a useful construction because it suggests that a project is experimental yet has finite edges and clear boundaries. It can be used to test, monitor, and set the groundwork for future, and hopefully, expanded project parameters.

Gulf refinery fire on Schuylkill River. 1977

ERIC
That's a clever way to sort of smuggle innovation into a regulatory process. The way you've mobilized citizens is also impressive — as you have said, we should build a public instead of a project, which resonates with us. A lot of our early work was done in the public realm and we often found ourselves trespassing into other disciplines. A more recent example would be FloatLab. The project requires permission from multiple agencies because it falls outside of normal categories for buildings and vessels. We're talking about whether we need a boat mooring permit or a dock structure permit.

KATE
Do you need to dock it?

ERIC
Yes, we do. We need to build a dock and gangway and we also had to figure out what the

Light Drift. Höweler + Yoon. Philadelphia,
Pennsylvania. 2011

FloatLab. Höweler + Yoon. Philadelphia,
Pennsylvania. 2016

AHJ (Authority Having Jurisdiction) is. Is it the
Department of Licenses and Inspections, the
Coast Guard, the Art Commission, or is it Parks
and Recreation? FloatLab resonates with work
you've been doing in terms of postindustrial
landscapes, finding nature already touched
by humans. As we researched the project,
we learned that the Schuylkill had caught on
fire at some point because it was so polluted.
When you go there now, it doesn't appear to be
polluted. It looks quite nice, but getting to the
actual waterfront was not always easy because
so much industry was located along the river.
Before the cleanup efforts, the city turned its
back to the riverfront. Now the question is: how
do we reverse that? The Philadelphia Mural
Arts Organization and Bartram's Garden have
been sponsoring interventions and programs
in and along the river to bring attention to
the ecological issues surrounding it. Before
FloatLab, we did a 'mural' in the river called
Light Drift that was a set of floating orbs with
interactive lights that communicated with
people on the shore, so that's when we started
thinking about the river as a kind of urban
nature, but also as a site of environmental
education.

KATE
FloatLab shines a spotlight on sea-level rise
and climate change alongside the adaptation of
buildings, edges, and shorelines. In many cases,
whether it's industrial or residential, you see
structures that go all the way to the shoreline
eliminating public access. We are also trying
to address the diminishing public realm at the
water's edge in our work on the Gowanus Canal
in our Lowlands Master Plan. At Gowanus, there's
an incredible desire for communities to go, touch,
and be in the space of the canal. In many cases
it's illegal because private properties go all the
way to the edge of the canal and to get there
you have to trespass. So, I love this concept of
getting the boat mooring permit because you're
hacking an existing set of permissible structures
and enabling public right-of-way in the more
immediate term.

ERIC
In Amsterdam, you can moor a boat along all
the edges of a waterway. If you need to get your

boat to shore, you can moor and cross private property — even walk over someone else's boat — to get to a public way. It's just a different idea of the public realm, what counts as a common resource.

Attitudes about the waterfront are codified at the city level as regulations, codes, or rules that create these ideas of publicness. Both of these projects create an architectural experience coupled with a programming agenda. In the case of FloatLab, Bartram's Garden will program events in the outdoor classroom.

MEEJIN
There's a lot of energy invested in public outreach, to build and educate a public. As a visitor, you're not only experiencing the river life yourself but there will be someone to help you interpret it, performing water pollution testing, and teaching you how to create a healthy river ecology.

KATE
We also feel the desire to invest in public outreach. You need to meet people where they are in both a literal and figurative way. I feel it's a challenge that no designers have fully mastered. It's a challenge of listening and translating our listening into a formal response.

MEEJIN
I notice you are doing multiple publications with your project, one set for a professional audience and one set for school kids, connecting with each audience graphically. That's very unusual! How would you compare the level of engagement and power in your field (landscape, planning, and urbanism) to a more academic architecture discipline? It's clear that architecture has oscillated between engagement and autonomy, and in this moment an expanded perspective of the discipline is critical.

KATE
We tried to make the *Toward an Urban Ecology* book broadly accessible, and not just focused on a professional audience of our peers or clients. At the same time, the *Oyster Gardening Manual*, the *Bird Safe Building Guidelines*, and a lot of our community charrettes and activities are really about reaching a

Toward an Urban Ecology. Kate Orff. 2016

younger or very different audience. There are broader landscapes that we don't traditionally consider as landscape architects, like agricultural landscapes, national parks, riverbeds, wildlife corridors, and marine landscapes, and I feel like that is where academia needs to start making a big difference. There is a growing interest in regenerative agricultural practices, methods, and broader policies that impact the landscape, but we do need to go beyond the typical studio model. I think landscape architecture could play an expanded role in addressing disappearing biodiversity, shifting eco-regions, and distressed smaller towns and cities in the broader American landscape that are home to populations who have been left behind by the current economy.

MEEJIN
I'm curious, did the Rising Currents project at MoMA enable you to have more exposure in relationship to local, state, or federal government — or did those develop in parallel?

KATE
Rising Currents was important for the office because we were able to experiment with what we were already looking at in a more public context. It helped us to instantly reach a wide audience with design on the critical topic of climate change. Typically, a designer's work is filtered through many formats, whether they are glossy magazines, agencies, or power structures.

MEEJIN
In Rising Currents, your project stood out because you were trying to make a point. It wasn't trying to erase our problems by designing new habitats for ourselves but was calling attention to the ecological history of the Gowanus Canal. By showing the canal as a marine habitat which was once a thriving oyster bed, we learned that a deeper understanding of our ecology could provide a path toward a more resilient future. That was the objective of your wall. You made it loud and clear.

KATE
I realized over the course of the eight months of work that whereas we could generate thousands of tiny little sections with all the things you would typically geek out about, in the case of the MoMA

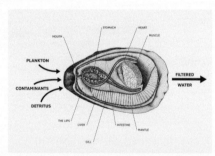

Oyster Gardening Manual. SCAPE

exhibition we really had one big moment to capture someone's attention in-full. We designed our space in the museum to be legible from fifty feet away, from five feet away, and five inches away so the information and design work at many scales. That's why, in the end, that body of work got pretty deep into the public consciousness. We were trying to hit at an emotional level.

> MEEJIN
> You're able to balance the technocratic with the ecological; man-made solutions with the natural environment. I think that's why your work is now the authority — you are the expert.

KATE
Well, if I'm not, then the people at SCAPE are. Although, the very notion of the expert is changing. Moving forward, we really have to facilitate climate expertise in everyone.

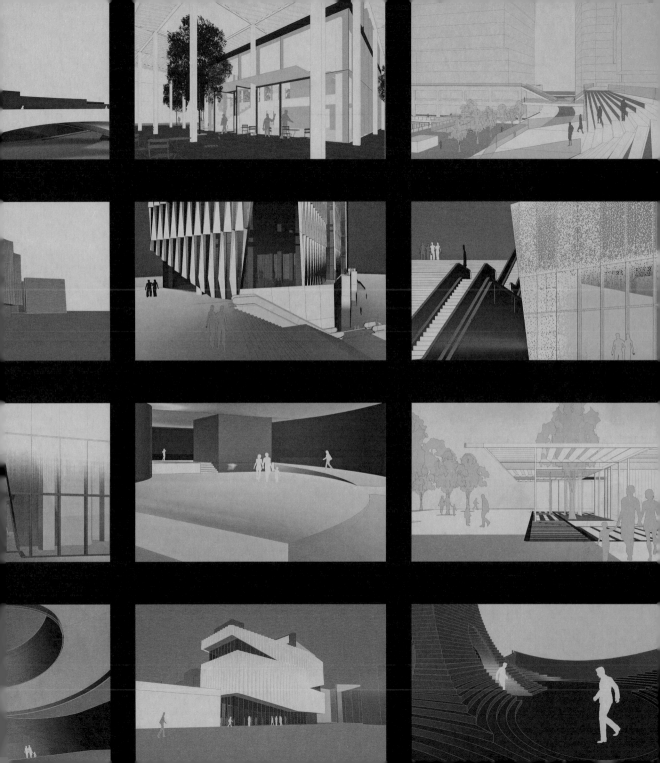

Chapter IV   Under the Weather

Unlike weather, climate is, by definition, a statistical phenomenon, a set of records, data points, and averages collected over long periods of time. Climate is what you expect, and weather is what you get. Philosopher Timothy Morton points out that weather is the "sensual impression of climate," whereas climate is a "higher dimensional being," something he calls a "hyperobject."[1] A hyperobject is a super-phenomenon, something so large and distributed across time and space that it is almost imperceptible.

Architecture exists in both weather and climate. It is an immediate response to phenomena, rain, wind, and snow — shielding and sheltering from the elements. Architecture also impacts the future of climate both in the energy consumed by its mechanical systems and the embodied energy stored in its materials. Architecture could be defined by both weather and weathering — its ability to resist hurricane-force winds or provide an air-conditioned interior. Even the slow erosion of materials over time (the weathering of stone, or the corrosion of steel, for example) define aspects of architecture. The title of this chapter suggests that architecture is always already under the weather, subject to its frictions and forces, but also complicit in the carbon economy of extraction and urbanization that have impacts at scales ranging from the local to the planetary.

How to design for or with climate in the twenty-first century? How does design impact larger phenomena in measurable ways? What is the scope of climate design? Of ecosystem design? Of environmental design? Projects in "Under the Weather" engage with various fields and discourses by making energy visible as a means for making our energy footprints legible, creating microclimates through the design of specifically tailored solar analysis thinking about renewable materials and embodied energy, and creating outdoor places for ecological teaching and environmental experiences.

We have inherited a twentieth-century model of oppositions between nature and culture — inside versus outside, conditioned versus unconditioned. So much of the built environment is understood as a hermetically sealed and mechanically conditioned interior, isolated from the larger environmental context through barriers, membranes, insulation, and sheathing. Architecture has come to be understood as an atmosphere apart.

An early application of a hermetically sealed and mechanically conditioned building was employed by Le Corbusier at the Cité de Refuge in 1933. An early advocate for mechanical conditioning, Le Corbusier was quick to embrace the emerging technologies of air conditioning and the curtain wall. Cité de Refuge performed well in the winter when solar radiation was trapped by the glass façade to retain heat but was unbearable in the summer when the building's mechanical systems could not keep up with solar heat gain, and the sealed curtain wall made natural ventilation impossible. After the war, Le Corbusier redesigned the south façade to incorporate brise soleil as an exterior sun screen. The brise soleil blocks solar radiation before it enters the building, reducing the demand for mechanical conditioning.

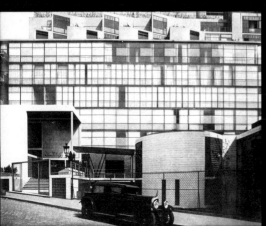 

employed by Le Corbusier for the rest of his career at sites as diverse in climate as Marseilles, Chandigarh, Algiers, and Cambridge, Massachusetts. Architectural historian Daniel Barber has argued that "the brise soleil is the moment when modern architecture became global."

The brise soleil acts as a discrete interface between building and climate. Its necessary separateness from the building makes it a pre-shelter, deflecting the rays of the sun before they reach the building. It is a kind of architecture for architecture. By rotating the brise soleil ninety degrees into a canopy, Helio House creates a shaded microclimate that reduces the mechanical load on a glass pavilion in Qianhai Park in hot, subtropical Shenzhen. The expansive canopy makes place by creating shade.

Conceived with Bryant Park as a precedent, Qianhai Park is a central green lawn that sits between high rises. Helio House, a mixed-use amenity structure, defines the western edge while plantings mark the lawn's perimeter. The building contains a café and bookstore, bathrooms, and a shaded terrace for small functions. The canopy structure is independent of the building and extends beyond the footprint significantly, creating a large, shaded area that produces a microclimate around the structure. The canopy and shading create a gradual transition from inside to outside and buffer the interior from the full brunt of the sun.

Solar control canopy spans program volumes and creates a shaded microclimate below.

The canopy around Helio House consists of a steel frame supported on tall steel columns infilled with extruded aluminum baffles that diffuse the sun. Because the building is surrounded by tall buildings that provide some shading, the optimal orientation of the solar baffles varies from bay to bay.

The baffles themselves are designed to bounce light between two concave profiles, allowing indirect light to filter through the canopy. The concave profiles of the solar baffles learn from the daylighting system used at The Menil Collection designed by Renzo Piano. The Menil's interior allows indirect light to illuminate the exhibited artworks while protecting them from the sun's harmful UV rays. For Helio House, the intent is to introduce light without heat. The underside of the canopy appears light and airy without the heat typically associated with direct sunlight.

The design of Helio House entailed extensive 3D modeling and sun angle studies. The simulation studies employed daylighting software to calculate optimal angles for blocking the most direct rays while permitting indirect rays. The use of simulation software in the design process allowed for the fine-tuning of environmental effects, which allowed Helio House to adapt to extremely localized climatic conditions.

The solar canopy surrounding Helio House is climate-responsive, intercepting the sun's rays before they reach the building to improve the comfort of the occupants and reduce the cost of its conditioning. As such, its efforts are both qualitative and quantitative. It is more pleasant in the shade, and it is simultaneously easier to cool the building as it is buffered from the direct solar heat gain.

Architect Kiel Moe describes the physical building as an "isolated object-instance" within a

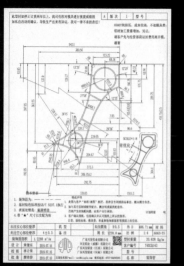

Extrusion shop drawings for concave solar control louvers.

much larger network of linkages, processes, and flows of materials and labor. [2] The materials used to construct buildings are extracted, processed, formed, and assembled to provide functional utility throughout the lifespan of the building. The longer view of these materials includes hundreds of thousands of years of formation prior to their becoming architecture, a brief moment as a building, and potentially hundreds of thousands of years as landfill after demolition. The embodied energy in our buildings and cities is an essential lens through which to view the built environment today. As architects and designers, our agency in specifying a material or system is one of the most significant decisions we make. The upstream procurement paths of a material or system as well as the downstream effects of our choices are critical considerations in the material ecologies of architecture.

At the same time, material selections for building systems are understood as having a significant impact on the environmental footprint of a building. Building with renewable materials, such as mass timber, has other benefits including carbon sequestration and impacts on land use and forestry practices.

As part of our research into mass timber as a building system, we developed a stacked mass timber structure for a public art piece in Spokane, Washington. Timber Stepwell is one of many sculptural projects to occupy the urban riverfront that was also once the site of the 1974 World's Fair. The project consists of sixty-eight blocks of stacked, glue-laminated Alaskan Yellow Cedar. The use of solid blocks of timber recalls the material history of

Historical photos of the timber

Spokane, a city that was for decades a significant resource for timber production and processing, and speculates on a material future that includes both traditional and innovative uses of timber.

Timber Stepwell uses glulam elements that are formed and milled to be assembled in a volumetric way, rather than the more typical application as columns, beams, and slabs. The volumetric use of mass timber to form the steps and walls of the project suggest monolithic construction that is more akin to masonry. Indeed, the concept is a cantilevered, monolithic shell with a tension ring at the top that operates as a simple, structural diagram of unit-to-unit load transfer. While the Collier Memorial at MIT is understood as a compression vault, approximating a dome, held together by tension members in the grade beam, Timber Stepwell is a bowl shape that relies on a tension tie around the upper ring to hold the structure together. In each case, the shell system of load transfer occurs from unit-to-unit through the planes that are shared. The design for the Collier Memorial requires load transfer between adjacent stones in the arch. For Timber Stepwell, load is transferred from woodblock to woodblock with compression while screws hold the cantilevered blocks together to ensure the continuity of the load path.

The block shell structure of the project presents an alternative to frame and skin applications. Most engineered wood construction is limited to the use of beams and panels as a substitute for steel or concrete columns, beams, and slabs. The volumetric use of mass timber

learns from the Collier Memorial's volumetric use of stone, where the fabrication envelope of a robotic mill is employed to arrive at a solution that is *inherently* volumetric. Timber Stepwell is understood as a stereotomic volume that produces spatial and structural configurations analogous to vaults and shells, rather than frames and skins.

The use of mass timber in a truly massive way reveals new expressive potential for engineered wood, not simply as a substitute for steel and concrete, but as an alternative to previous construction modes that architect Elisa Iturbe fits within the concept of "carbon modernity."[3] Finding alternatives to "carbon form" requires prototyping with materials that sequester carbon, developing rapidly renewable resources, and finding new applications and forms of expression for those new and hybrid materials. By accounting for the embodied energy of materials, Timber Stepwell offers alternative material flows that impact energy footprints. Thinking through material, its qualities and quantities, procurement and processes, allows us to imagine an approach to building with the earth in mind. What Bruno Latour would call "earthly accounts of buildings," or an architecture of accountability.[4]

Accountability requires awareness, measurement, and verification. The false opposition of the natural and the man-made is a result of our inherited understanding of the environment as something untouched by the human hand. This dichotomy promotes a double falsehood. On the one hand, the premise that there is a pristine nature untouched by human activity, and on the other, the idea that humans can somehow stand outside of natural systems. Today, we can see how our actions impact ecosystems, weather patterns, and global temperatures — and, how these actions are integrated into systems that are much larger than ourselves.

The consequences of these actions are often difficult to perceive, and many of these phenomena remain unseen. The raw materials

Robotic milling of mass timber units for Timber Stepwell.

that make up our buildings and the fossil fuels extracted to operate them remain remote and abstract. The history of the extraction industry, its impact on the environment, and efforts to regulate and remediate polluted waterways, is largely untold. Many urban rivers used for transporting people and goods were polluted by the industrial sites that developed along them. These waterways, which were left neglected as cities turned their backs to the riverfronts and developed away from them, are now experiencing a moment of rediscovery. Cities and citizens are recognizing neglected waterfronts as resources for recreation and sites of environmental education. This is the context for the FloatLab project sited on the Schuylkill River.

The City of Philadelphia is framed by two waterways, the Delaware and Schuylkill rivers, that have served as a transportation network enabling the city to flourish and become an extraction hub for coal, oil, and natural gas. The tributary area of the Schuylkill River encompasses much of what is known as anthracite coal country, a place where coal was mined and sent downstream by barge. The Schuylkill River, once considered the purest drinking water in the region, eventually earned the title of the most polluted river in the country, actually catching fire in November, 1892.

The Schuylkill River was the original superfund site. In 1945, before such designations existed, the state and federal governments spent millions of dollars to dredge and remediate the river and restore its ecosystems. Our proposal for FloatLab aims to tell the story of the river's transformation. FloatLab is a submersible barge that allows visitors to observe the river from an uncommon vantage point — from *within* the river. Visitors to FloatLab perceive the river from eye-level. This shift in perspective provides the opportunity for intimate observation of the urban waterway. FloatLab seeks to transform the city's relationship to the river and guide behaviors and choices that affect the urban ecosystem. By design, visitors become participants, citizen scientists, and co-producers.

FloatLab features a platform that serves as an outdoor classroom for environmental education, and the project's form follows with a trench-like circuit that ramps down 5' (150 cm) below the surface of the water before rising back up to the deck level. The program for FloatLab includes recreational kayaking, a mussel hatchery, and educational programming designed to cultivate a broader understanding of the urban waterway ecosystem, its history, and its remediated condition.

The direct experience of the Schuylkill River provided by FloatLab offers a new vantage point from which to view a dynamic urban ecosystem and assess the river ecology. Ultimately, FloatLab aims to support and increase eco-literacy by providing an accessible space for close observation that allows visitors to survey, confirm, and verify qualities specific to the relationship between urban and natural environments.

In the introduction to our 2009 book, *Expanded Practice*, we recounted the events of the Chernobyl nuclear disaster of 1986. As is well-known, the explosion of a nuclear reactor in what was then the U.S.S.R. sent a plume of radioactive particles across parts of Western Europe. Weather patterns distributed the radioactive cloud across national and political boundaries, resulting in widespread contamination and environmental damage. The Chernobyl disaster marked a moment in environmental consciousness that was tied to a local catastrophe but felt globally. Weather patterns and ecosystems are interconnected — irrespective of political borders and

FloatLab concept model.

cultural systems. Radioactivity, pollution, storms, and fronts continue to connect us across distances and differences. The Chernobyl disaster serves as a reminder of how we have all become increasingly aware of the interconnectedness of ecological systems, the environment, and how our activities span regional, continental, and planetary scales.

Fast forward to our contemporary moment. The science around global warming and climate change is staggering. The built environment is a significant contributor to greenhouse gas emissions and a consumer of raw materials. We know that business as usual cannot be sustained, and urgent action is needed. Or, as climate activist Greta Thunberg says, we need to behave "like our house is on fire."

As designers, we need to ask: how do we make visible the everyday practices that contribute to climate change? How to create a sense of urgency that catalyzes awareness and translates into action? Or, how do we redesign the house while it is on fire?

The abstract qualities of climate — its short-term fluctuations, and its long-term transformations — make it maddeningly difficult to perceive as a tangible reality and even more so to conceptualize as a problem with a solution built on the choices we make every day. Projects in "Under the Weather" work to build eco-literacy. They heighten environmental consciousness by expanding our capacity to see nature, decode its signals, and interpret its phenomena. The work aims to change *perceptions* of energy and environment so that the ethereal qualities of our interrelated systems and lives can be understood physically, materially, and empirically. Only then can we construct a future where we see ourselves embedded within a complex concept of our environment and accept our responsibility to design with weather *and* climate in mind.

1 Timothy Morton, *Hyperobjects, Philosophy and Ecology after the End of the World*, University of Minnesota Press, 2013, p.74–5.

2 Kiel Moe, *Empire, State & Building*, Actar Publishers, 2017 p.19.

3 Elisa Iturbe, "Architecture and the Death of Carbon Modernity," *Log 47*, Fall 2019, Anyone Corporation, p.11.

4 Bruno Latour, Albena Yaneva, "An Ant's View of Architecture," in *Explorations in Architecture, Teaching Design Research*, ed. Reto Geiser, Birkhäuser, 2008, p.88.

Helio House

Subject to the frictions and forces of both weather and climate, architecture can produce highly specific solutions to negotiate climate and comfort.

Shenzhen, Guangdong Province   (22.5286, 113.8856)

50m 100m   250m

Shenzhen, in the Pearl River Delta in southern China, is located in a
humid subtropical climate zone and experiences high temperatures
from May to October, upwards of 90°F/32°C. Helio House creates a
sense of place by making shade with a generous canopy that extends
well beyond the building footprint. While the surrounding towers shade
some of the site, the pavilion has significant solar exposure. Based
on a precise vector graph of solar exposure, louvers in the canopy are
arranged to address anticipated solar exposures throughout the day.

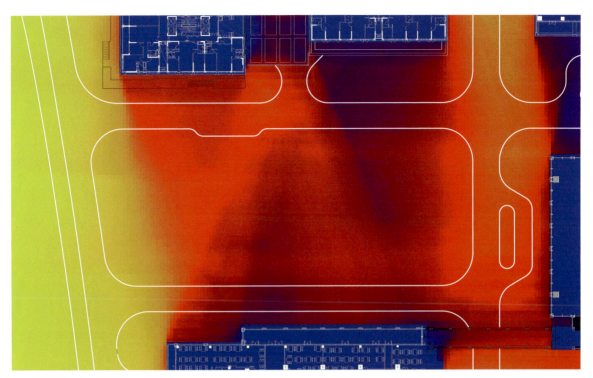

Solar exposure

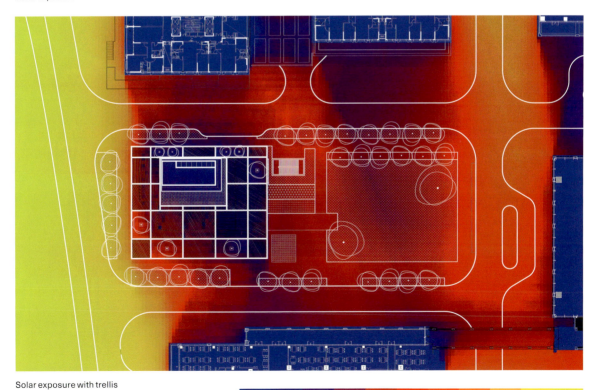

Solar exposure with trellis

10m   20m   50m

3 hours   1000 hours   2000 hours

Solar exposure (May–October)

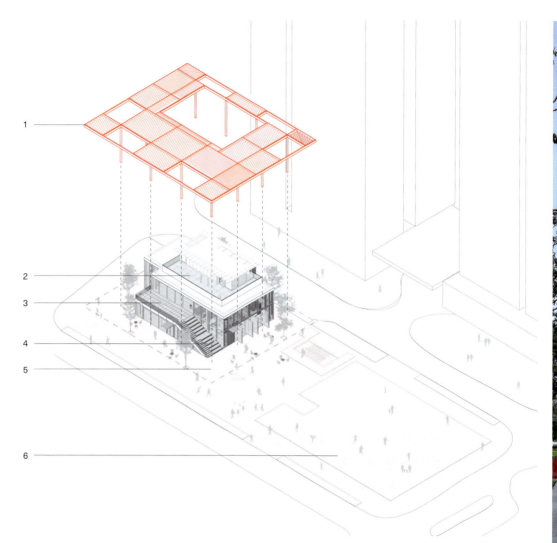

1 Trellis
2 Roof deck
3 Mezzanine deck
4 Grand stair
5 Shaded area under canopy
6 Great lawn

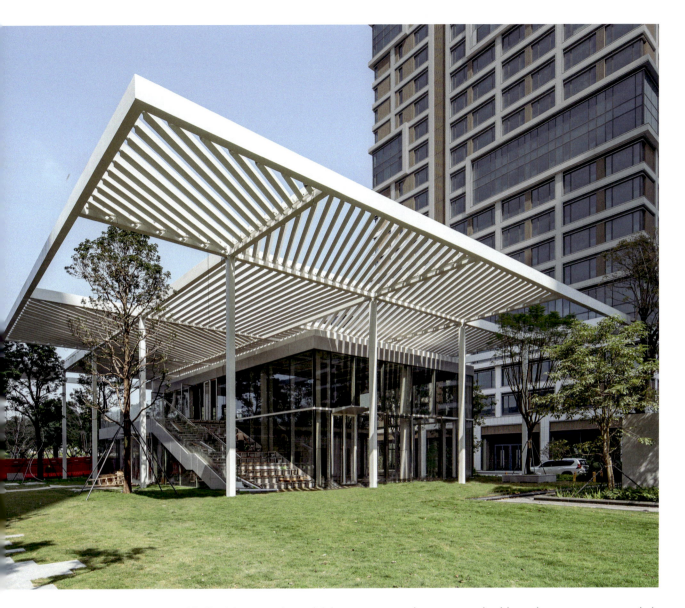

Helio House sits within a new park surrounded by a large commercial development in Shenzhen's third Central Business District. An expansive trellis extends over the transparent pavilion that houses a café, event space, and public restrooms, creating a shaded space for outdoor activities and café seating.

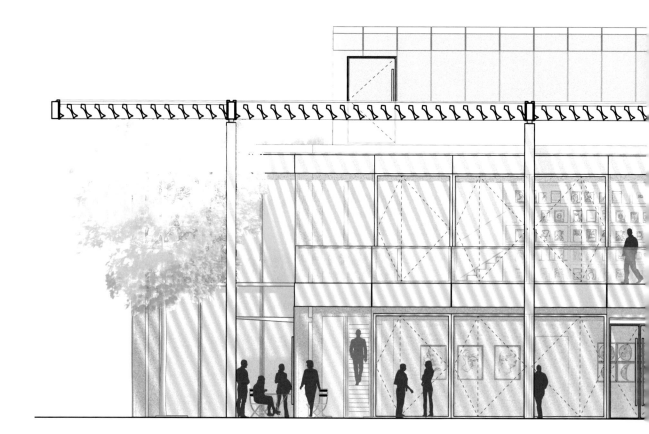

As the building's defining feature, the trellis not only shades inhabitants below, but extends the activities hosted by the pavilion into the park, balancing shaded and unshaded areas. Anchored by the glass box, the area around the pavilion becomes a shared public realm defined by shade. The grand stair provides access to the upper terrace level and serves as a small amphitheater for public events.

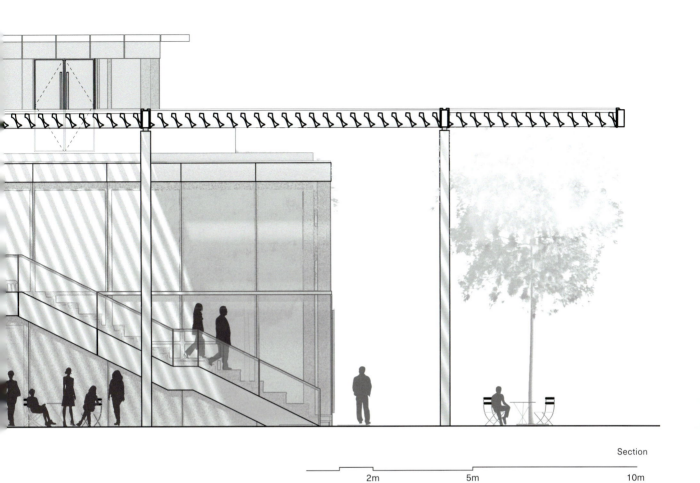

Section

2m   5m   10m

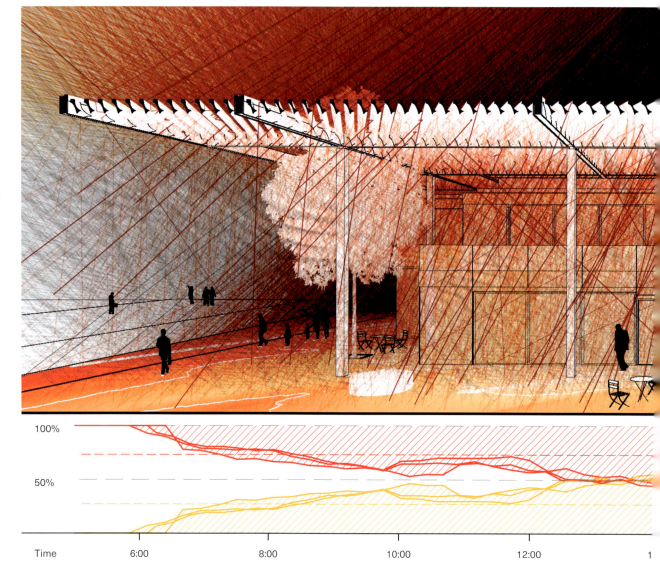

Using parametric tools, the diffuse and direct light hitting the ground and building surfaces below the trellis can be measured throughout the day. The geometry of the louver profile impacts paths of light reflection beneath the canopy. Iterative testing confirms the hypothesis that a convex louver profile provides twice as much diffuse light below the canopy while also blocking direct light and reducing heat. Helio House leverages computational tools to calibrate a specific solar performance that informs the process of designing a unique architectural microclimate.

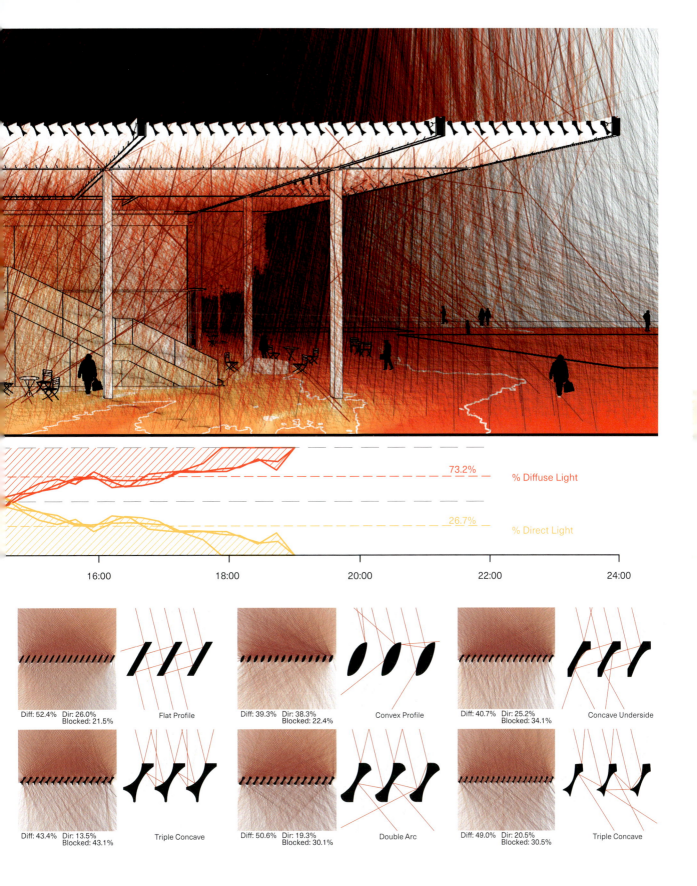

73.2% % Diffuse Light

26.7% % Direct Light

16:00 18:00 20:00 22:00 24:00

Diff: 52.4% Dir: 26.0%
Blocked: 21.5%

Flat Profile

Diff: 39.3% Dir: 38.3%
Blocked: 22.4%

Convex Profile

Diff: 40.7% Dir: 25.2%
Blocked: 34.1%

Concave Underside

Diff: 43.4% Dir: 13.5%
Blocked: 43.1%

Triple Concave

Diff: 50.6% Dir: 19.3%
Blocked: 30.1%

Double Arc

Diff: 49.0% Dir: 20.5%
Blocked: 30.5%

Triple Concave

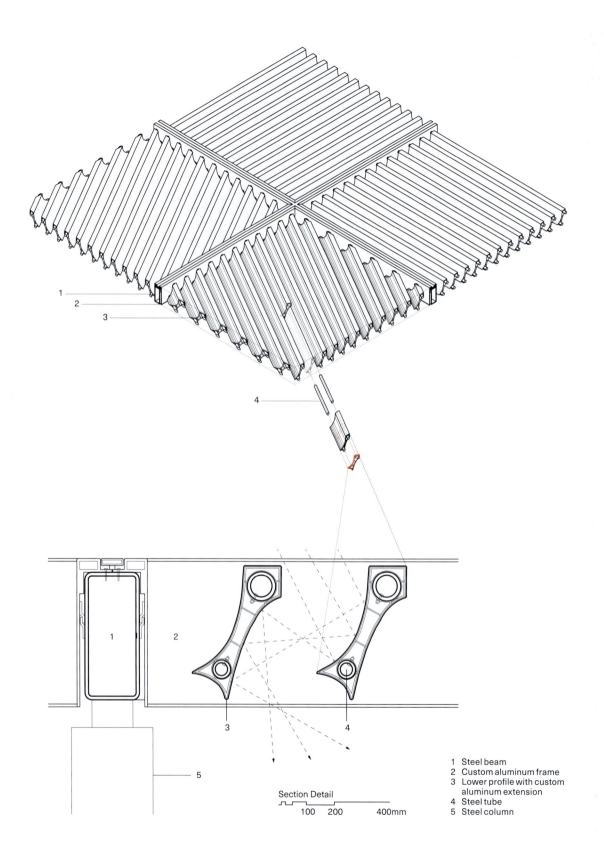

1 Steel beam
2 Custom aluminum frame
3 Lower profile with custom
   aluminum extension
4 Steel tube
5 Steel column

Section Detail

100   200   400mm

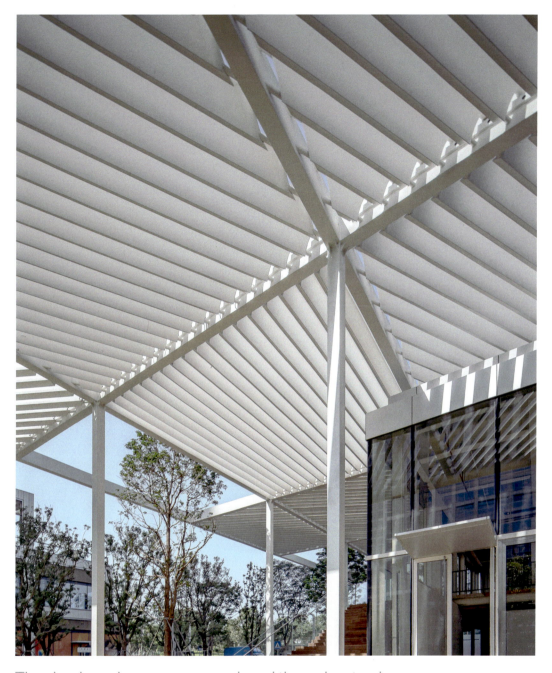

The aluminum louvers were produced through extrusion from a custom die and cropped to precise angles and lengths to fit within the trellis frame. The orientation of the louvers is specific to the direction of most solar gain, resulting in a quilt-like pattern. Because of the large size of the trellis cells, the aluminum is reinforced with steel tubes that are welded to the trellis frame.

Typical convex louver profiles have a dark underside that reflect most incidental light upwards. The unique concave louver profile of Helio House blocks direct sunlight while admitting indirect light, giving the pavilion a light and airy appearance.

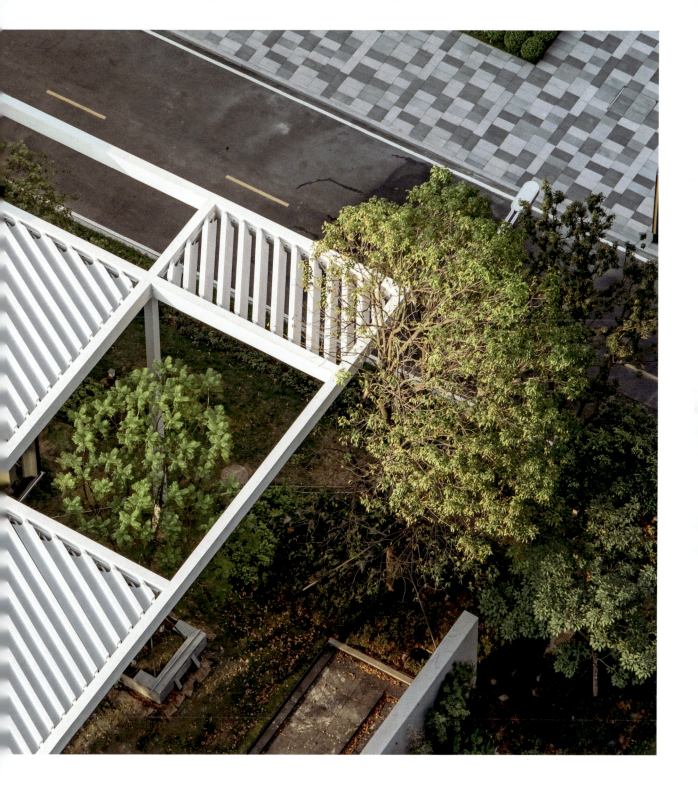

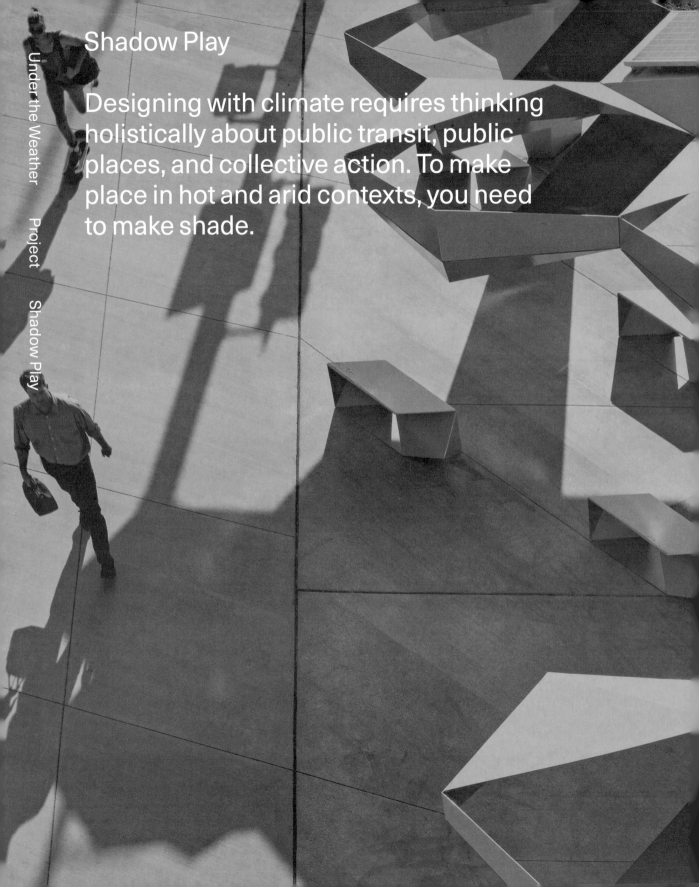

Shadow Play

Designing with climate requires thinking holistically about public transit, public places, and collective action. To make place in hot and arid contexts, you need to make shade.

Pheonix, Arizona   (33.458863, -112.069468)

0 50' 100'   300'   600'

1   Central Avenue light rail
2   Roosevelt Row Arts District

As part of the City of Phoenix's initiative to encourage the use of public transit and improve the pedestrian experience, the reconstructed streetscape of a multiblock section of Roosevelt Row narrows the road, adds bike lanes, and widens sidewalks. Shadow Play is a public art installation that integrates this streetscape improvement project with the creation of comfortable public space in the context of Phoenix's hot and arid climate. Conceptualized as a series of 'public parasols,' Shadow Play makes place by making shade. The shade structures are distributed along Roosevelt Row between 4th Street and the light rail station on Central Avenue, creating microclimates of respite along the urban route.

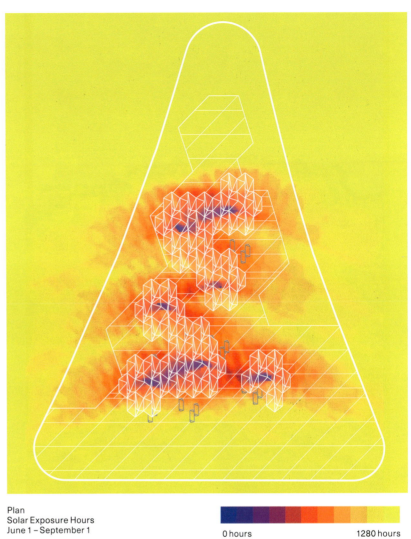

Plan
Solar Exposure Hours
June 1 – September 1

0 hours   1280 hours

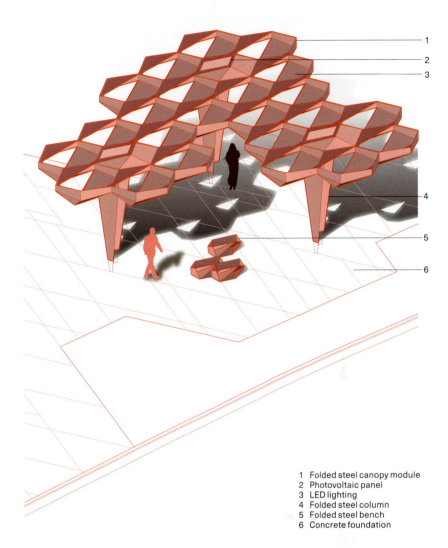

1 Folded steel canopy module
2 Photovoltaic panel
3 LED lighting
4 Folded steel column
5 Folded steel bench
6 Concrete foundation

The central Shadow Play shade structure on 4th Street transforms a former traffic island into a shaded plaza. The design of the shade structure and its geometries are calibrated to create both shade and shadows to reduce heat, enable air flow, and frame patterns of light that change throughout the day. Shadow Play uses an aggregation of geometric modules that cluster to form a canopy. The open modules of the canopy link together, spanning vertical supports to create transfer loads.

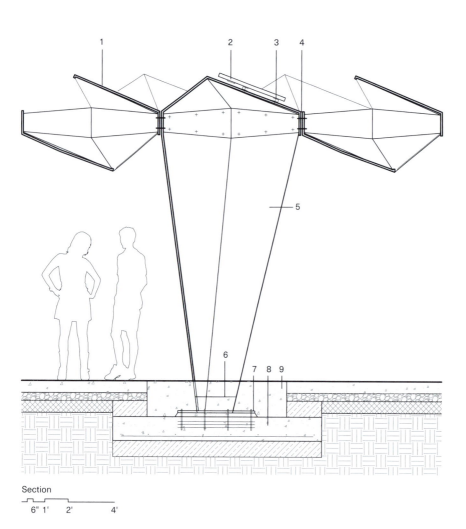

Section

6" 1' 2'   4'

The canopy is constructed out of 1/4" (6 mm) steel plate, which is folded to maximize shade from the south while encouraging natural airflow. The cellular modules are geometrically optimized to create maximum rigidity with minimal material. Photovoltaic panels are mounted to the top surface of the canopy, taking advantage of the optimally oriented geometry of the cells.

1 ¼" Steel plate canopy cell
2 Photovoltaic panel
3 Connection bracket
4 Bolted connection
   between cells
5 Folded steel column
6 Steel stiffener
7 Steel base plate
8 Concrete footing
9 Site-cast concrete

After dark, the solar power generated by the photovoltaic panels illuminates the interior of the canopy cells, creating a well-lit plaza for pedestrians to use at night.

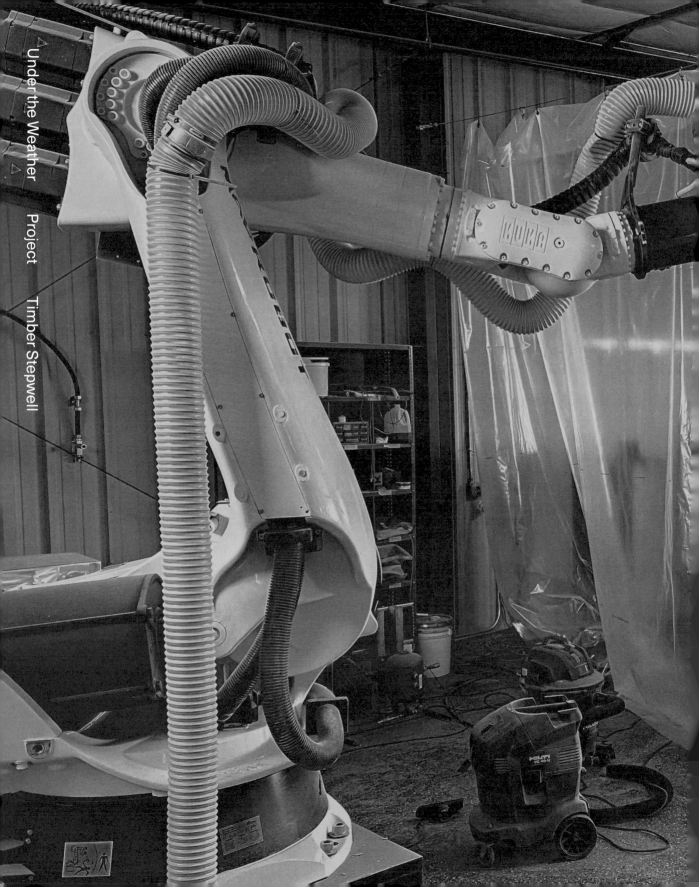

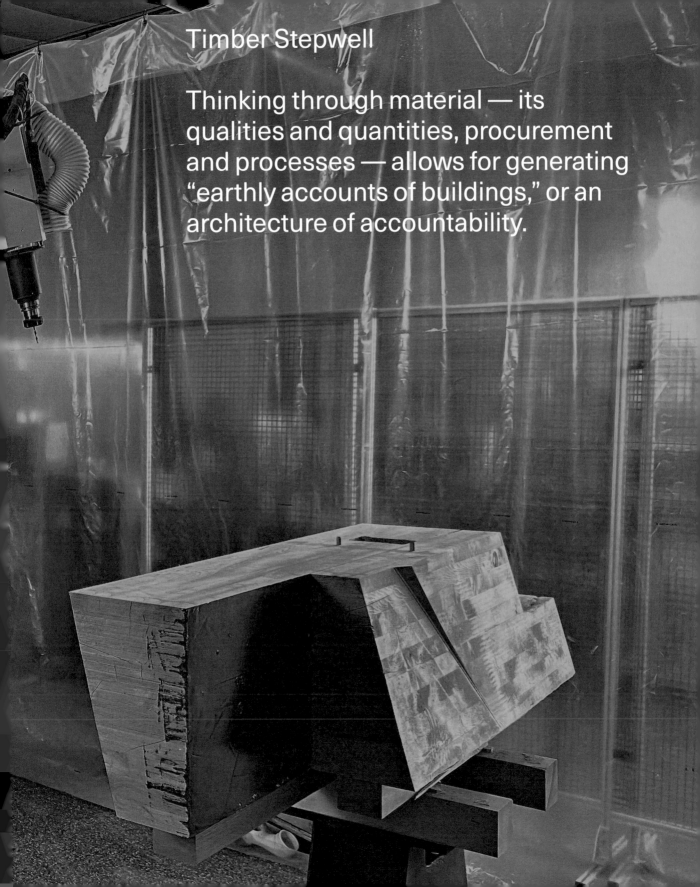

Timber Stepwell

Thinking through material — its qualities and quantities, procurement and processes — allows for generating "earthly accounts of buildings," or an architecture of accountability.

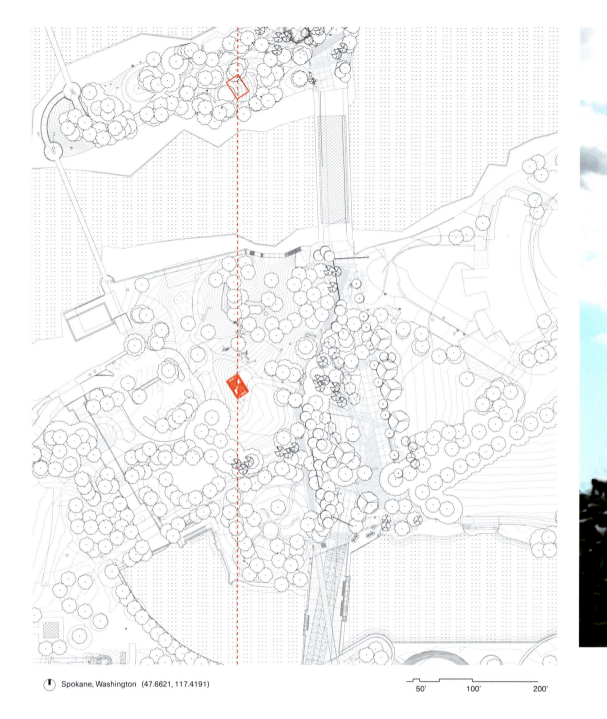

Spokane, Washington (47.6621, 117.4191)

50'   100'   200'

Sited on a high point overlooking the Spokane Falls, Timber Stepwell is both a lookout point and a viewing device. The inhabitable sculpture frames views across the landscape while also creating an intimate space for gathering. Conceived as part of a larger public art master plan, the project references the legacy of environmental activism dating back to the Spokane World Expo of 1974.

Timber Stepwell's sculptural silhouette features smooth and continuous geometry on the exterior and a stepped seating area on the interior. Precisely CNC-milled, glue-laminated solid blocks of wood form the massive assembly. Laminated wood tiers corbel to create the tapering profile.

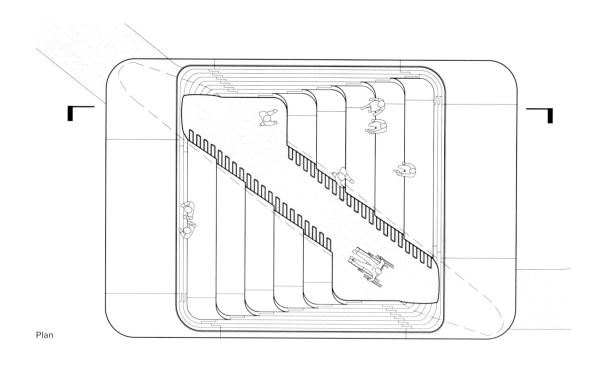

Plan

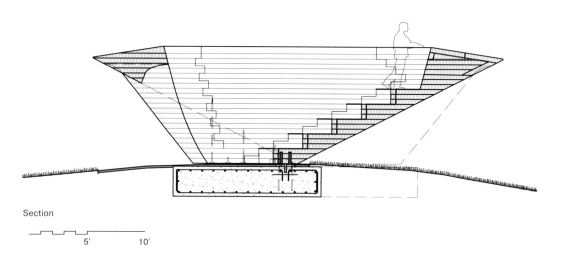

Section

5'   10'

The high precision of digital fabrication facilitates the use of mass timber not only for framing, but to create volume. Mass timber is precisely machined in the shop rather than cut in the field. Having fewer and larger parts reduces on-site installation time and labor. The diagram at right shows half of the project's sixty-eight timber components.

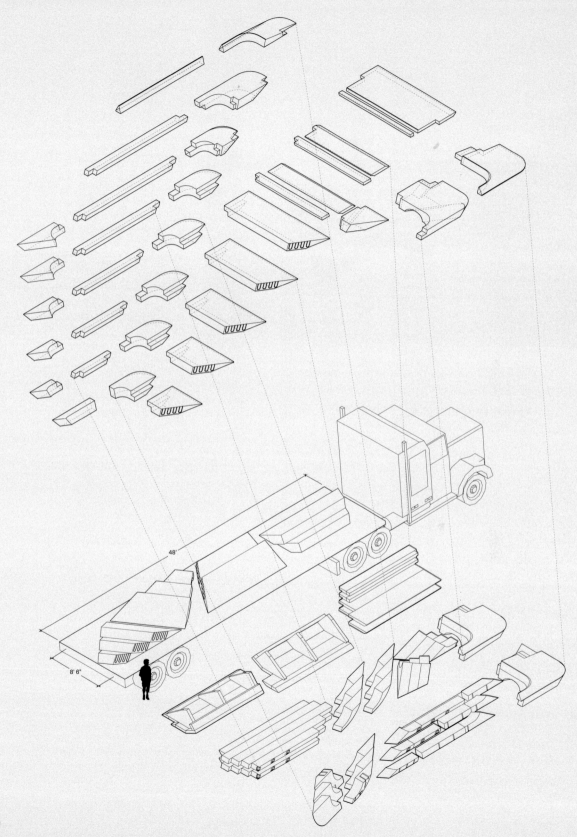

48'

8' 6"

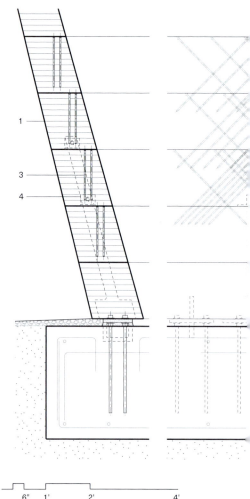

Timber Stepwell uses mass timber as a sculptural construction material assembled from a relatively small number of parts. Solid glulam billets are assembled and milled off site, transported to the site, and set in place on a concrete foundation with custom steel knife plates. The large prefabricated wood blocks are set with scaffolding and mechanically connected to adjacent blocks with long fasteners and pre-drilled pilot holes. By maximizing shop preassembly with robotic equipment, the on-site time is minimized.

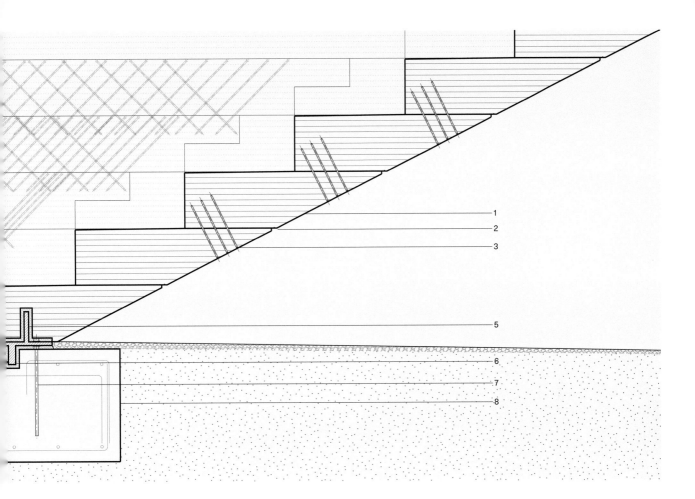

1 Alaskan Yellow Cedar glulam
2 Drip edge
3 Fasteners
4 Steel knife plate behind
5 Steel fin plate
6 Steel baseplate with shear lug
7 Anchor bolt
8 Concrete foundation

The dramatic cantilever and sculptural volume demonstrate new modes of expression for mass timber products that are typically used as substitutes for steel or concrete building elements that require more energy to produce.

Solar Veil

The brise soleil acts as a discrete interface between building and climate. Its separateness from the building makes it a "pre-shelter," deflecting the sun's rays before they reach the building — a kind of architecture for architecture.

The City of Haikou, on the island of Hainan in the South China Sea, has a humid subtropical climate. Building code in Haikou sets minimum standards for solar exposure, while the architecture simultaneously seeks strategies for solar control. The Solar Veil building orients the double-loaded segment of the bar on a north-south axis and employs vertical louvers to screen eastern and western exposures from the low angle of the sun.

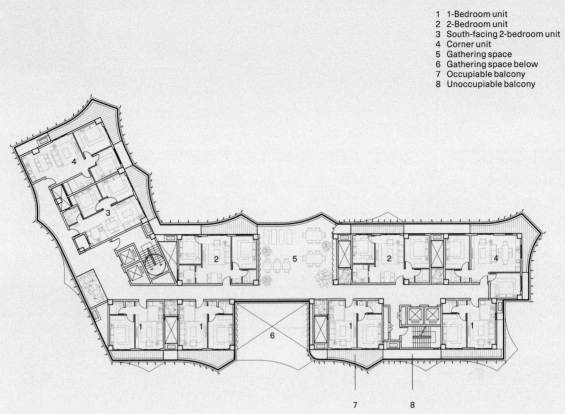

1 1-Bedroom unit
2 2-Bedroom unit
3 South-facing 2-bedroom unit
4 Corner unit
5 Gathering space
6 Gathering space below
7 Occupiable balcony
8 Unoccupiable balcony

Plan Level 04

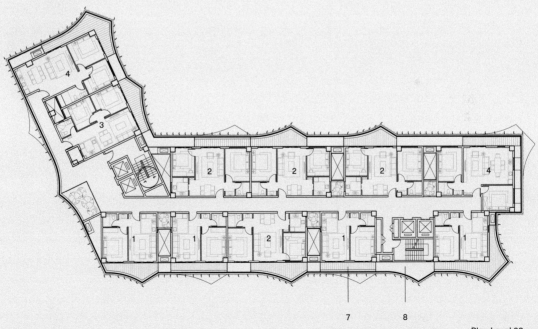

Plan Level 02

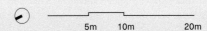

5m   10m   20m

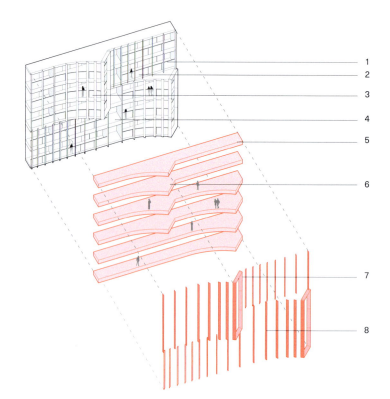

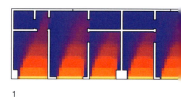

1

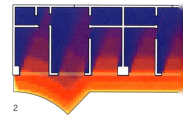

2

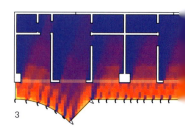

3

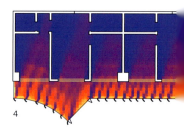

4

1 Guardrail
2 Straight balcony
3 Peel balcony
4 AC gap
5 Straight slab
6 Peel slab
7 Chamfered frame
8 Colored louver

All units in the Solar Veil building benefit from outdoor balconies that extend living spaces and create solar shading. The saw-toothed slab edge varies, forming multistory bay window projections that appear to peel open and create the impression of a rippling façade.

Sun exposure in summer

1 No balcony
   16% sun exposure
2 Balcony
   11.1% sun exposure
3 Straight louvers
   9.2% sun exposure
4 Tilted louvers
   8.2% sun exposure

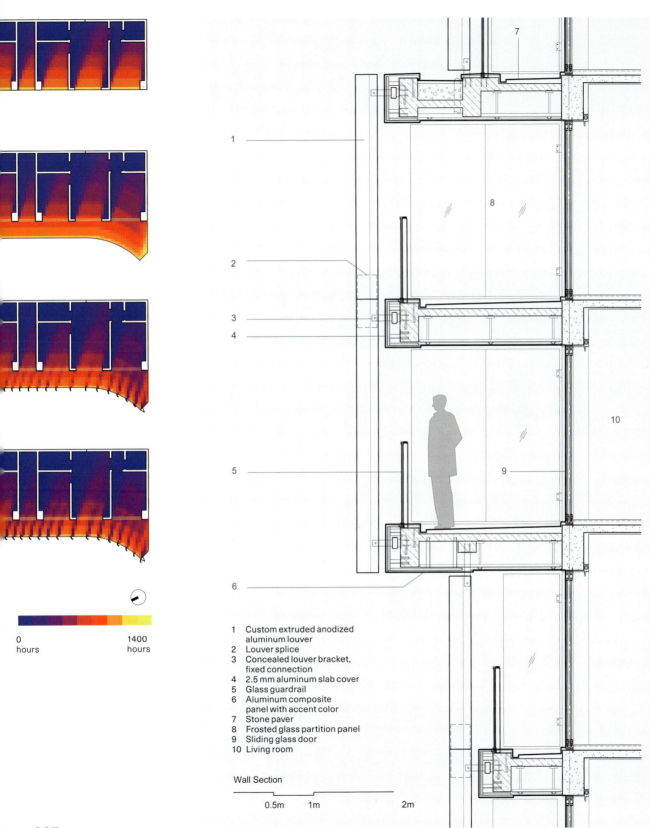

0 hours

1400 hours

1 Custom extruded anodized
   aluminum louver
2 Louver splice
3 Concealed louver bracket,
   fixed connection
4 2.5 mm aluminum slab cover
5 Glass guardrail
6 Aluminum composite
   panel with accent color
7 Stone paver
8 Frosted glass partition panel
9 Sliding glass door
10 Living room

Wall Section

0.5m   1m   2m

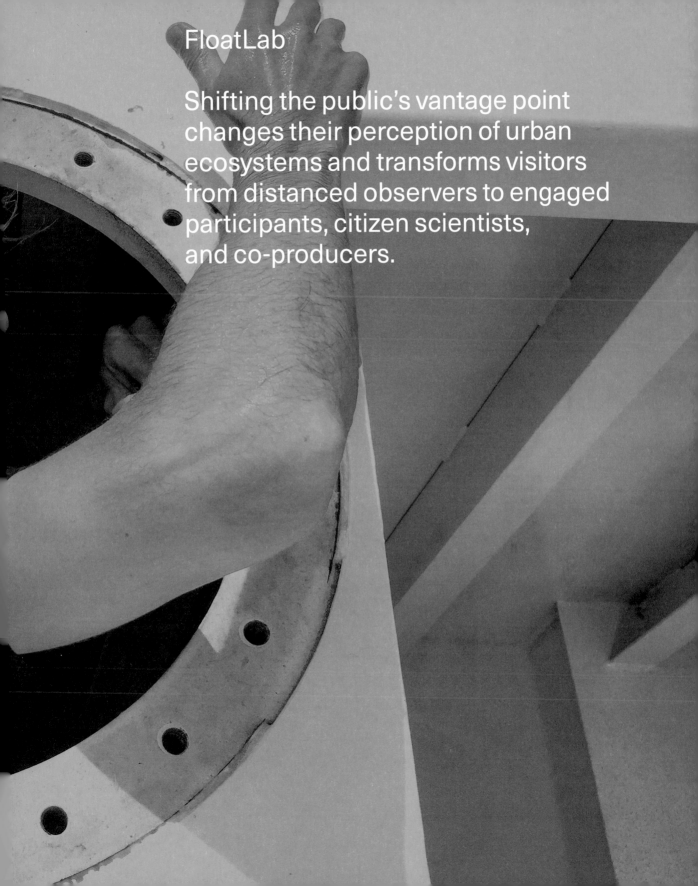

FloatLab

Shifting the public's vantage point changes their perception of urban ecosystems and transforms visitors from distanced observers to engaged participants, citizen scientists, and co-producers.

Throughout the city's history, Philadelphia has thrived in part due to two main waterways: the Delaware and Schuylkill rivers. Often referred to as a city between two rivers, Philadelphia has relied on the Schuylkill River from the time of its founding through the Industrial Revolution. The discovery of anthracite coal in the river's headwaters would transform the waterway, once celebrated for its uncommon purity, into the most polluted river in the country.

Over several decades, coal mining operations added millions of tons of silt annually to the river while industrial and manufacturing plants along the riverfront further polluted the waterway. By the 1940s, the river required extensive remediation. One of the earliest environmental cleanup efforts in the U.S., the restoration of the Schuylkill River to a healthy waterway was critical for the city. The Schuylkill River remains of vital importance to the urban ecology of Philadelphia.

FloatLab

Schuylkill River

Passyunk Avenue

Penrose Avenue

Schuylkill Expressway

Delaware Expressway

Delaware River

5000'   10,000'

Philadelphia, Pennsylvania (39.9291, -72.2119)

50' 100'   200'

FloatLab, a partnership between Bartram's Gardens and Philadelphia Mural Arts, is a public community platform designed to connect Philadelphians and visitors to the city to the Schuylkill River and promote environmental awareness and stewardship. As a new kind of laboratory within the city, FloatLab focuses on the health of Philadelphia's riverfront. The platform extends into the Schuylkill from the tidal wetlands of Bartram's Garden, the oldest surviving botanical garden in the country. Bartram's Garden, a 45-acre (18 ha) historic landmark, has long been a gateway to the river and its habitat.

FloatLab extends the garden into the water, offering both a platform for environmental learning and new vantage points from which to observe the ecology of the Schuylkill River, subject to daily tides, seasonal changes, and forces like erosion and climate change.

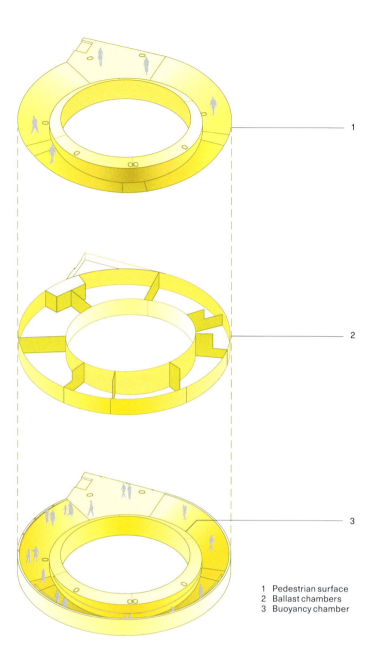

1 Pedestrian surface
2 Ballast chambers
3 Buoyancy chamber

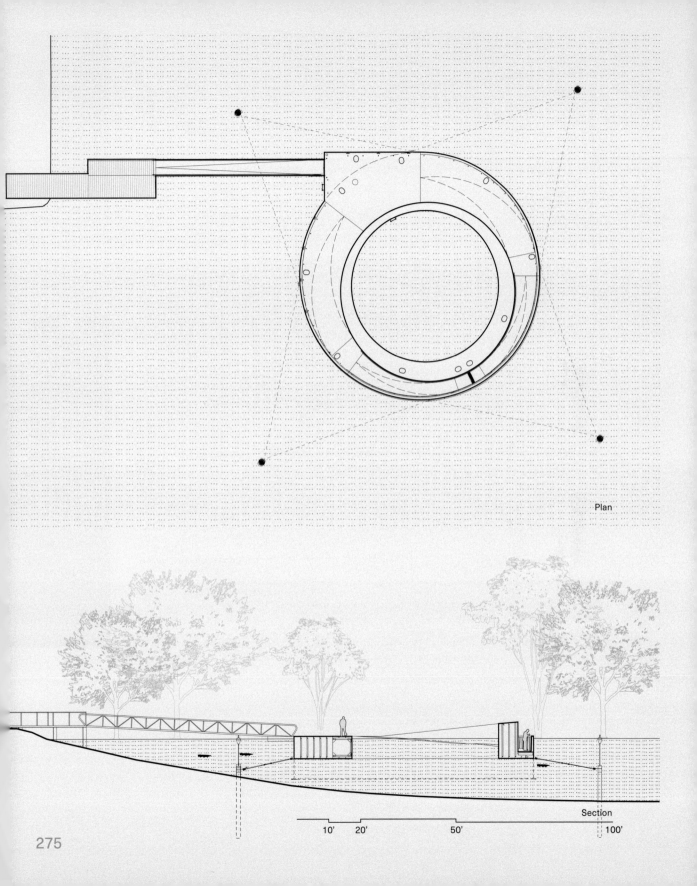

Plan

Section

10' 20'   50'   100'

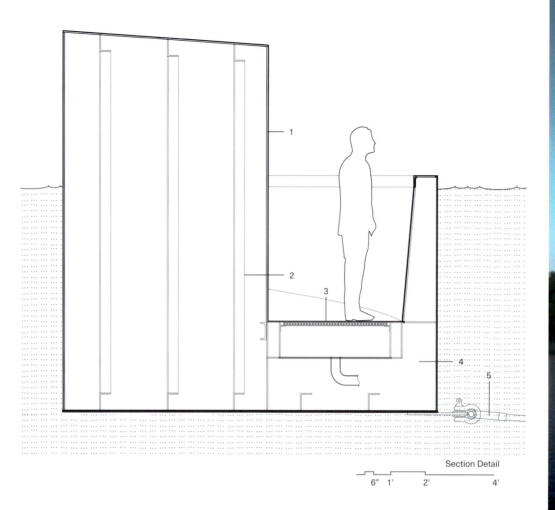

Section Detail

6"   1'   2'   4'

The FloatLab structure is a
submersible platform that uses
a series of engineered ballast
chambers to float just above the
surface of the water.

1 Steel plate barge construction
2 Stiffener ribs beyond
3 Metal grate
4 Ballast chamber
5 Tie

The structure widens in plan to form a gathering area and provides a ramp around the circumference that narrows to form a sunken path for viewing the water at eye-level. This simple form accommodates myriad programs for Bartram's Garden, ranging from an outdoor classroom on the platform to a mussel hatchery in the central body of water, to a dock for kayaks around its perimeter.

FloatLab provides a surreal immersive experience of the Schuylkill River, allowing visitors to observe the river's ecology in relationship to the industrial landscape. A full-scale submersible mockup with stairs that descend to the water level demonstrates the efficacy of the ballast system and tests the intended effect for visitors.

The mockup simulates sensory and perceptual experience and allows for a thorough test of the buoyancy chamber to ensure that the structure could not sink, thus demonstrating a proof of concept for the full installation.

Helio House	Shadow Play	Timber Stepwell	Solar Veil	FloatLab
Location	Location	Location	Location	Location
Shenzhen, Guangdong Province, China	Phoenix, Arizona, USA	Spokane, Washington, USA	Haikou, Hainan Province, China	Philadelphia, Pennsylvania, USA
Team Members	Team Members	Team Members	Team Members	Team Members
Eric Höweler	Eric Höweler	Eric Höweler	Eric Höweler	Eric Höweler
J. Meejin Yoon	J. Meejin Yoon	J. Meejin Yoon	J. Meejin Yoon	J. Meejin Yoon
Kyle Coburn	Alex Marshall	Nancy Nichols	Sungwoo Jang	David Hamm
Alexander Porter	Paul Cattaneo	Neil Legband	Di Wang	Jonathan Fournier
Gillian Schaffer	Yushiro Okamoto	David Tarcali	Bernard Peng	Max Jarosz
Ching Ying Ngan		Hari Priya Rangarajan	Vanille Fricker	Zach Seibold
Sarah Martos		Alexander Porter	Mengzhe Ye	Max Wong
Daniel Haidermota	Collaborators	Ching Ying Ngan	Gideon Schwartzman	Elle Gerdeman
Caleb Hawkins	Waibel & Associates Landscape (Landscape Architect)	Kevin Marblestone	Estelle Yoon	Alexander Porter
			Jacob Bruce	
Collaborators				
Kohn Pedersen Fox (Masterplan)				
Adrian L Norman Ltd (Landscape Architect)				
A+E Design (Local Design Institute)				

Degrowth Industry
Conversation
with Daniel Barber

Daniel A. Barber, Associate Professor and Chair of the Graduate Group in Architecture at the University of Pennsylvania Stuart Weitzman School of Design, discusses the challenges and opportunities that come with designing in this moment of climate crisis.

ERIC

Daniel, when I read your work, it makes me think about the complexity of comfort. Comfort is a cultural expectation, as much as a product of the natural climate. We design not for a universal man or woman, but for someone who has very specific cultural expectations of a comfortable environment. On top of that, everyone experiences comfort differently, and this seemed like the route to a design solution a couple of years ago: that a building would tailor its microclimate to a user through personalized technology. But this idea raises the question of architecture's role in the conditions for comfort.

DANIEL

It's an abstract notion, but I wonder how the culture of architecture sees an opportunity to play a game with the thermal interior as a space for creativity in anticipation of that soon becoming a growth industry?

MEEJIN

The assumption that we have an abundance of energy has determined our current relationship to the climate and set up our cultural expectations around comfort. This assumption has kept architecture from having challenging and meaningful conversations about climate for many decades.

ERIC

A few years ago, when Iñaki Abalos was chair at the GSD, he introduced a whole different agenda about thermodynamics. Kiel Moe and Salmaan Craig introduced thermally active surfaces and thermal mass in first-year core studios. There was hope that we could think about architectural form and thermal conditions at the same time, and it led students to consider passive and premodern strategies. Through mechanical systems, we've overcome thermal discomfort with brute force for so long.

Jimmy Carter's report to the American people on energy. 1977

DANIEL

The brute force approach to thermal comfort is being displaced by an ambition to operate a bit more intelligently, by a recognition that such a system always had winners and losers. There is interest in overcoming an embedded resistance in our field, an assumption that if it was premodern, it has been

Edifício Mamãe. MMM Roberto. Rio de Janeiro, Brazil. 1945

figured out better since then. I often refer to Jimmy Carter's sweater speech, his Fireside Chat on energy in 1977, where he suggested that Americans could put on a sweater rather than rely on heating houses with imported oil from the Middle East. This is one of those moments in history that suddenly seems a lot more relevant to architecture, especially when we think about the concurrent debates about postmodernism that seemingly had nothing to do with energy, or climate, or heating — but are significant in how aggressively these issues were ignored or deemed irrelevant. It was a moment that clarified the relationship between geopolitics and air conditioners or thermal comfort — demonstrating that there is a relationship, and that architects are involved. Still a bit abstract today. If the preset were shifted down one degree (i.e., if the occupant put on a sweater) how much carbon would be saved? What is the cost in terms of discomfort? And what is the qualitative effect?

MEEJIN
This is why I was curious about your notion of designing for discomfort, which you've spoken about in several places including *Log 47*. Do you mean designing architectural form? Architecture designed to solve problems is at times not the same as architecture designed to project the values of a society. But it seems like it is possible to do both. You've made the point that the brise soleil was a form of media that brought the ideology of modernism to the Global South, where otherwise modernism may not have caught on the way it did.

Shadow Play. Höweler + Yoon. Phoenix, Arizona. 2015

DANIEL
I think it's part of the project of the design fields to encounter climate. The task is not simply the technical efficiency of the well-managed thermal interior, but also making it a cultural space of creativity and innovation. Bringing climate to the forefront of individual, cultural, and spatial experience — these spaces are tied to a broader set of relations.

What really struck me about some of your urban-scale, pavilion-esque projects — I'm thinking of Swing Time and Helio House, and to some extent Shadow Play as well — what you're modeling is a changing experience of the urban environment, a novel set of behaviors. There's not one fixed condition, either because the sun's moving or because you're moving. You're placing yourself in a dynamic relationship with the designed space, and with the city; to the environment. I see this same issue of behavior, of forming new habits, as a question of external conditioning, or the possibility for outdoor public spaces to use architectural interventions to bring people together and make them more comfortable. And I mean this in the best way possible — the simplicity of some of those gestures, the swing being such an obvious object to perform that dynamism — really helps to adjust our perspective to the notion that things will be moving, things will be adjusting. We see a condition in the near future where that capacity to adjust to different environments might be required.

This also plays out, in different ways, in the Schuylkill FloatLab project and the UVA Memorial — spatial experience that questions everyday behaviors in order to reveal and bring experiences or issues that are hidden, or otherwise hard to see, to the foreground. Relationships to nature, awareness of the violence of our shared history, of course these are very different experiences to be revealed, but the design premise of shaping behavior and exploring the unseen is a crucial aspect of climate as well, of bringing these issues into the cultural dialogue, of framing space for a new kind of awareness.

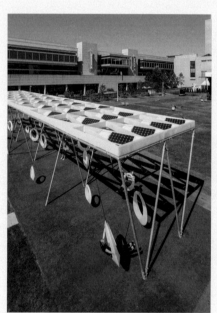

Swing Time at the Lawn on D. Höweler + Yoon. Boston, Massachusetts. 2014

Helio House. Höweler + Yoon. Shenzhen, China. 2020

ERIC

This extended network of relationships that are provoked by climate will change what it means to design as an individual, as a team, and as a community. I think those are exciting challenges for how we might expand the role of design beyond simply form or intent. Many of our questions concern how you design a process, not just how you design a building. This isn't just what you design, but who designs, and how they do so. So much of what we do as architects is manage expertise from all different sectors — structural, mechanical, and electrical. These big questions are not to be solved single-handedly.

DANIEL

In our field, there are so many obstacles to feeling the urgency and recognizing the violence that goes on as a result of excessive energy use. We know that our islands are sinking, that disasters are occurring, and people are suffering and it's very real. And, we are all complicit just by getting up in the morning and making coffee and doing regular things. Whether we're talking about commissioning a building with a certain type of comfort spectrum or taking the bus versus driving a car to work — these are decisions that seem to have no consequence, but of course we know about the chain of cause and effects that amplifies threats, harm, or discomfort elsewhere. But I get encouraged thinking that, increasingly, our cultural discourse is about adding value to a set of decisions that have historically been treated as neutral.

We're starting to think about carbon and comfort in terms of currency — where we invest a lot of resources, and where we hold back. Designing the thermal interior becomes another place to produce affect. An architect can produce different kinds of conditions in different parts of the building — one can imagine an entryway should feel different than a bedroom, maybe the bedroom has a bit of power assist, like an e-bike, you flip it on as needed. We are just beginning to imagine a role for design to help us live with a changed carbon economy — where buildings are as much about the production of energy, working through a kind of metabolic balance, as they are simply about use.

MEEJIN
I think it's interesting that climate experts are trying to educate architects and designers about these ranges of temperature variation. Before, it seemed to me that thermal consultants would study a design and offer a choice between several systems, usually recommending the best solution for consumer comfort. Now, they recommend multiple systems working together. Using multiple systems, you might try to reduce the heating or cooling load from the beginning through some other strategy. This is more complex and therefore more difficult to sell and guarantee a certain performance. I think architects are excited to embrace gradients and differences because having multiple and layered systems allows for nuanced solutions to reconcile different conditions through design.

ERIC
We've been looking at Victor and Aladar Olgyay's 1963 book *Design with Climate* again and it seems like this thinking is coming back today. I was just flipping through the section on Miami — prevailing winds come in here, so plant

Design with Climate. Victor Olgyay. 1963

shade trees there so that wind coming through the building will be pre-tempered a few degrees because it's been blowing across a cool area. A lot of these thoughtful premodern strategies could be recuperated in contemporary work.

MEEJIN
What comes to the fore, especially among those studying architecture, is whether we position architecture as part of the solution or as part of the problem.

DANIEL
Given that we are all also involved in educational institutions, I think we want to draw our students into this discussion about future generations, whether architects are part of the problem or part of the solution, and help them recognize that we're going through a process of adjusting our expectations of the future. I was having a discussion with a colleague about young architects who say that in order to take these issues on, maybe our aspirations for the 'model project' or the 'model practice,' as a professional in this new world, might require some adjustments. We are no longer trying to educate the next starchitect, with some sort of ineffable talent for novel design. Instead, we are focused on how to prepare architects for a life of collaboration — with engineers, sociologists, policymakers, and on and on — to prepare them to think a bit more broadly about the relationship of buildings to social and ecological systems. Even coming to terms with the possibility that 'not building' in some scenarios may be a better choice, an innovation more relevant to the future of architecture. With the restriction of resources rather than its profligacy relative to economic growth, what activities should students expect to have the most impact?

MEEJIN
So you're suggesting that instead of building, architects should be — not building?

DANIEL
To some extent, yes. I imagine the question of retrofitting will be a huge growth industry (I like to call it a degrowth industry) in the coming decades as building owners want to adapt existing structures — if we assume some form of carbon cost or some social condition whereby carbon becomes functionally more expensive. Then it is likely that

people will say, 'Let's hire someone to figure out the windows and do all the work to make this building energy-efficient.' How can we see that as a space for creativity? It's not just a set of technical solutions or negotiating R-values. Reimagining the energy future also has to happen at the building scale. I'm thinking about the proposed legislation for the Green New Deal, HR-109, which calls for 'upgrading all existing buildings in the United States and building new buildings to achieve maximum energy efficiency' — all existing buildings! If we don't train architects to take this on, someone else will get in ahead. How does energy retrofitting become a space for creativity?

MEEJIN
How do we reposition design problems in school to reimagine our existing building stock and think about adaptive reuse and circular construction in innovative ways?

DANIEL
I'm not quite advocating that we teach design students to be renovators, but I think we need to encourage students to see their futures differently and find opportunities for the kinds of dynamism that design can provide. Given our generation's background and training, what are the tools we have left to provide young architects with skills and hope? What aspirations do we start to feed them or discuss with them, and what ideas can we help them think through? We should articulate a way of engaging with the project of building that helps architects incorporate new forms of knowledge into these complex urban, spatial, and climatic considerations. We need to seriously consider what young architects need to know. I think it would be interesting to speculate on the curriculum ten years into the future, or about what your list of consultants might look like in ten years. Will MoMA's next half-billion-dollar renovation involve more space, or, a transformation of itself into the first carbon-free museum? What are the terms of innovation or design excellence? And how can architects lead this discussion, or at least develop the tools to participate in it effectively?

ERIC
I led an options studio at the GSD, with Corey Zehngebot, on Adapting Miami. That's one place that climate change is already causing effects.

Miami options studio review, Graduate School of Design. 2019

The solutions weren't only architectural — they had to take on questions of density, flexibility, mobility, and land use. One idea tested in the studio is how to get people to want things other than the single-family house on a parcel of land. This is tied to notions of the American Dream, of utopian images, and a cultural imaginary. Our premise was: in order to change the urban landscape toward more climate-responsive approaches, we first have to redesign the American Dream.

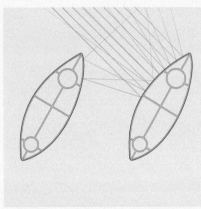

DANIEL
Architecture as a field has a pretty compelling set of opportunities for providing value to novel experience — for soliciting and cultivating new kinds of desire. The next generation is looking for opportunities for hope, for how to think about the world they're entering into a different way. It's not about the end of the world, but about how we reframe our practices and values to build a new one. In architecture schools, we can start to map different trajectories for them to do so.

ERIC
Today, designers have different capacities to simulate, visualize, and make things legible than we had in the past. We should acknowledge the superpower of visualization — we can turn climate intelligence into media, into communicable information, and broadcast it in different ways. We have the capacity to design desire — that's powerful.

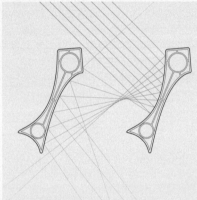

Simulations developed for Helio House show that a concave louver profile reflects more indirect light below than the typical convex louver.

DANIEL
We look at the appeal of renderings in schools, exhibitions, and biennials. We've constructed a media apparatus in architecture (and in landscape, too), for reasons that appear quite obvious — as a field, we make beautiful pictures. Really stunning. And a lot of our discourse, certainly at the pedagogical level where I spend most of my time, is about how to make the images look even better! We're talking at a midterm, and most juries are like: this image could look better if you change the contrast, or add some elements here or there — that's effectively what's being discussed. It's as much about the representation as it is about the architecture itself, if not more so. I find it surprising how we look at the field and our operations relative to this question of inducing desire, and the skills

we are developing and tools we are using, yet we don't always see this as part of the project.

More broadly, I'm trying to encourage us all to consider carbon in the production of desire. How do we change the culture so that people want something else? Whether that's a bike lane, a dense high-rise tower, or a type of urban experience that's not so familiar, obvious, or desired today. When we consider the theories of the '80s and '90s — and the production of desire and desiring machines — we're prepared for this! In architecture, we've thought this through and have the tools at the ready. There tends to be a lot of normativity in our field because we're under the pressure of capital, insurance, and ASHRAE. But amidst the perpetuation of existing conditions, it's exciting to recognize that we have this space of creativity that's well-attuned to the challenge ahead of us.

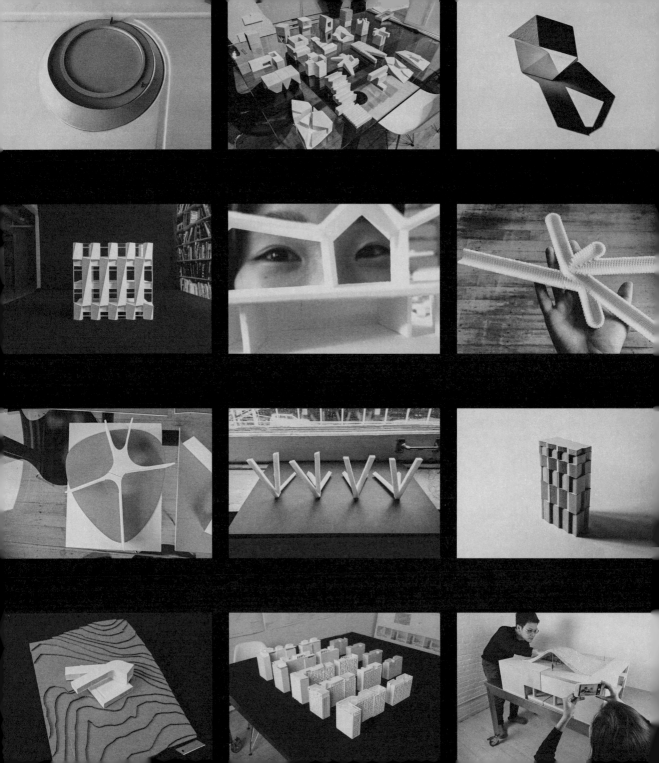

"Architecture starts when you carefully place two bricks together," wrote Mies van der Rohe in his 1959 editorial, *On Restraint in Design*. "There it begins." For Mies, architecture is a matter of relationships between parts — material details, which come together to make a larger whole — a building. "God is in the details," he famously added, turning the way two material components come together into a question of right and wrong. By this standard, part-to-whole relationships become a question of morality.

Whether it is God — or the devil — in the details, the questions they raise — around scale and ornament, affect and perception — continue to haunt the discipline. How components meet to produce different conditions that represent ethical positions about the use of materials, how their qualities are either revealed or concealed, and what the detail communicates are all subjects of continuing debate and speculation.

The legacy of the tectonic detail is rooted in the *correctness* of architectural assemblies that allow the components of a building or space to express how they come together. Paradoxes surrounding Mies's applied I-beam in the Seagram Building suggest that the detail can be more discursive than functional, more theatrical than essential, and more obscuring than transparent.

"No money, no detail," is Rem Koolhaas's irreverent response to detail obsession. For Koolhaas, attitudes about detailing are positioned against the preciousness of propriety. The Seattle Central Library conveys this in its diagrid steel members that turn corners in irregular ways and converge at vertices that appear unresolved. In the building's reading room, the transition between a midspan brace and the sloped diagrid façade is resolved by simply doubling the steel members in an area where added depth is needed. Koolhaas's design for the detail results in a fried-egg shape figure, a mat of steel beams, that acts as a column capital, distributing loads and eliminating punching shear. In this case, the detail is a means to an end, an opportunity to articulate a concept with a sense of no-nonsense authenticity. Ironically, Mies's applied I-beams on the Seagram Building are derided as decorative, whereas Koolhaas's applied beams on the Seattle Central Library are understood as a necessity.

As architectural historian Robin Evans has pointed out, "architects do not make buildings; they make drawings of buildings."[1] For Evans, the task of translation from drawing to building is how architecture is articulated. The translation of design intent to construction relies on the detail. The detail is not about scale; it is about how design intent is implemented and articulated. The detail is how attitudes toward materials, systems, and assemblies are organized — and how those attitudes are either made legible or obscured. The detail is the inertia of an idea as it is translated from concept to construction. It is a response to a series of questions: what is it made of? How thick is it? Will it expand and contract? How is it attached? Can it be cut in the shop? Can it be cut in the field? What is its finish? Who will install it? How will

Applied I-beams on Mies van der Rohe's Seagram Building.

Applied I-beams on OMA's Seattle Central Library.

it be maintained? How will it be replaced if it fails? How will it weather? And importantly, what effects does it produce?

While traditional approaches to detailing, understood through the lens of tectonics, insist on the correctness of a material expression through the articulation of parts and wholes, we see detailing as a means to follow through on a concept at multiple scales while addressing the hierarchy of intent, material, and perception. Often, details participate in perceptual effects, revealing or concealing conditions that encourage the viewer to look more carefully. The steel plate stair at the BSA Space is only 3/4" (19 mm) thick, and its detailing suggests that it is hanging from the ceiling above. The curved profiles of the stair accentuate the continuity between horizontal tread and vertical stringer while expressing the thinness of the materials. In an entirely different usage, the image of Isabella Gibbons carved into the stone surface of the Memorial to Enslaved Laborers at UVA is only visible under certain lighting conditions and from specific points of view. Visitors to the memorial are invited to look carefully at the surface of the exterior to see the image. As an optical device, the colossal portrait enlists the viewer in a kind of perceptual play; it asks visitors to walk around the memorial and to not only look, but to look again. Both the BSA Space and the UVA memorial projects employ details to articulate perceptual effects that represent evolving attitudes about material culture and the means of translating those into architecture.

"...In the Details," presents a case study of one detail developed across three projects. The condition is an

The steel plate stair at the BSA Space appears impossibly thin.

outside corner and a transition between a wall, a roof, and a window. The jointing of an outer corner, revealing the size or thickness of materials and their assembly, is a fundamental detail in architecture. From wall to window, the transition from surface to opening hints at questions of structure or load transfer and supporting versus supported. This detail is developed in three projects and explores three different materials in three different conditions, yet with the same intent — the articulated transition that masks the true dimensions of the wall and roof.

The three projects included here are all houses, though the articulation of this particular detail might apply to other building types. Each house is set in a wooded area where views from the interior to the exterior drive design decisions. And, each house is understood as a viewing device, framing particular views while masking others.

The detail of the articulated frame is achieved with a tapered profile and is articulated in different ways to achieve different effects. Bridge House consists of three aluminum-clad volumes that appear to be stacked on top of one another. The volumes are articulated as square tubes, with a shared orientation, as if the house has an open grain from front to back. The articulation of outside corners reinforces the grain of the house and is articulated with a tapered aluminum profile. The aluminum cladding is an interlocking rain

Mockup of v-carve technique with Isabella Gibbons' eyes for the Memorial to Enslaved Laborers.

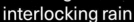

Miter joint at the ridge line of the Memorial to Enslaved Laborers.

screen system with a clear natural anodized finish that gives the frame a bright metallic appearance. The frame's infill materials are floor-to-ceiling glass and a dark bronze anodized aluminum panel intended to recede visually and allow the opaque metal panels to group with the glazing. The use of a knife-edge detail on all four sides of the frame conceals the thickness of the walls, floors, and roof as the leading edge has no thickness. The angle of the tapered profile varies with each condition, as they each respond to a different thickness. The wall construction consists of a 2x8 wood framing, sheathing, and an aluminum rainscreen resulting in a 10" (25 cm) thickness and an acute angle of the taper. The floor package consists of 12" (30 cm) LVLs, sheathing, and an aluminum rainscreen soffit, resulting in a shallower tapered profile. The roof construction considers the same 12" (30 cm) LVL structure and sheathing but also accounts for tapered insulation, the pitch of a low-sloped roof, and the construction of the parapet coping. The resulting roof package is nearly 2'-6" (76 cm) thick, making the tapered profile quite shallow. While each angle is different, they align on their leading edge to give the volume its sharp, tube-like appearance.

Bridge House is arranged to frame a view that passes through the house to the surrounding wooded area. When viewed at an angle, the wall appears impossibly thin, giving the illusion that it is a two-dimensional plane. An interplay between the material and immaterial qualities of Bridge House is also found in the anodized aluminum panels that reflect natural light and blend the diffused greens and blues of the trees and sky. The subtle optical effects and geometry of the tapered panel profile again dematerialize the wall, making it appear like a rendering — or a texture map

The knife-edge detail finds precedent in the work of artist James Turrell, whose constructions rendered in immersive, colored light suspend perception. For his aperture installations, Turrell tapers a 6" (15 cm) interior partition to a point, using the knife-edge detail to make the opening within the wall appear two-dimensional and the space behind the wall appear depthless. The same knife-edge detail is also used in his Skyspace projects that frame the sky with a plane of seemingly zero dimension. The architecture of the frame dissolves, rendering the sky a depthless field of abstract color. For Turrell, the work of art is not an object hanging on the wall or a sculpture on a pedestal. Rather, the work is a perceptual effect located in the retina of the viewer. Turrell constructs the viewer as he constructs the installation.

Architect Yoshio Taniguchi employs a similar set of details to conceal the thickness of the materials used for his MoMA expansion project. By refusing to express the thickness of the material — drywall, brick, or glass — the MoMA expansion appears weightless. The typical gallery wall details are articulated with a knife-edge profile at the wall base and at transitions around portals. The wall's surface is denied its thickness and appears to float, suspended in a plane, hovering above the floor. Taniguchi's subtle use of the knife-edge profile transforms the primary planes of his architecture into dimensionless surfaces. The surface qualities of the materials are present in the textures, reflectivity, and

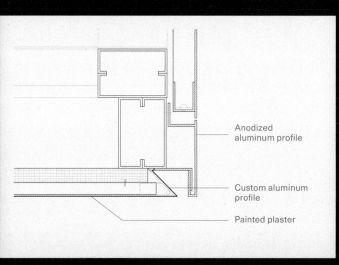

Anodized
aluminum profile

Custom aluminum
profile

Painted plaster

jointing, but they are denied their thickness, rendering them ambiguous. Taniguchi seems to be assembling a building, not with materials, but with images of materials.[2]

Much like Bridge House, Oblique House is made of volumes that frame and direct views, provide privacy, and protect from solar exposure. Oblique House also employs a similar perceptual detail where materials meet. The Oblique House façade consists of a matte charcoal gray rainscreen system made of 1/4" (6 mm)-thick recycled paper panels. The 4'×8' panel module is legible on the façade as 3/8" (9 mm) joints and the 1/4" (6 mm) thickness of the panel is exposed as it turns the corner. Unlike Bridge House, where the aluminum panel turns the corner with a sharp knife-edge detail, the recycled paper panel detail is lapped so that one panel takes precedence over the other. Yet, the outer corner is nonetheless expressed as a tapered geometry and blunted profile. Though the 1/4" (6 mm) panel dimension does not allow for the sharpness of a true knife-edge profile, tapering effectively hides the significant dimension and weight of the cantilevered overhang and achieves a kind of visual paradox.

Plus House's tapered profiles again use the knife-edge detail that gives a deceptively stark first impression. In this case, the house conforms to strict orthogonal geometry, and it is the two intersecting wings of the house that are articulated with knife-edge wall, roof, and floor profiles. The geometries of Plus House define the outer faces as orthogonal while extending the tapered profiles of the walls and ceilings into the house as thick poché zones. The house's interior consists of oblique walls and thickened zones, concealing structure, embedding fireplaces, and carving out storage and closet spaces. In section, the knife-edge geometry transitions from the double-height glazed wall facing the pond to the kitchen's single-story height. The sloped surface of the living room soffit conceals the playroom above and forms an inverted attic section with a sloped floor rather than a sloped roof.

Plus House is clad in 3/4" (19 mm)-thick charred wood siding, or shou sugi ban, in a rain screen system of 6" (150 mm) vertical boards. The blackened wood absorbs light and conceals joints when seen from a distance, making the house appear monolithic from specific vantage points. Upon closer inspection, the vertical grain of the boards that march around the house becomes perceptible, and the rich texture of the charred wood is revealed. The shou sugi ban technique protects against weathering and insects and gives the house a black-on-black iridescence with light flickering across the surface that is at times reflective and, at others, matte.

The thickness of charred wood cladding is challenging at corners where the siding transitions to aluminum plate at the edge to ensure a sharp profile while maintaining a straight and true line. At its corners where the wall, roof, and floor meet, Plus House combines the perceptual effects of the tapered profile and adds the environmental benefits of a sun-shading overhang, all while producing a series of thick poché spaces within the house. In this case, the interior space's thickness renders the knife-edge profile inhabitable. The taper — its geometry and effect — extends the logic of the corner deep into the house.

Each of the houses discussed is constructed with a relatively standard set of

Knife-edge detail from Plus House.

and siding. Traditional detailing in residential construction tends to accentuate transitions around windows, making the elements and materials visible while protecting edges and managing water. Eaves, trim, sill, and drip edges all play a role in articulating normative residential building conditions. In the three cases shown, normative wood frame and siding systems are employed, though the precise design of a critical detail produces unexpected effects. The articulation of the knife-edge profile presents the viewer with a visual paradox. A thick wall appears impossibly thin. A roof overhang appears to float without any apparent thickness. The visual effects of the details dematerialize the buildings, making them appear weightless. Material textures without thickness appear like texture maps in a rendering, as if the houses were assembled from images.

Making buildings that take on the appearance of a rendering is like coming full circle in the process of tectonic material articulation, digital workflows, and detailing intent. If Mies van der Rohe insisted on the moral imperative of detailing *correctness*, then the discipline's investment in the *appropriateness* of material articulation as expressed in details is inverted when physical structures mask their actual material dimensions in favor of a perceptual effect. As the handling of a single detail across three houses demonstrates, accounting for thickness is a critical task in the translation from drawing to building, and from digital modeling's surfaces, curves, and NURBS, to material like dimensional lumber, rainscreen systems, and

Bridge House photograph and rendering.

lap joints. A key difference between the digital modeling environment and the material realities of the world has everything to do with thickness. How to manage it? How to turn a corner when it is revealed? Thickness, weight, and mass are all qualities of matter. And managing these qualities architecturally, matters.

When all design workflows begin in a digital environment as surfaces, thinking through thickness is essential to the translation from concept to construction. If we are truly rethinking material after media — after the material has been modeled, specified, and engineered — and after we have reconfigured, milled, surveyed, post-occupancy evaluated it, and, after it is posted on social media as either rendering or building or both — then what do these practices tell us about this particular moment? What is the status of material in culture? What is the status of material in an image-based culture? And by extension, what is the status of the image in culture?

These details reflect a material and image culture, where details that mask material speak to the status of the rendered image and to the culture of which it is part. Where once architectural renderings aspired to realism by articulating material properties and textures, today, the real aspires to renderings by masking material thickness and provoking the viewer to look carefully, or perhaps to look again. The double-take is a kind of verification in the realm of perception. Designing "in the details" today demands a different kind of viewership, a visual and material literacy for the age of inattention.

1   Evans, Robin. 1997. *Translations from Drawing to Building.* Cambridge, Mass: MIT Press

2   We are indebted to Stephen Rustow's excellent reading of Taniguchi's architecture published in *Praxis Magazine.* Stephen Rustow, "MoMA's Minimalist Baroque," *Praxis 7,* Untitled Number Seven, 2005, p.6.

Bridge House

Materializing architecture today may involve detailing that renders materials unfamiliar, appearing without thickness, dimension, or depth, as if assembled from images.

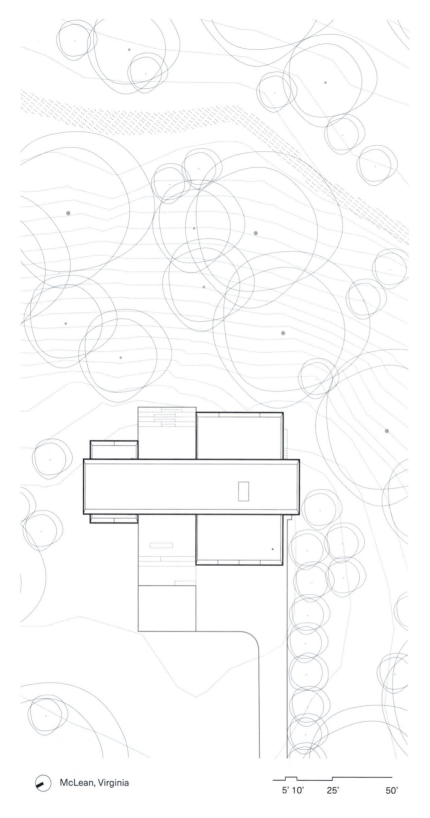

McLean, Virginia

5' 10'   25'   50'

Bridge House is a framing device for the surrounding landscape. Three volumes frame a view through the house that looks onto the dramatically sloped, wooded site.

Bridge House is a home for intergenerational living.
Each volume contains carefully organized private and
public areas that correspond to the family's generational
structure. The smallest volume on the ground floor is a
private suite for the grandparents, the larger is a shared
central area, and a long block that houses the family's
second and third generations bridges the two.

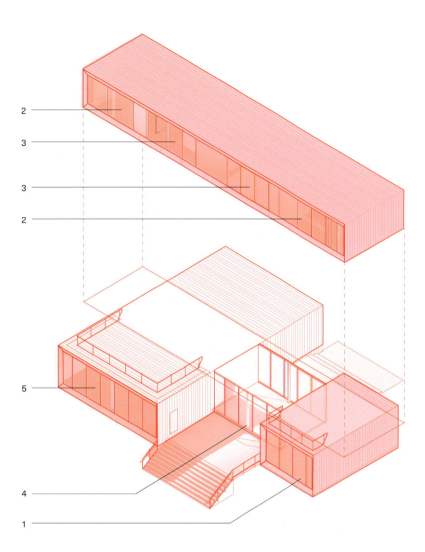

1 Sleeping quarters for first
  generation of family (grandparents)
2 Sleeping quarters for second
  generation of family (parents)
3 Sleeping quarters for third
  generation of family (children)
4 Shared family room
5 Living spaces, shared by all
  members of family

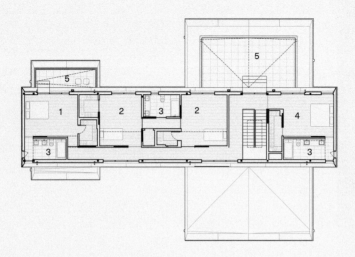

Plan Level 02

1   Primary bedroom
2   Child's bedroom
3   Bathroom
4   Guest bedroom
5   Deck

Plan Level 01

1   Living room
2   Dining room
3   Family room
4   Kitchen
5   Pantry
6   Laundry
7   Primary bedroom
8   Bathroom
9   Garage

5' 10'   25'   50'

The plan is organized around a central living space shared between the family's three generations. Glazed on both sides, the breezeway appears completely porous to the landscape.

Optimized for the solar angles of the site, beveled exterior edges allow for low winter sun to enter the house while protecting the residence from solar heat gain in the summer. In addition to the solar advantage of the overhang, the knife-edge detail denies the appearance of material thickness, reducing the house's exterior to a dematerialized diagram and its interior to an unencumbered picture plane.

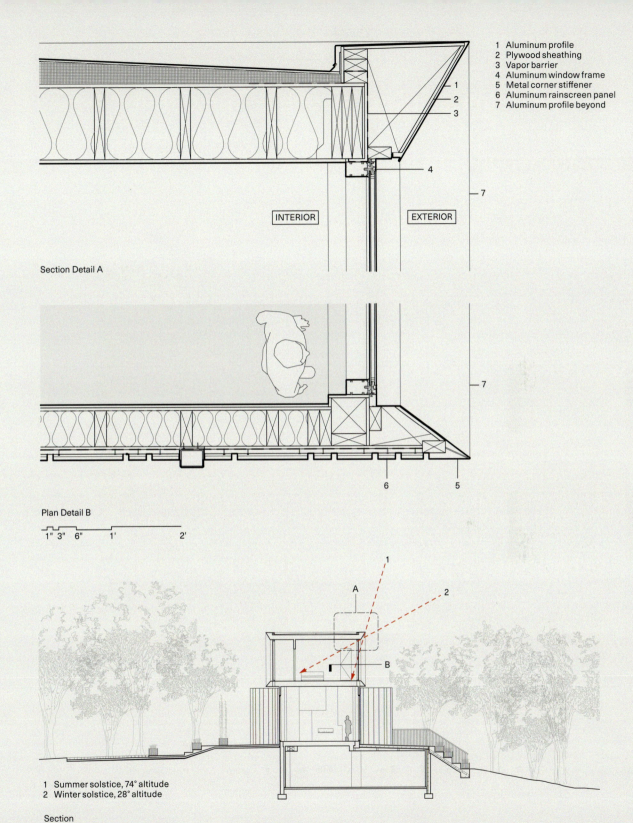

1 Aluminum profile
2 Plywood sheathing
3 Vapor barrier
4 Aluminum window frame
5 Metal corner stiffener
6 Aluminum rainscreen panel
7 Aluminum profile beyond

INTERIOR

EXTERIOR

Section Detail A

Plan Detail B

1" 3" 6"   1'   2'

1 Summer solstice, 74° altitude
2 Winter solstice, 28° altitude

Section

5' 10'   20'   50'

Oblique House

The detail is not about scale. The detail
is the inertia of an idea as it is translated
from concept to construction.

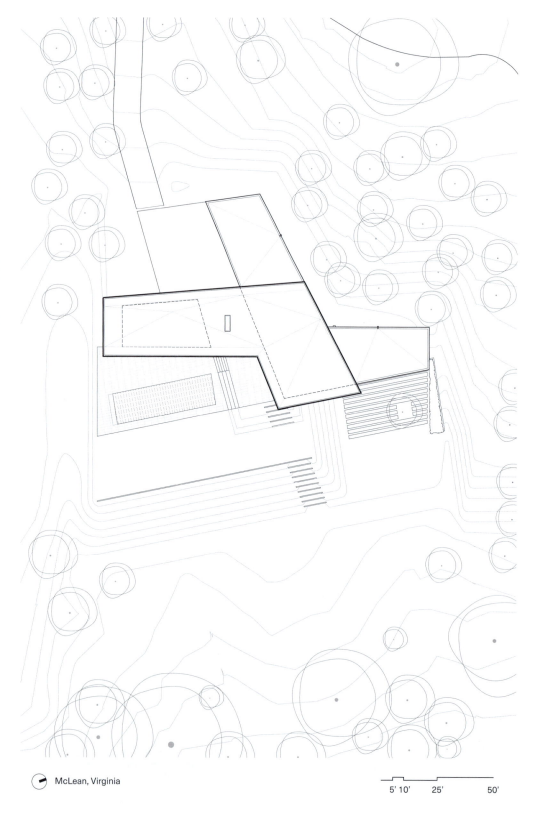

McLean, Virginia

5' 10'   25'   50'

Nestled in Virginia's deciduous woodlands, Oblique House is formed by two stacked L-shaped bars. The oblique geometry of the house frames views to the east and south while integrating with the topography to the north of the building. Due to the oblique angles and stark contrast of cladding materials, the house presents distinct characters from its different sides. The charcoal gray rainscreen panels clad the primary volumes of the house, and red cedar siding creates warm infill panels between full-height glazing.

At the point where the building's two wings meet, a
breezeway creates an entrance and a gathering space
that frames the surrounding woods from the approach.
The lower L-shaped bar houses living, family, and
entertaining spaces. Bedrooms and a guest room
comprise the upper level. The upper and lower volumes
interlock around a double-height living space which
opens to views and southern exposures. The opaque
north-facing walls screen the home's private functions
from the view of the street. Supported by steel beams,
the tapered visor-edge cantilevers 6' (180 cm) to create
an effective sun shade for the double-height living
space against the high-altitude summer sun.

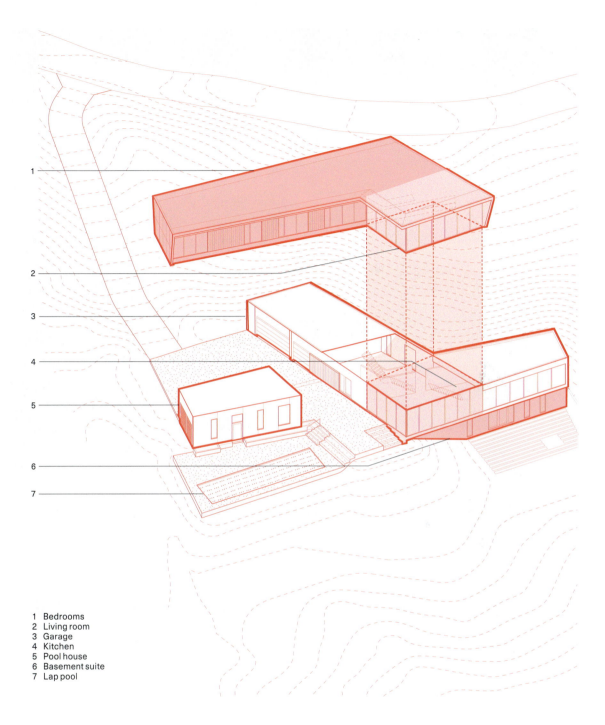

1 Bedrooms
2 Living room
3 Garage
4 Kitchen
5 Pool house
6 Basement suite
7 Lap pool

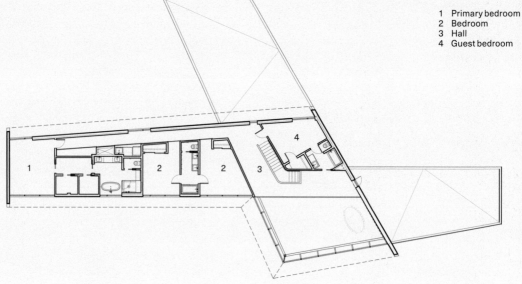

Plan Level 02

1 Primary bedroom
2 Bedroom
3 Hall
4 Guest bedroom

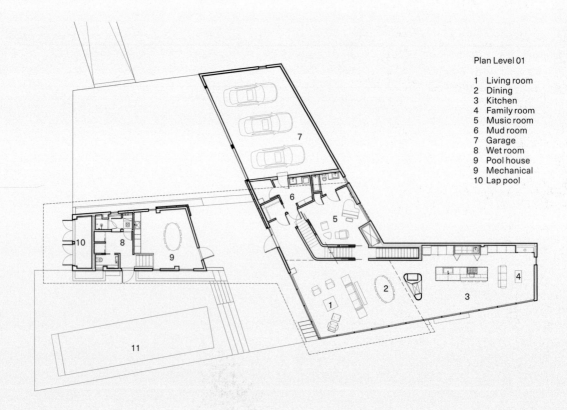

Plan Level 01

1 Living room
2 Dining
3 Kitchen
4 Family room
5 Music room
6 Mud room
7 Garage
8 Wet room
9 Pool house
9 Mechanical
10 Lap pool

5' 10'   25'   50'

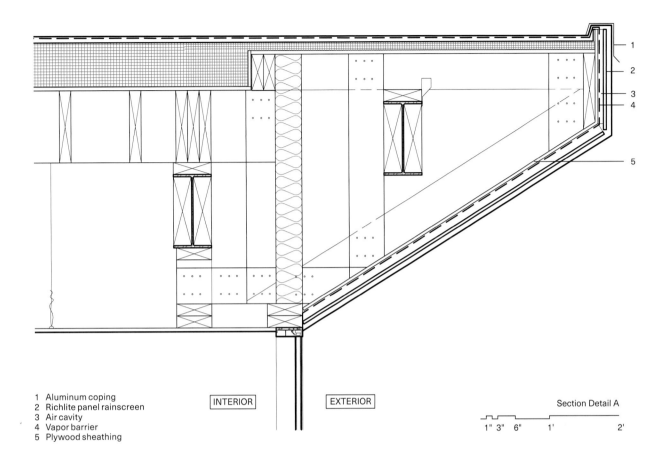

1 Aluminum coping
2 Richlite panel rainscreen
3 Air cavity
4 Vapor barrier
5 Plywood sheathing

INTERIOR   EXTERIOR

Section Detail A

1" 3" 6"   1'   2'

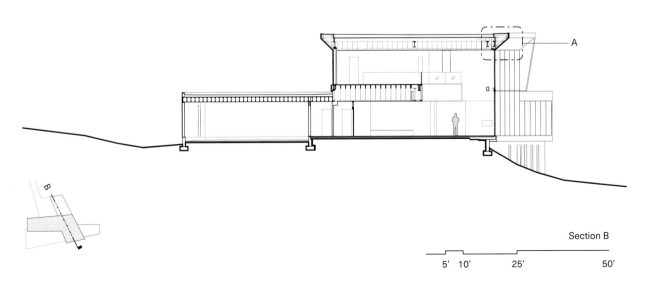

A

Section B

5' 10'   25'   50'

Plus House

Details that mask materiality while producing material effects of lightness, thinness, and surface reveal the status of the image in contemporary culture.

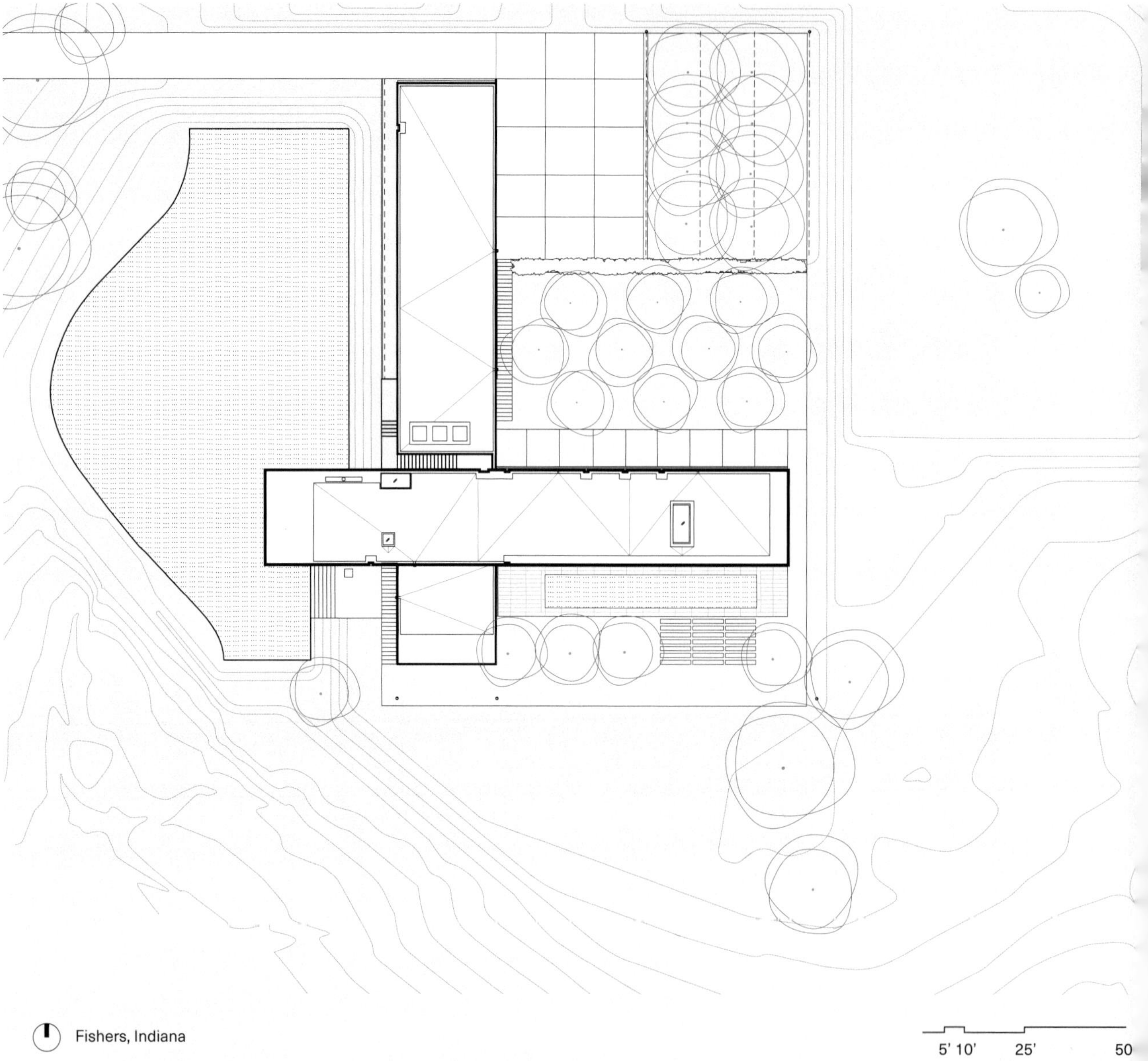

Fishers, Indiana

5' 10'   25'   50

Plus House, located outside of Indianapolis, Indiana sits on a flat, wooded site that borders a pond. The cruciform plan organization subdivides the site into quadrants: the approach and view of the pond to the northwest, the orchard grove to the northeast, a lap pool to the southeast, and an outdoor patio to the southwest. A decidedly Cartesian diagram, this gesture emphasizes a connection between the plan's abstract geometry and the natural landscape.

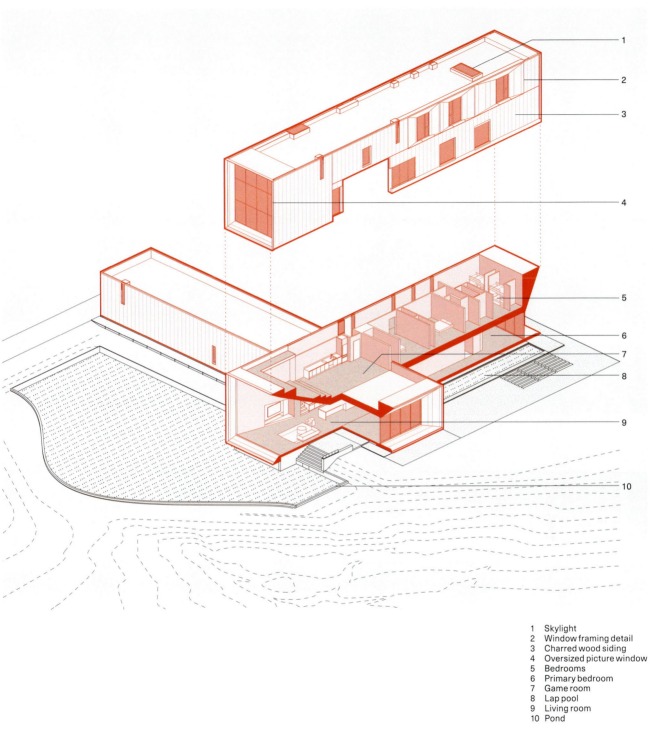

1 Skylight
2 Window framing detail
3 Charred wood siding
4 Oversized picture window
5 Bedrooms
6 Primary bedroom
7 Game room
8 Lap pool
9 Living room
10 Pond

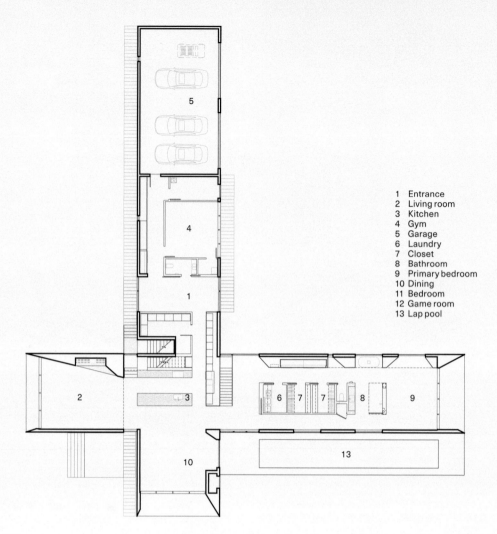

1	Entrance
2	Living room
3	Kitchen
4	Gym
5	Garage
6	Laundry
7	Closet
8	Bathroom
9	Primary bedroom
10	Dining
11	Bedroom
12	Game room
13	Lap pool

Plan Level 01

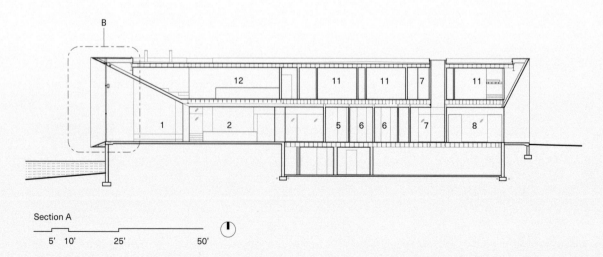

Section A

5' 10' 25'   50'

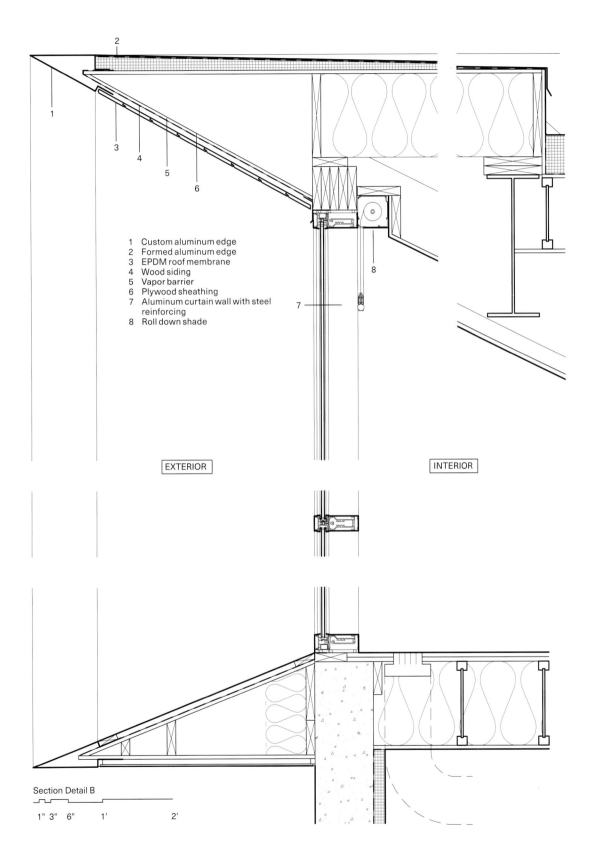

1   Custom aluminum edge
2   Formed aluminum edge
3   EPDM roof membrane
4   Wood siding
5   Vapor barrier
6   Plywood sheathing
7   Aluminum curtain wall with steel
     reinforcing
8   Roll down shade

EXTERIOR

INTERIOR

Section Detail B

1" 3" 6"   1'   2'

327

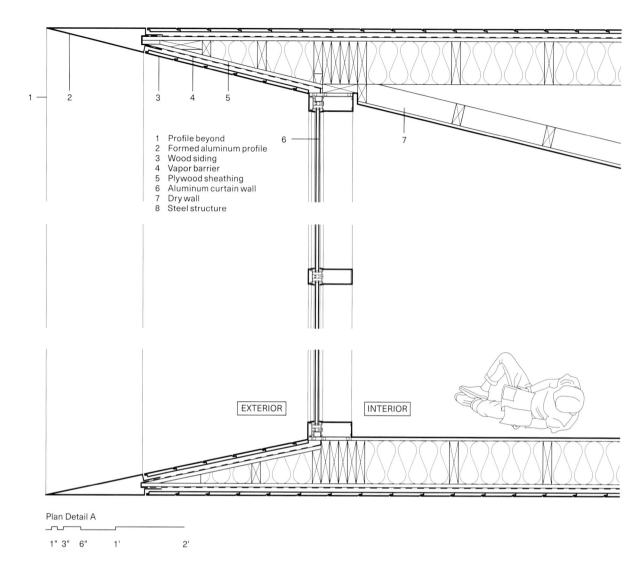

1 Profile beyond
2 Formed aluminum profile
3 Wood siding
4 Vapor barrier
5 Plywood sheathing
6 Aluminum curtain wall
7 Dry wall
8 Steel structure

EXTERIOR

INTERIOR

Plan Detail A

1" 3" 6"   1'   2'

The outer geometry of the house is strictly orthogonal and the ends
are articulated with a knife-edge profile, creating the visual effect of
dematerialization that makes the walls appear impossibly thin. The tapered
edge extends into the house to form thickened poché zones that contain
fireplaces, closets, and service spaces. The sloped ceiling surface in the
living room conceals the second-floor alcove, forming an inverted attic
with a sloped floor rather than a sloped roof.

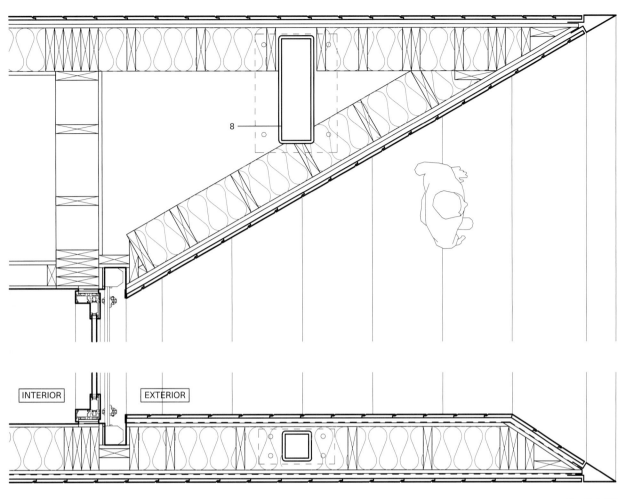

8

INTERIOR

EXTERIOR

Plan Detail B

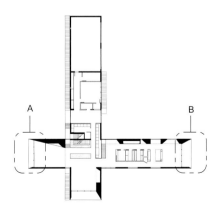

A   B

From the interior, Plus House frames specific views with cardinal
orientations. The tapered frames of the building edges bracket
views, while the knife-edge profile masks the material as well as
the actual dimensions of the walls and roof assemblies.

Bridge House

Location
McLean, Virginia, USA

Team Members
Eric Höweler
J. Meejin Yoon
Yoonhee Cho
Meredith Miller
Ryan Murphy
Parker Lee
Jennifer Chuong
Cyrus Dochow
Thena Tak
Sungwoo Jang
Casey Renner
Matthew Chua

Oblique House

Location
McLean, Virginia, USA

Team Members
Eric Höweler
J. Meejin Yoon
Neil Legband
Max Jarosz
Sungwoo Jang

Collaborators
Gregg Bleam
(Landscape Architect)

Plus House

Location
Fishers, Indiana, USA

Team Members
Eric Höweler
J. Meejin Yoon
Elle Gerdeman
Jonathan Fournier
Daniel Fougere
Max Jarosz

Collaborators
Gregg Bleam
(Landscape Architect)

Conversation with Ana Miljački

Ana Miljački, Associate Professor of Architecture at MIT and Director of the Critical Broadcasting Lab, discusses the effects of image circulation on notions of originality, ownership, knowledge, and innovation in design practice.

ERIC

Our age is characterized by the superabundance
and accessibility of information, especially
images. The fact that we can type a question
into Google and get an answer instantaneously
changes what it means to *know* something. So
much of our knowledge is outsourced to external
reference points. Likewise, our contemporary
glut of information changes what it means to
imagine something. And it changes the way we
design. After doing a sketch, I often think: did I
come up with that? Or, did I see that somewhere?
There is this kind of peripheral vision around
our imagination that is linked to images that
surround us, for example, on social media. We
are constantly scanning — always considering
what's already out there.

ANA

I think contemporary image flow does not just
occupy our peripheral vision; we also seek it out.
We are constantly and willingly consuming it,
and in the last decade the flow has become even
more rapid and harder to avoid. Academia and the
discipline are beginning to contend with this. I like
David Joselit's description of the image explosion in
relation to his notion of knowledge and image. He
talks about how there was a time (a more analog
time) when images were witnesses to history
whereas now, they constitute its currency. Images
transform thus from an index to a form of currency.
He talks about the irreversibility of the explosion
of images as something we must contend with,
as something that has produced a qualitative
transformation. It is not enough to mash up the
things you have seen. It is not enough to consider
an idea in terms of imagination and creativity,
maybe even originality. We have learned to see
image flow as a base.

ERIC

In architecture education, we celebrate
originality, newness, and invention. Innovation
seems to have never had a higher value than
it does today. We demand it of culture, of
technology, and of our students. Yet at the same
time, we acknowledge that we and our students
are all immersed in this media-dense world.
This moment foregrounds the role of the editor,
the curator, and the influencer. To take all this
content, distill it, and highlight the elements that

are important: that is the role of the curator, and, of the designer in the attention economy.

ANA
I like that. The world may not always have been as saturated with images as it is now. We couldn't have always found our peers as easily as we do now, or the things that we like. But at any given point in history, designers and architects were looking at others and curating the information available to them.

I think it is important to transfer an understanding of what it means to innovate in a particular historical moment to our students. Today, the constant barrage and flow of images define our experience. Newness, which was largely a modernist position on progress, was a significant underpinning of our education. I prefer to think that now we are not only seeking novelty, but also — alongside important political transformations and effects of estrangement — a way to produce pause or interest in the moment, within the constant flow of images.

In his important book *Patterns of Intention*, art historian Michael Baxandall suggests that 'influence' was not a very useful analytical concept. When we think in terms of influence, we are likely to imagine things (and people) in history having agency upon us. But instead, Baxandall would prefer us (and I agree with him) to think of agency as belonging to you, the new author, rather than the historical object or even the contemporary object that you are ingesting, because indeed you are the one processing it. So, as you ingest multiple influences you might do something entirely different with each of them, and this 'doing' is the register of real, even historical, agency.

BSA Space. Höweler + Yoon. Boston, Massachusetts

ERIC
One thing that differentiates this moment from the past is that now there are different channels. Before, we relied on *El Croquis* and *Progressive Architecture* to tell us who the important architects were, and now people are finding their own channels and promoting themselves through platforms like social media. The means of producing cultural currency have changed: as soon as you conceive an idea, you put it out into the world, and it starts to have a life of its own. In our own work on the BSA Space, the presence

of the rendering in the public realm ensured the outcome. When we had to value engineer the project, we couldn't consider removing elements like the stair because the image had already gained 'currency' and circulated, and there was an expectation that the project would be realized in a manner consistent with the image.

MEEJIN
Before now, an understanding of history and the direct experience of visiting buildings and structures to analyze them was how you learned about architecture. Today, we live in a world where architecture is constantly subject to new influences as it operates across different registers and channels. There is a desire to influence what flows back out too, which is why architects and designers participate in these channels.

Swing Time at the Lawn on D. Höweler + Yoon. Boston, Massachusetts. 2014

ANA
In terms of the way architects operate in culture, there's a superficiality of knowledge that comes with the flow of images. The architect is saturated with images today, whereas in the past one had to find a piece of architecture or inspiration and understand it on its own terms, as a full-fledged architectural object. Now, we have a very different understanding. You can search for your images and feel like you know something, but that is not the same as disciplinary knowledge.

ERIC
The next generation of architects consumes images at an unprecedented rate, replacing the need to go to the library to find the plans and other drawings needed to explain the image. So, there is a 'money shot' approach to architecture; a single image that has to speak instantaneously and compellingly: the 'image-basis' of architecture. David Joselit argues that an image has a different valuation when taken out of its context. Some images have more bang than others, and they gain currency in their ability to circulate. The more points of contact the image enables, the more valuable it is, the greater its power.

ANA
I know you have decided not to take issue with some bodies of work that seem to be influenced by

— or, in conversation with, your work. And yet you have also taken steps to protect some work, right?

MEEJIN
I think you're talking about Swing Time — this project has a set of demands that is much different than any we've done before because of its exposure on social media.

ERIC
Its popularity as a place for selfies on Instagram has created a demand. We are often asked to reproduce it for others, and because we choose not to meet those requests, somebody else does. In fact, on Alibaba, you can see our photographs of our swing used illegally by others to market and sell their knockoffs. It's an explicit copy at the scale of the product. It doesn't seem right that the copiers would be able to profit from it, and so in this case we did file a design patent and brought a formal complaint to Alibaba.

MEEJIN
When we see buildings learn from each other and employ similar techniques, that feels like influence and idea exchange. On the other hand, when a developer copies the Chengdu Sky Courts project and places it next to the original, that is a bit more uncomfortable.

ANA
Since the 1990 AWCPA, the Architectural Works Copyright Protections Act, developers have been taking each other to court to defend their right to the reproducibility of something, but you seldom see architects taking architects to court for the copy of a piece of architecture.

MEEJIN
We find ourselves being asked to sign over more and more of the intellectual property of our work in every client contract.

ERIC
It seems that the court cases are struggling to catch up to the contemporary design process, and they haven't gotten there yet.

ANA
The law has its way of describing what is original, what isn't original, what is sufficiently original.

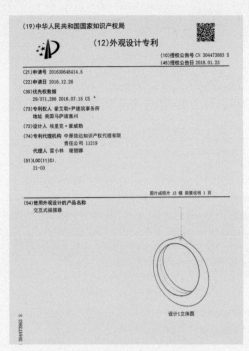

Chinese Patent for Swing Time

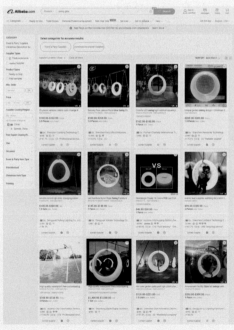

Pirated image of Swing Time on Alibaba

But do we really want the law to catch up with the design process? I think the reason we don't have architects taking each other to court all the time is because architects understand the design process.

> ERIC
> Also, because they are not necessarily the ones who would see a financial benefit. The owner has the money to gain from that IP, so the owners defend their trademarks or their copyrights.

ANA
Or, the architect's name has currency.

> MEEJIN
> I think it is still critics and historians who create lasting cultural currency. If a certain project has a lot of currency among students and young architects, especially on social media, but if it is never adopted into the canon, then what?

ANA
I think what you're talking about is a longer process of legitimation, of the production of the starchitect. Timothy Hyde has a great text in the book *Terms of Appropriation*, edited by Amanda Reeser Lawrence and myself, where he writes about the architect's persona — differentiating between and complicating the notions of author as person, author as persona, and author as signature. These are all very different ways of existing in the historical and cultural continuum. And at some point, the signature is something that is detachable from the person.

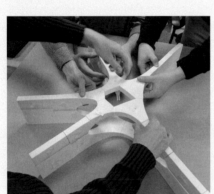

Collaborative design for Collier Memorial. Höweler + Yoon.

> ERIC
> Mark Wigley said the secret of the master architect is that every architect's office has people in it that are able to do the work of the master better than the master can. You cannot be a successful architect if you cannot find someone who could do your own thing better than you. Not just like you, but better than you. I think that is a really interesting statement, and it says something about our culture of creativity. There are people in Zaha's office that do Zaha better than Zaha, in a way...

Stuart St. façade mockup. Höweler + Yoon.

ANA
...and *still* do Zaha today. How would you say the perspective of the younger generation of HYA designers affects your process?

Memorial to Enslaved Laborers section test.
Höweler + Yoon.

MEEJIN

We were just looking back on a project and Eric said, "I don't remember where that project idea came from." In my recollection, Eric prompted the initial conversation with a sketch and everyone around the table evolved it — pushed and pulled on it, transformed it — re-synthesized it, and a design emerged organically with the team at that particular time. We are still very much influenced by everybody in the studio and their interests and obsessions.

ERIC

There is a process in the studio that is intentionally *not* top-down. The conversation is more along the lines of: what do we have to say about this? What's interesting about it? It reminds me of this or, bring that to the table. And then we start sketching; we produce six, eight, ten ideas. We pin them to the wall and talk about them. We reorganize them, hybridize them. That is the messy work of design today. It is horizontal and multi-authored.

ANA

If you think about the distance between your process and the things you have looked at, they are multiple. The idea of influence is also connected to the image. The flow of images is relentless, and it is irreversible. Is there a way to slow down? To put some friction into the flow that exposes the work of the process in such a way that it is not as simple as taking an image of the outcome. There is so much more that happens. I think this book might already be doing some of that.

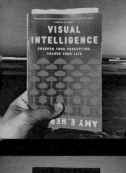

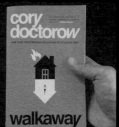

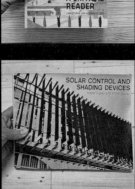

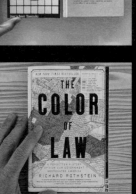

Why write a book in the age of Instagram? If one medium renders the prior obsolete, why bother with archaic media? It turns out that the printing press did not kill the cathedral. Instead, it added another channel to a dense web of communication formats and technologies. Even as they coexist, each technology has specifics and nuances in terms of medium, audience, and reach that differentiate them. A visit to the cathedral may have required a pilgrimage to access the content within. A paper bible, produced with the modern printing press, became abundant and ubiquitous, occupying drawers in motel rooms everywhere. The digital image posted on Instagram flickers under your thumb for a brief instant before being replaced by the next and the next, forming an endless image stream. With the introduction of new channels and the explosion of content comes the fierce competition for visibility, saturation, and distraction that corresponds to the mechanics of the attention economy.

An Instagram feed is an endless stream of images, hashtags, and data points. It is tailored to the modes of reception and access of the medium: distracted browsing, anytime, anywhere. Instagram's currency consists of likes and reposts, comments and emojis, while its algorithms for sequencing and suggestions produce feedback loops and reinforce behavioral patterns and political beliefs. The logics of social media work within the framework of the attention economy: an at-a-glance aesthetic, and the logic of the thumbnail image. The format rewards certain kinds of images and reinforces posting patterns, skewing content toward the seemingly superficial that eschews subtlety in exchange for splash. The instantaneous image produces its own aesthetic imprint. Nuance is lost in constant swiping through the Instagram scroll. On the other hand, the brevity of a well-written caption and a clever hashtag has produced a new sub-sub-genre of architectural writing within the constrained logics of the feed.

A physical and printed book is distinct from a website and distinct from a social media feed. The work compiled in this book, *Verify in Field*, has been carefully selected, the texts are edited, and conversations are curated. It is distinct and finite, with a beginning and end. It invites attention, a close read, maybe even study. The physicality of the book, the texture of the paper, and the quality of the binding contribute to the book as object and artifact. It is conceived as a design object unto itself. It is media as material.

Verify in Field follows our previous book, *Expanded Practice* by twelve years. As part of a series, the book could also be understood as a kind of very slow feed. Instead of social media killing the book, or the building, new media formats recast our relationship to old media. New media formats reach different audiences, have their own tempo, and produce different modes of reception and production. Old media, like books and buildings, are now reread relative to new media. The book is no longer a fast building. It is a slow feed.

Contemporary cultural production can be understood as a question of signal and noise, where the signal is the new content produced against the backdrop of all other content screaming for our attention. The logics of attention and visibility are altered by the structures and algorithms of our contemporary image

Our contemporary culture is characterized by
device dependency and image superabundance.

economy. Writing about contemporary art practices, critic David Joselit has argued that "images produce power — a current or currency," through their circulation, producing image value, as they are shared, reposted, and recirculated in a networked media ecosystem.[1] Instead of *aura*, today we have *buzz*.

In our own experience with design and social media, the Swing Time project illustrates many of the issues around design, contemporary image circulation, and the intellectual property questions that surround them. Originally intended as a temporary public art installation, Swing Time became a social media phenomenon as thousands of users posted images of themselves in the swings on Instagram, Twitter, and Tinder.

The illuminated and interactive swings quickly became a popular selfie spot with the glowing swing creating an illuminated frame. Swing Time selfies contributed to the dissemination of the project as the multi-user sharing and networking expanded the project's reach well beyond any single broadcast that originated with the designers.

As a photogenic public art installation, Swing Time also became a poster child for creative placemaking and innovation culture. Although the swings were designed and fabricated as a site-specific project, the demand for reproducing the project has continued and we have received requests to purchase, rent, and install Swing Time in city parks, residential developments, museums, and even music videos.

As a side effect of social media success, the dissemination of Swing Time produced a raft of copycat projects. We learned that

Social media posts of #swingtime and #lawnond circulated widely as part of a selfie phenomenon.

Images of our swings were being used to sell knockoffs on the Chinese platform Alibaba. In an effort to protect the intellectual property of our design, we filed for design patents in the U.S., China, and Europe. We also filed an official complaint through alibaba.com to take down listings that used our images to sell knockoffs. The visual currency of Swing Time highlights many aspects of our contemporary image culture; the image's ability to circulate through posting and reposting, and the pitfalls of reproducibility manifesting as so many knockoff imitations.

The imageability of architecture has evolved in parallel with media formats, from yesterday's curb appeal, which referred to a vantage point from the street, to today's *Instagrammable* as a new adjective referring to its dissemination. Architecture and design are now an integral part of the social-media-fueled attention economy, where the work of architecture in the age of its social media *circulability* has rewritten the brief for architectural aspiration. It is not uncommon for a client brief to include a list of requirements and attributes for a new project: 120,000 square feet (11,000 sq m) of core and shell retail, loading from the rear, flexible interior demarcation between tenants — and, make sure it's Instagrammable.

Scholar and critic Beatriz Colomina has highlighted the interrelationship between modern architecture and mass

Social media practices have not only altered how we share images, but fundamentally reshaped how we see architecture. #seeingseeing.

media, where modern architecture is inconceivable without a media campaign to broadcast its message. For Colomina, the "site of architectural production — no longer exclusively located on the construction site, but more and more displaced into the rather immaterial sites of architectural publication, exhibition, and journals."[2] If magazines like *L'esprit Nouveau* and *G* were essential in the broadcasting of modern architecture, did they also affect its reception? If modern architecture found its feed in the avant-garde journals of the moment, how might we think about the present moment, with its proliferation of formats and feeds? And what sort of intertwining of projects and publicity might the contemporary social media ecosystem present?

There is no doubt that social media culture alters how projects are disseminated, circulated, and consumed. The reception of design through images follows the logic of digital media currency. What about the experience of buildings? A built project might have had a pre-life on social media as process #wip images circulate in advance of the building's completion. Social media feeds also change the reception of built work, in that the work is often *pre-experienced* via feeds.

Often, when construction is complete, the physical building has an uncanny presence. A completed building often looks eerily like the renderings and models that preceded it. The Collier Memorial at MIT produced a distinct feeling of *déjà vu* when it was

Projects shared as work in progress #wip, produce familiarity, fundamentally altering the experience and

finally completed. The form of the memorial was familiar yet strange. We were accustomed to the curved profiles and intersecting geometries from the digital model that had orbited on our computer screens for a year leading up to the construction. Standing on the corner of Vassar and Main Streets, the nearly 200 tons (180,000 kg) of stone suspended in midair in the form of an arch looked just like the Rhino model, only different.

If architecture is pre-figured by its digital workflows and anticipatory instruments — models, renderings, technical datasheets, toolpaths — then how are digital workflows affected by the constant din of the image ecosystem of social media? If the proliferation of social media feeds affects the reception of design, how does it affect its conception? Years ago, as Google was marketing its Google Glass product, a spokesperson for the company remarked that instant access to information flickering inches away from your eyes might change what it means to *know* something. Google's instant search function would presumably free up memory in the human brain, and, make mountains of data available on demand. The act of knowing would be altered by instant search. Following this line of thinking for a moment, we might also ask: if images are streaming in from social media, how might it alter what it means to *imagine* something? With the proliferation of channels and feeds, and images ricocheting in the echo chamber of social media, video clips go viral, memes

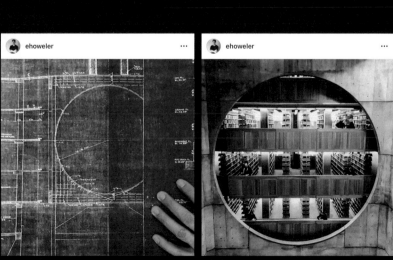

come and go, and trends accelerate through cycles of cool and cliché with incredible speed. Questions of originality and influence are an inevitable aspect of contemporary cultural production. If postmodern architecture can be characterized by a return of history via motifs and quotations, then the present moment might also be understood as a period of rapid returns. The trend of pseudo axonometric parallel projection drawings produced by Make2D commands and Choisy perspectives were popular in architecture schools circa 2015. Derez pixelated forms circa 2010. Single-surface floor, wall, and roof projects circa 2005. Trendspotting and feed surfing has become a perpetual pursuit to grasp and apprehend the contemporary before it passes into cliché.

How then to conceptualize social media as another channel in cultural production? Could social media be used to expand knowledge or to broaden an audience? As an alternative to traditional media or institutional channels, the individual channel that social media represents offers some optimism. Could Instagram serve as an extension of teaching or have a pedagogical dimension? I have been told that the university is not a MOOC, and certainly, a feed is not a lecture, just as a tweet is not an essay. On the other hand, a series of thoughtful posts, observations, and reflections can accumulate over time to form a following, or elaborate a line of inquiry and start to form a long-distance, drawn-out conversation among strangers. A series of posts under the hashtag #strangedetails elaborate on questions initially posed by architect Michael Cadwell in

The filtering of information on #fireexitplans highlights essential elements of buildings, often revealing what is not shown. #aquatower #mercedesbenzmuseum

his book of the same title. Images and commentary with the #strangedetails hashtag now circulate on Instagram as an extended appendix to the book, crowdsourced and collected by multiple contributors.

Another Instagram series of posts collected with hashtags like #escapeplan, #fireexitplan, or #egressplan collect the posted plans of significant buildings through their code-required exit plans. These plans inform the viewer of their location relative to the closest means of egress. Because the plans are diagrammatic and highlight only essential components like corridors and stairs, they offer a distilled reading of the building. For example, the exit plan for Aqua Tower in Chicago illustrates the elevators and stairs but does not feature the curvilinear slab edge that provides the building's distinct architectural image. Other egress plans present the complex information in diagrammatic form. The exit plan for the Mercedes-Benz Museum in Stuttgart manages to distill a complex plan down to the critical information: its basic organizational and essential circulation logic of cores and stairs. While collecting and posting egress plans may be understood as an eccentric activity, it arguably also contributes to an expansion of disciplinary knowledge.

The significance of social media feeds is threefold: its timeliness, its reach, and its accumulation. The "insta" in

Work-in-progress posts of the curtain wall for the Luxelakes office building façade tracks the development from massing to wall type to mockup. #wip #luxelakes #façademodel #fullscalemockup

Instagram refers to its liveness, its of-the-moment-ness. Surveying Instagram feeds in real time offers a glimpse of a visual cross-section of design culture at any moment: exhibition openings, books published, buildings previewed, construction completed, work-in-progress. Instagram's reach is its ability to circulate well beyond the network of the initial post through a network. It is not uncommon for images to be reposted by feeds that do not produce work, but simply aggregate it and make it available to tens and hundreds of thousands. And finally, social media feeds accumulate over time to form a resource: a live archive. Unlike the work of traditional archives that involve collecting, cataloguing, and safeguarding selected works, the social media archive is crowdsourced, collected over time, sorted, and tagged — and searchable from anywhere.

Can a hashtag serve to take the temperature of the age and register a moment? Does the live archive accumulate actively? Can a feed serve as a call to action? Yes, yes, and yes. Social media, like traditional media, register a moment in time. Hashtags like #blacklivesmatter, #saytheirnames, #bethechangeyouwanttosee, and #goodtrouble served to rally a movement in the months after the murder of George Floyd. The Black Lives Matter movement brought greater attention to the systemic racism that exists in institutions, planning policies, and the built environment, among many facets of American life. Social media amplified this message beyond traditional platforms of place and protest.

Our contemporary moment is also characterized by the traumas that were amplified during the Trump presidency,

ehoweler

Full-scale plot of detail drawings from GSD course, Cases in Contemporary Construction. Drawing by Benjamin DiNapoli. #handscale #gsd6230

the emergence of Post-truth in the Age of Information, political polarization, wildfires, COVID-19, social distancing, the brutality of police killings of Black Americans, and an emerging mainstream consciousness of structural and systemic racism, the acceleration of the wealth gap, and the indisputable evidence of global warming as the result of human actions. How is social media affecting each of these indicators of the contemporary, either as medium or accelerant? Trump was the first reality TV president and social media was his medium of choice. Inflammatory speech and conspiracy theories have fueled the Post-truth phenomenon and political polarization. Social media is not innocent of amplifying hate speech and spreading conspiracy theories. The echo chamber of self-similar political beliefs is one of the mechanisms that has contributed to the fractured state of political discourse at the end of 2020.

Overlapping and cumulative traumas make stocktaking of the contemporary moment almost too much to bear. Doom-scrolling social media and news feeds in search of some shred of positive news has become a contemporary mode of being. Italian philosopher Giorgio Agamben describes the challenge of recognizing the contemporary moment while being embedded in it. Agamben sketches out the persona of "the contemporary" as someone who is able to gaze upon their own time,

Posts of the Hancock building, including a review of Harry Cobb's book, *Words & Work*, and a detail of the building as it meets the ground contribute to the 'live archive.' #harrycobb #hancockbuilding

"so as to perceive not its light, but rather its darkness." The present is always obscure, only to be revealed in hindsight. For Agamben, the contemporary writes by "dipping his pen in the obscurity of the present," detecting its outlines by tracing its darkness.[3]

Agamben's was yesterday's contemporary. The present is not so much obscured by darkness, but drowning in a blinding blizzard of content. It is not an absence of light, but an overabundance of stimuli. How to detect the signal in the noise? Decoding the contemporary moment requires filtering, editing, and curating. Adding friction to the flow so as to gauge its composition, velocity, or disposition.

How then to characterize the present moment relative to politics, technology, and culture? There is no turning back. Posting is a mode of being in time and also outside of time, offering commentary on the moment with an eye to a future repository of a live archive. Perhaps posting is a way to detect the dim profile of the present in the torrent of noise, an attempt to make sense of our chaotic contemporary.

Eric Höweler
January 2021

 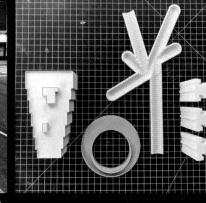

One reading of the contemporary is a ratio of signal to noise, where cultural production is the signal, and noise is the messy backdrop of contemporary culture and politics. #signaltonoise

1 Joselit, David. 2013. *After Art.*
   Princeton, NJ: Princeton
   University Press, p.xvi.

2 Colomina, Beatriz. 1994.
   *Privacy and Publicity: Modern
   Architecture as Mass Media.*
   Cambridge, Mass: MIT Press, p.14.

3 Agamben, Giorgio. 2009.
   *"What is Contemporary?" in
   What is an Apparatus? and
   Other Essays.* Stanford:
   Stanford University Press, p.44.

Acknowledgments

This book has been years in the making. We need to thank our exceptional in-house book team, Rae Pozdro and Alexander Porter, for their thoughtfulness, organizational talents, and sheep-dogging skills to move VIF over the finish line. Thanks to the book's early concept team — Elle Gerdeman, Chloe Conceicao, and Gina Ciancone — for kicking off this project many years ago. Without this group, we would never have gotten from concept to completion. Thanks to Edith Fikes for careful copy edits over many rounds of revisions.

Earlier drafts of some of the essay texts appeared in *Perspecta*, *Log* and the conference proceedings from Exactitude. We would like to acknowledge the editors of *Perspecta* 42, Matthew Roman and Tal Schori, as well as Cynthia Davidson of *Log*, and Pari Riahi from University of Massachusetts Amherst, who prompted us to develop ideas included in this book in prior publications.

The Graham Foundation for Advanced Studies in the Fine Arts provided generous support for this publication. The Harvard Graduate School of Design, and the Massachusetts Institute of Technology, Center for Advanced Urbanism (CAU), Center for Art, Science & Technology (CAST), and SA+P have all supported our design research over many years.

We are grateful to the talented and dedicated members of our studio, whose efforts have brought the projects featured in VIF into being. Current members of the studio include: Jacob Bruce, Kyle Coburn, Daniel Fougere, Jonathan Fournier, David Hamm, Karl Heckman, Sungwoo Jang, David Mora, Ching Ying Ngan, Bernard Peng, Rae Pozdro, Hari Priya Rangarajan, Gideon Schwartzman, Caroline Shannon, Katie Wolochowicz, Mengzhe Ye, Estelle Yoon, and Shunfan Zheng. Former members of the studio include: Stephanie Amato, Boris Angelov, Emily Ashby, Sofia Balters, Travis Bost, Paul Cattaneo, Beining Chen, Yoonhee Cho, Ihwa Choi, Matt Chua, Jennifer Chuong, Gina Ciancone, Chloe Conceicao, David Costanza, Cyrus Dochow, Evan Farley, Joann Feng, Vanille Fricker, Julian Funk, Elle Gerdeman, Daniel Haidermota, Caleb Hawkins, Max Jarosz, Jeremy Jih, Sophie Juneau, Anna Kaertner, Aryan Khalighy, Min Sung Kim, Namjoo Kim, Parker Lee, Neal Legband, Alex Li, Yujun Mao, Kevin Marblestone, Alex Marshall, Sarah Martos, Elisa Medina-Jaudes, Ian Miley, Meredith Miller, Ryan Murphy, Nancy Nichols, Yushiro Okamoto, Nerijus Petrokas, Alexander Porter, Casey Renner, Julia Roberts, Zach Seibold, Gillian Shaffer, Yanfei Shui, Lisa Smith, Carl Solander, Thena Tak, David Tarcali, Cheyenne Vandevoorde, Kate van Heusen, Di Wang, Audrey Watkins, Paul Wood, and Nan Xiang.

A special thanks is owed to our friends and colleagues who participated in the included conversations: Adam Greenfield, Nader Tehrani, Kate Orff, Daniel Barber, and Ana Miljački.

We would also like to thank our exceptional collaborators and co-creators over the years who shared their expertise, experience, and brilliance with incredible fearlessness and generosity: Gregg Bleam, Skip

Burke, Frank Dukes, Jim Durham, Devon Henry, Hauke Jungjohann, Pat McCafferty, John Ochsendorf, Eto Otitigbe, Ryan and Annie Page, Will Pickering, Ian Schmellick, Shari Sharafi, Brian Streb, Mohammad Vatan, Victor Vizgaitis, Mabel O. Wilson, and Philip Yuan. This work is also their work.

We also acknowledge the support of clients without which these projects would not be possible: Alice Raucher, Mary Hughes, Sarita Herman and Ted Nelson of the University of Virginia; Dick Amster, Paul Murphy, Jon Alvarez and Thayer Donham from MIT Facilities; John Durant and Gary van Zante of the MIT Museum; Neal Howard, Peter Spellios, and Bryan Lee of Transom Real Estate; Kathy Tallman, Michael Maynard, Gary Stoloff, and Barbara Stein of the Coolidge Corner Theater; Mr. Luo and Jie Jiao of Wide Horizon; Tony Pangaro and Kathy MacNeil of Millennium Partners Boston; Eric White of the Boston Society of Architects; Elizabeth Grajales and Ed Lebow of the City of Phoenix Arts and Culture, Hua Kuok of Kerry Properties; Melissa Huggins of Spokane Arts and Berry Ellison of Spokane Parks and Recreation; Jane Golden, Magda Martinez, and Judy Hellman of Philadelphia Mural Arts and Maitreyi Roy of Bartram's Garden; Mr. and Mrs. Chung, Eunnice Eun and Patrick Kim, and Dan and Lucy Neely.

Ideas don't happen in a vacuum, so we need to acknowledge our mentors, colleagues, and friends: Iñaki Abalos, Lucia Allais, Amale Andraos, Frank Barkow, Martin Bechthold, Tatiana Bilbao, Eric Bunge, Yung Ho Chang, Preston Scott Cohen, Milton Curry, Thomas de Monchaux, Liz Diller, Rodolphe el-Khoury, Jeanne Gang, Rosalie Genevro, Ben Gilmartin, Michael Hays, Mimi Hoang, Andrew Holder, Timothy Hyde, Mariana Ibañez, Mark Jarzombek, Sheila Kennedy, Simon Kim, Jeannette Kuo, Grace La, Amanda Reeser Lawrence, Mark Lee, Andrea Leers, Andres Lepik, Paul Lewis, Jon Lott, John May, Michael Meredith, Lee Moreau, Toshiko Mori, Mohsen Mostafavi, Neri Oxman, Mark Pasnik, Antoine Picon, Monica Ponce de Leon, Charles Renfro, Anne Rieselbach, Hilary Sample, Adèle Naudé Santos, Ric Scofidio, Mack Scogin, Brigette Shim, John Shnier, Jorge Silvetti, Filip Tejchman, Lily Tsai, Billie Tsien, Gediminas Urbonas, Franco Vairani, Jamie von Klemperer, Sarah Whiting, Beth Whittaker, Dan Wood, Kim Yao, and Ed Young.

A special thanks to our publisher, Thomas Kramer of Park Books, and our book designers, Ken Meier and Yoonjai Choi of Common Name.

A special shout out and immense gratitude to Ana Miljački for her critical intelligence, impeccable eye, and the numerous crits sessions, pep rallies, and reality checks that helped us find our voice and keep things in perspective.

We need to thank our families for the love and support over a lifetime: Ichun Jane Höweler and Reinhardt Höweler, Mike Höweler and Kim Dupcak, Jason (Heung-lho) Yoon, Hannah (Young-ai) Yoon, Gene Yoon, and Steve Yoon.

This book is dedicated to Kaya Miae Höweler, with love.

Acervo do Núcleo de Pesquisa
e Documentação. FAU/UFRJ.
Brazil
   283 (top)
Baan, Iwan
   82, 84, 92, cover (aerial:
   Collier Memorial)
Boston Public Library, Rare
Books and Manuscripts
   40 (portrait)
Brick Visual (c/o HYA)
   273, 277, 278
Chao, Zhang (c/o HYA)
   222 (photo), 235, 237
   (photo), 241, 242, 243, 284
Cordera, Rik (c/o HYA)
   52 (process shots)
Dobens, Samuel (c/o HYA)
   160, 166
Fondation Le Corbusier;
Birkhäuser. From Le Corbusier:
Oeuvre Complete
   221 (left)
GLUCK+
   153 (diagrams)
Graves, Kris. The Living
   153 (Hy-fi)
Harris, Britni
(@brucegoffworld)
   148
Horner, John (c/o HYA)
   7 (left), 59, 86, 87, 94–95,
   162, 169, 171, 172, 175
   (photo),186–187, 189, 194,
   284 (top), 336 (photo)
Hu, Yihuai (c/o HYA)
   127, 132-133
Jones, Lou. Millennium
Partners.
   161 (right)
Karchmer, Alan (c/o HYA)
   38–39, 43 (photo), 53
Knight, Justin
   287
Library of Congress, Prints and
Photographs Division,
Washington, D.C.
   161 (left)
Library of Congress. Sequioa
Log, Sequioa National Park,
California, ca. 1910.

Public domain.
https://bit.ly/3vGBM0V
   224
Library of Virginia, Richmond,
VA. A List of Slaves and Free
persons of color received in the
Penitentiary of Virginia for Sale
and transportation from the
25th June 1816 to the 4th
February 1842. 1842.
   40
Lin, Jonathan. Castelvecchio
Museum. CC BY-SA 2.0.
https://bit.ly/3xLAjs7
   149
Luxigon (c/o HYA)
   99 (rendering), 100, 137,
   138 (rendering), 141
Martinez, Daniel. Aerial View of
Port Arthur and Beaumont
Texas after Hurricane Harvey.
Air Nat'l Guard. Public domain.
https://bit.ly/33doGvQ
   210
Museum of History and
Industry. Stacks of lumber
drying at the Seattle Cedar
Lumber Manufacturing
Company's mill in Ballard,
ca.1919.
   224
NADAAA
   150, 151
Neely, Dan
   322–323, cover (aerial: Plus
   House)
Olgyay, Victor. From Design
with Climate
   285
OPERA Architectes;
Chatillon & Associates
   221 (right)
Otitigbe, Eto
   25
Page, Ryan
   330, 331
Prince, Bart
   148
Public domain
   282
Quarra Stone (c/o HYA)

61, 225, 226, 254–255
Ravenscrodt, Tom. Seagram
Building. CC BY 2.0
https://bit.ly/3nURMKg
   295 (left)
Ryan, Andy (c/o HYA)
   181, 182, 335 (photo)
SC Johnson.1937
   69
SCAPE
   211 (drawing), 213
Shanghai Landscape-
Architecture Design and
Research Institute Co., Ltd.
(c/o HYA)
   198–199, 207
Shining (c/o HYA)
   112
SHoP
   152
Shurtleff, Andrew
   6, 27
Squared Design Lab (c/o HYA)
   201, 203 (rendering),
   204, 206
Maria Acconci
   159
Suchak, Sanjay
   17, 18 (vigil), 23 (memory
   marks), 34, 40 (timeline,
   memory marks), 42, 54–55
Tiedemann, George.
Temple University Libraries,
Special Collections Research
Center. Philadelphia, PA.
Floating oil from a sunken
barge at Gulf Oil Co burns on
the Schuylkill River. 1977.
   211
University of Virginia Library,
Special Collections,
Charlottesville, VA. Garden
walls. 1972.
   18
University of Virginia Library,
Special Collections,
Charlottesville, VA. Rotunda
and Lawn, B. Tanner Engraving
from Boye's Map of Virginia.
1826.
   30–31

Vairani, Franco (c/o HYA)
    7 (right)
Van der Wal, Gijsbert
    343
VCG
    124
Winquist, Matt (c/o HYA)
    244–245, 247 (photo), 248,
    249, 251, 252–253, 283
Wolfram, Jeff (c/o HYA)
    212 (top), 302 (photo), 307,
    308, 311, 312, 314–315,
    317, 318

Agamben, Giorgio. 2009. "What is Contemporary?" in *What is an Apparatus? and Other Essays*. Stanford: Stanford University Press.

Alexander Çelik, Zaynep, and John May, eds. 2020. *Design Technics: Archaeologies of Architectural Practice*. Minneapolis: University of Minnesota Press.

Banham, Reyner. 1969. *The Architecture of the Well-tempered Environment*. Chicago: The University Of Chicago Press.

Barber, Daniel. 2020. *Modern Architecture and Climate: Design Before Air Conditioning*. Princeton, NJ: Princeton University Press.

Beck, Ulrich. 1992. *Risk Society: Towards a New Modernity*. London: Sage Publications.

Borden, Gail Peter, and Meredith Michael, eds. 2012. *Matter: Material Processes in Architectural Production*. New York: Routledge.

Borden, Gail Peter, and Meredith Michael, eds. 2018. *Lineament: Material, Representation and the Physical Figure in Architectural Production*. New York: Routledge.

Bridle, James. 2018. *New Dark Age: Technology and the End of the Future*. London: Verso.

Cadwell, Michael. 2007. *Strange Details*. Cambridge, Mass: MIT Press.

Carpo, Mario. 2017. *The Second Digital Turn: Design Beyond Intelligence*. Cambridge, Mass: MIT Press.

Cheng, Irene, Charles L. Davis, and Mabel O. Wilson. 2020. *Race and Modern Architecture: A Critical History from the Enlightenment to the Present*. Pittsburgh: University of Pittsburgh Press.

Colomina, Beatriz. 1994. *Privacy and Publicity: Modern Architecture as Mass Media*. Cambridge, Mass: MIT Press.

Daston, Lorraine. 2019. *Against Nature*. Cambridge, Mass: MIT Press.

Deamer, Peggy, and Phillip G. Bernstein. 2010. *Building (in) the Future: Recasting Labor in Architecture*. Princeton, NJ: Princeton University Press.

Evans, Robin. 1997. *Translations from Drawing to Building*. Cambridge, Mass: MIT Press.

Ford, Edward R. 1998. *The Details of Modern Architecture, Volume 2: 1928 to 1988*. Cambridge, Mass: MIT Press.

Ford, Edward R. 2011. *The Architectural Detail*. Hudson, NY: Princeton Architectural Press.

Foster, Hal. 2009. *The Return of the Real. An October Book*. Cambridge, Mass: MIT Press.

Foster, Hal. 2020. *What Comes After Farce? Art and Criticism at a Time of Debacle*. London, New York: Verso.

Gelpi, Nick. 2020. *The Architecture of Full-scale Mock-ups: from Representation to Reality*. New York: Routledge.

Ghosh, Amitav. 2017. *The Great Derangement: Climate Change and the Unthinkable*. Chicago: The University of Chicago Press.

Goodhouse, Andrew. 2016. *When is the Digital in Architecture?* Montréal: Canadian Centre For Architecture.

Graham, James. 2016. *Climates: Architecture and the Planetary Imaginary*. Zurich: Lars Muller.

Greenfield, Adam. 2018. *Radical Technologies: the Design of Everyday Life*. Brooklyn, NY: Verso.

Hughes, Francesca. 2014. *The Architecture of Error: Matter, Measure, and the Misadventures of Precision*. Cambridge, Mass: MIT Press.

Hulme, Mike. 2017. *Weathered: Cultures of Climate*. London: Sage Publications Ltd.

Hutton, Margaret-anne. 2018. *The Contemporary Condition: on Writing a Literary History of the Contemporary, or What Is or Was, "The Contemporary," and Should We Keep Calling it That?* Berlin: Sternberg Press.

Ibañez, Daniel, Jane Hutton, and Kiel Moe. 2019. *Wood

Urbanism: from the Molecular to the Territorial. New York: Actar D.

Iturbe, Elisa. 2019. "Architecture and the Death of Carbon Modernity," in Log 47. Anyone Corporation.

Joselit, David. 2013. After Art. Princeton, NJ: Princeton University Press.

Kayden, Jerold S. 2000. Privately Owned Public Space: The New York City Experience. New York: John Wiley & Sons.

Lanham, Richard A. 2007. The Economics of Attention: Style And Substance in the Age of Information. Chicago: University of Chicago Press.

Latour, Bruno, and Catherine Porter. 2019. Down To Earth: Politics in the New Climatic Regime. Cambridge, UK: Polity.

Lawrence, Amanda Reeser, and Ana Miljački. 2018. Terms of Appropriation: Modern Architecture and Global Exchange. New York: Routledge.

May, John. 2019. Signal. Image. Architecture: (Everything is Already an Image). New York: Columbia Books on Architecture and the City.

McCullough, Malcolm. 2013. Ambient Commons: Attention in the Age of Embodied Information. Cambridge, Mass: MIT Press.

McInnis, Maurie Dee, and Louis P. Nelson, eds. 2019. Educated in Tyranny: Slavery at Thomas Jefferson's University. Charlottesville, VA: University of Virginia Press.

McIntyre, Lee. 2018. Post-truth. Cambridge, Mass: MIT Press.

Miljački, Ana. 2014. Under the Influence: Symposium. Cambridge, Mass: SA+P Press.

Moe, Kiel. 2017. Empire, State & Building. New York: Actar D.

Moe, Kiel. 2020. Unless: the Seagram Building Construction Ecology. New York: Actar D.

Morton, Timothy. 2017. Hyperobjects: Philosophy and Ecology After the End of the World. Minneapolis: University of Minnesota Press.

Mostafavi, Mohsen, and David Leatherbarrow. 1993. On Weathering: The Life of Buildings in Time. Cambridge, Mass: The MIT Press.

Olgyay, Victor, and Aladar Olgyay. 1963. Design with Climate: Bioclimatic Approach to Architectural Regionalism. Princeton, NJ: Princeton University Press.

Orff, Kate. 2016. Toward an Urban Ecology. New York: The Monacelli Press.

Picon, Antoine. 2020. The Materiality of Architecture. Minneapolis: University of Minnesota Press.

Rustow, Stephen. 2005. "MoMA's Minimalist Baroque," Praxis: Journal of Writing + Building 7.

Steyerl, Hito, and Franco Berardi. 2012. Hito Steyerl: The Wretched of the Screen. Berlin: Sternberg Press.

Tehrani, Nader. 2011. "Difficult Synthesis," in Material Design: Informing Architecture by Materiality, ed. Thomas Schröpfer and James Carpenter, Basel: Birkhäuser.

Urbonas, Gediminas, Ann Lui, and Lucas Freeman. 2017. Public Space? Lost and Found. Cambridge, Mass: SA+P Press.

Wapner, Paul. 2010. Living Through the End of Nature: The Future of American Environmentalism. Cambridge, Mass: MIT Press.

Wilson, Mabel O. 2019. "White By Design," in Among Others: Blackness at MoMA, ed. Darby English, Charlotte Barat, Mabel Olivia Wilson, and Glenn D. Lowry, New York: The Museum of Modern Art.

Windeck, Georg, Lisa Larson-walker, Sean Gaffney, and Will Shapiro. 2016. Construction Matters. Brooklyn, NY: Powerhouse Books.

Yoon, J. Meejin, and Eric Höweler. 2009. Expanded Practice: Höweler + Yoon Architecture/MY Studio. Hudson, NY: Princeton Architectural Press.